The Debated Mind

Dedicated to Jorun

The Debated Mind

Evolutionary Psychology versus Ethnography

Edited by
Harvey Whitehouse

Oxford • New York

First published in 2001 by
Berg
Editorial offices:
150 Cowley Road, Oxford, OX4 1JJ, UK
838 Broadway, Third Floor, New York, NY 10003-4812, USA

Berg is an imprint of Oxford International Publishers Ltd.

Library of Congress Cataloging-in-Publication Data
A catalogue record for this book is available from the Library of Congress.

British Library Cataloguing-in-Publication Data
A catalogue record for this book is available from the British Library.

ISBN 1 85973 427 8 (Cloth)
     1 85973 432 4 (Paper)

Typeset by JS Typesetting, Wellingborough, Northants.
Printed in the United Kingdom by Biddles Ltd, Guildford and King's Lynn.

Contents

List of Contributors   vii

Acknowledgements   ix

Introduction
Harvey Whitehouse   1

PART ONE

1 Mental Modularity and Cultural Diversity
   Dan Sperber   23
2 Cultural Inheritance Tracks and Cognitive Predispositions:
   The Example of Religious Concepts
   Pascal Boyer   57
3 Some Elements of a Science of Culture
   Henry Plotkin   91

PART TWO

4 From the Transmission of Representations to the
   Education of Attention
   Tim Ingold   113
5 The Child in Mind
   Christina Toren   155
6 Steps to an Integration of Developmental Cognitivism and
   Depth Psychology
   Charles W. Nuckolls   181

Conclusion: Towards a Reconciliation
Harvey Whitehouse   203

Index   225

List of Contributors

Dan Sperber (Chapter One) is Directeur de Recherche at the Centre National de la Recherche Scientifique, Paris. He is associated particularly with the fields of social anthropology and cognitive science. His previous books include *Rethinking Symbolism, On Anthropological Knowledge, Explaining Culture*, and, with Deirdre Wilson, *Relevance*.

Pascal Boyer (Chapter Two) is Chargé de Recherche at MRASH-Dynamiques du Langage, Lyon. He is associated particularly with the fields of religious anthropology and cognitive science. His previous books include *Barricades Mystérieuses et Pièges à Pensée, Tradition as Truth and Communication, The Naturalness of Religious Ideas*, and *Cognitive Aspects of Religious Symbolism*.

Henry Plotkin (Chapter Three) is Professor of Psychology at University College London. He is associated particularly with the fields of evolutionary psychology and philosophy of science. His previous books include *The Role of Behaviour in Evolution, Darwin Machines and The Nature of Knowledge*, and *Evolution in Mind*.

Tim Ingold (Chapter Four) is Professor of Social Anthropology at Aberdeen University. He is associated particularly with the fields of anthropology and evolutionary biology. His previous books include *Hunters, Pastoralists, and Ranchers, Evolution and Social Life, Companion Encyclopedia of Anthropology, Key Debates in Anthropology*, and, with David Riches and James Woodburn, *Hunters and Gatherers (Vols. 1 and 2)*.

Christina Toren (Chapter Five) is Reader in Social Anthropology at Brunel University. She is associated particularly with the fields of social anthropology and child cognitive development. Her previous books include *Making Sense of Hierarchy* and *Mind, Materiality and History*.

Charles Nuckolls (Chapter Six) is Professor of Anthropology at the University of Alabama. He is associated particularly with the fields of psychoanalytic anthropology and social theory. His previous books include *The Cultural Dynamics of Knowledge and Desire* and *Culture: A Problem That Cannot be solved.*

Harvey Whitehouse (Introduction and Conclusion) is a Reader in Social Anthropology at the Queen's University of Belfast. He is associated particularly with the fields of cognitive and religious anthropology. His previous books include *Inside the Cult* and *Arguments and Icons.*

Acknowledgements

This volume arose from a series of ESRC-funded seminars on 'Memory and Social Transmission', organized by Elizabeth Tonkin and myself at the Queen's University of Belfast. The planning and development of the book owes much to the efforts of those attending the meetings, especially those who eventually contributed chapters. The latter produced material of outstanding quality and responded swiftly and conscientiously to the criticisms of anonymous reviewers. To those who displayed considerable patience during the lengthy process of publication, I should like to express my deepest appreciation. I also owe a special debt of gratitude to Justin Barrett, Peter Bowler, Pascal Boyer, Tom Lawson, Bob McCauley, Brian Malley, Kay Milton, and Naomi Quinn for their insightful comments on the project as a whole and especially their constructive criticisms of my introductory and concluding chapters. Finally, all the contributors profited greatly from the recommendations of two anonymous reviewers.

Introduction

Harvey Whitehouse

Social scientists are notoriously scornful of the naive reductionism of socio-biological and psychological perspectives on culture while those working in fields of biology and cognitive science have often been exasperated at the reluctance of social/cultural theorists to recognize the explanatory power and relevance of naturalistic models in the study of human behaviour. One of the greatest controversies fuelling this unproductive situation has been the so-called nature/nurture debate. Crudely, if it could have been demonstrated that cultural phenomena are the infinitely variable consequences of 'learned' mental abilities then the social scientists would have been vindicated in their dismissal of most biological perspectives. Conversely, if it could have been shown that certain cultural things are shaped by 'innate' features of mental processing then the successful encroachment of biologists would have been assured.

The debate which unfolds in this volume is rather more subtle. The theories advanced in Part One are founded on conventional models in evolutionary psychology and cognitive science, in which the recognition of both genetic and environmental causes of neurological/mental development is axiomatic. At the 'nativist' end of the spectrum, some theorists (e.g. Sperber, this volume) argue that the mind-brain is richly endowed with genetically specified mechanisms for the discrimination and processing of inputs. Nevertheless, Sperber's notion of 'genetic specification' is not intended to mean a blueprint for mental activity but rather a set of instructions (rather like computer hardware) that must be augmented by information from the environment (the equivalent of computer software) in order to become operational. At the other end of the spectrum, there are 'empiricists' who envisage the neonate as a *tabula rasa*, bombarded by a flux of inputs that can only be discriminated and conceptualized through experience and learning, without the guidance of genetically specified equipment capable of anticipating some of that input. Between these two positions, cognitive science offers a vast array of competing perspectives, attributing varying degrees of importance to both genetic and environmental factors in relation to specific aspects of cognitive development.

In relation to some of the arguments put forward in Part One, however, the nativism/empiricism debate is tangential. Although both Sperber (Chapter One) and Boyer (Chapter Two), for instance, argue for genetic specification of at least some cognitive capacities, their explanations for patterns of cultural recurrence do not necessarily hinge on nativist assumptions. All they presuppose is the presence of globally convergent developmental schedules in human cognition that could, at least in principle, result from a *tabula rasa* starting point (e.g. relatively undifferentiated neural networks). They would argue that current evidence from cognitive science points to at least some innate biases but, even if that trend was reversed, their selectionist models of culture would still stand.

It is primarily with regard to the production of specific accounts of cognitive *evolution* that the question of innate capacities and dispositions becomes important to resolve. Here, the central question is whether distinct computational capacities are genetically specified, and thus outcomes of distinguishable evolutionary pressures under natural selection (as Sperber, in particular, suggests), or whether our task is to account for the evolution of rather more undifferentiated, general-purpose cognitive equipment. But, however we answer such questions, genes, environment, and culture stand in complex relations of mutual causation. As Plotkin points out (Chapter Three), not only are phenotypic properties only ever part-caused by genes, but these properties affect the natural selection of genes, and hence the phenotypic properties of future generations themselves. Perhaps the most obvious cultural innovation influencing the course of evolution was the development of language, but Plotkin also mentions migration, genocide, warfare, and agricultural technologies. Thus, according to Plotkin, biology and culture must be seen as a 'two-way street' of causation in evolution.

Meanwhile, the contributors to Part Two of this volume do not argue for a *tabula rasa* view of mind, still less for any form of nativism. They maintain that biological and psychological perspectives are vital for a fuller understanding of culture but that the conceptual frames within which these perspectives are conventionally expressed and developed require substantial modification. Ingold (Chapter Four) argues that cognitive science, along with certain concepts of neo-Darwinian evolutionary biology which it imports, are premised upon a circular but powerful ideology. Toren (Chapter Five) similarly focuses on the ideological character of what she calls 'Western science models of mind' but, for her, the main weakness of such models is their incapacity to reflect on the conditions of their own genesis. Among the alleged effects of this lack of reflexivity is the exclusion of emotion in cognitive models, a problem with cognitivism that also lies at the heart of Nuckolls' critique (Chapter Six) of Part One. According to Nuckolls, the hypotheses advanced in Part One with regard to the cognitive causes of cultural phenomena explain considerably less than they might due to the principled, but entirely unnecessary, neglect of unconscious emotional conflict and repression.

Boyer argues that there are two distinct but, to some extent, compatible projects being advanced in this volume. The projects of Part One, he suggests, are specifically concerned with producing cognitive and evolutionary explanations for the global recurrence of certain social/ cultural phenomena, whereas the Part-Two contributors are concerned with a more diverse set of issues. According to Boyer, however, problems arise when one theoretical agenda claims to be intrinsically superior to those being pursued in other fields, and thus seeks to replace them. He points out, for instance, that Toren's search for a 'phenomenologically valid' account of human mental life, while entirely legitimate, is not the only kind of project worth pursuing. The fact that much of what Toren has to say is incommensurable with work in cognitive science (witness Toren's decision to exclude critical engagement with such research from the main body of her text), is not in itself evidence of the incompatibility of Boyer's and Toren's projects. In general, the Part-One contributors favour a division of intellectual labour in the study of mental and cultural phenomena, allowing various projects, both naturalistic and humanistic, to proceed more or less independently. By contrast, Part-Two contributors express serious misgivings about the validity of the projects advanced in Part One, and argue that the latter need to be radically modified (Ingold and Nuckolls) or dispensed with altogether (Toren). Thus, at the root of the debate between contributors to Parts One and Two of this volume is a concern not about the relative salience of biological, psychological, and ethnographic perspectives on cultural transmission but about the way in which multidisciplinary research, and interdisciplinary cross-fertilization, should proceed.

Cognition and evolution

A point on which virtually all cognitive scientists agree is that people cognize different chunks (domains) of their environment in distinctive ways. In other words, cognition is 'domain specific'. For instance, from an early age, children conceptualize animals as possessing indefinable, invisible essences that are unalterable, but do not apply this principle to artefacts, as Keil (1989) has demonstrated:

[Keil] told children stories, for example about a skunk that was surgically altered to resemble a raccoon but still had the parents and internal structure of a skunk. By approximately the second grade, children reported that the animal was still a skunk, despite its outward appearances. They did not do so for artefacts, such as a coffeepot altered to resemble a birdfeeder (Hirschfeld and Gelman 1994: 14).

Hirschfeld and Gelman point out that the study of domain specificity in cognition has generated a bewildering diversity of candidate domains (1994: 12; see also Keil 1990: 139). Some researchers envisage domains as substantial areas of knowledge relating, for instance, to intuitive physics, mathematics, and linguistic computations (e.g. Karmiloff-Smith 1992), whereas other researchers regard comparatively narrow fields of knowledge, such as expertise in the game of chess, as distinct domains (e.g. Chase and Simon 1973). It follows, of course, that domain-specificity does not necessarily imply any sort of nativist argument. Nobody suggests that humans possess genetically specified cognitive equipment dedicated to solving chess problems, although chess may constitute a domain in the cognitive repertoires of those who are competent players of the game.

One possibility is that all forms of domain-specificity are products of a general learning device – that the cognitive architecture of the neonate is relatively undifferentiated and becomes structured through experience in the absence of genetically specified biases or discrete, dedicated structures. One of the most influential advocates of such a view in modern psychology was Jean Piaget, who argued that rich cognitive structures develop as a result of infants' exploration of their environments, by means of a *general* set of sensorimotor skills. Piagetians maintain, for instance, that infants' sensorimotor intelligence is sufficient for the building of syntactic and semantic representations necessary for speech learning. Thus, the syntactic principles of clause embedding would be learned through sensorimotor investigations of embedded objects (e.g. by playing with differently-sized containers). Similarly, the experientially discovered relations between agents, actions, and patients would provide the cognitive architecture for simple sentence structure (subject–verb–object). Piagetians hold that not only language but all aspects of cognition develop through domain-general processes of this sort.

Piagetian theories of development, however, are not the only domain-general, *tabula rasa* paradigms available in psychology. Behaviourism likewise pursues such a view of cognitive development, as Annette Karmiloff-Smith observes:

Neither the Piagetian nor the behaviourist theory grants the infant any innate structures or domain-specific knowledge. Each grants only some domain-general, biologically specified processes: for the Piagetians, a set of sensory reflexes and three functional processes (assimilation, accommodation, and equilibrium); for the behaviourists, inherited physiological sensory systems and a complex set of laws of association . . . The behaviourists saw the infant as a *tabula rasa* with no built-in knowledge . . .; Piaget's view of the young infant as assailed by 'undifferentiated and chaotic' inputs . . . is substantially the same (1992: 7).

Moreover, most recent models in neuroscience and artificial intelligence describe relatively domain-general processes of learning. The neurological theories of Gerald Edelman, which bear more than a passing resemblance to Skinner's behaviourism, are a striking case in point (see my conclusion to this volume), and some connectionist models of neural networks argue along similar lines (e.g. Sejnowski and Rosenberg 1987; for a broader overview, see Bechtel and Abrahamsen 1991).

What could a domain-general, *tabula rasa* theory of mind say about cognitive evolution, other than that such a mind must have appeared at some stage, as a result of unknown causes, during hominid evolution? A major problem with, say, the Piagetian theory of mind seems to be that it does not provide any clues as to why our primate cousins and early hominid ancestors are/were unable to develop the higher-level cognitive capacities of modern humans. Chimpanzees have sensorimotor intelligence similar to that in people, but even highly trained chimps cannot acquire the syntactic principles of parsing, clause embedding, subject–verb–object relations, and so on, that develop in children with remarkable speed and lack of deliberate training. Attempts have been made to square domain-general, *tabula rasa* approaches with an account of mind/brain evolution (e.g. Edelman 1992). Nevertheless, the postulation of genetically-specified cognitive mechanisms, dedicated to discrete computational tasks, is much more appealing to evolutionary psychologists, for a number of reasons.

To start with, mechanisms with phylogenetic histories give neo-Darwinian selectionist models something to work with. It becomes possible to speculate that particular mechanisms conferred reproductive advantages and therefore evolved under natural selection. In the domain of naive or intuitive physics, for instance, Spelke (1988, 1990) has postulated that certain principles underlying object perception are innately specified and at least some of these principles are likely to have contributed to survival in the general conditions in which humans evolved. An illuminating example is the evidence relating to infants' perceptions of object unity (Kellman and Spelke 1983), where a static object in the foreground partially occludes a moving display in the background. Due to the occlusion, infants are unable to determine whether the background display consisted of one unified object or two separate ones (the gap between them being obscured by the foregrounded object). Nevertheless, whenever the background display moves as if the visible elements are joined, it is interpreted as a unified object, even when the visible sections of the background display are very different in shape, colour, and texture. As Karmiloff-Smith observes, such inferences amount to 'an excellent survival mechanism, for if a tiger is running behind some trees, you had better realize that the simultaneously moving, perceptually different parts are the unitary body of one hungry tiger!' (1992: 70). Many similar stories of the evolution of a richly-structured mind/brain under natural selection have been told in relation to language (e.g. Pinker 1994, Dunbar 1993) and a range of other cognitive domains (e.g. Barkow, Cosmides and Tooby 1992; Boyer, Chapter Two, and Sperber, Chapter One of this volume).

Moreover, the postulation of genetically-specified, domain-specific cognitive mechanisms fits rather well with the piecemeal, incremental character of evolutionary change. Evolutionary biology envisages natural selection as short-sighted, favouring genetic mutations that confer immediate, not necessarily long-term, advantages. Consequently, one might expect cognitive capacities to evolve in relatively small parcels – that is, in the form of special-purpose mechanisms. In this view, evolution operates on the brain rather as a computer scientist in the field of artificial intelligence operates on automata: the concern is not with how a given modification works or whether it is the most aesthetic (e.g. economical) design alteration, but that it *does* work. Such modifications, adding complexity (in their inelegant fashion) to the existing equipment, have come to be known as 'kludges' (Clark 1987). Some scholars (e.g. Sperber, Chapter One) argue that cognitive research increasingly supports a view of the mind as constructed substantially out of kludges.

The notion of highly compartmentalized cognitive architecture predates evolutionary theory. Such a model of the mind was proposed, for instance, by the eighteenth-century anatomist Franz Joseph Gall. The most influential contemporary version of this argument takes the form of 'modularity' theory. The concept of modularity was pioneered by Noam Chomsky, who argued that humans are endowed with specially evolved cognitive architecture for processing language – an innate 'Language Acquisition Device' (LAD). Evidence for the innateness of Chomsky's LAD takes three main forms. First, certain aspects of language development in children are undetermined by experience. For instance, certain logically possible (and from the viewpoint of mental economy, highly expectable) grammatical errors are never in fact made by native speakers, irrespective of their stage of development. Since the non-occurrence of such errors cannot be explained by environmental input, it must be explained (so the argument goes) by the presence of a mechanism (or mechanisms) at least partially specified in advance of the process of language acquisition. Recent research has supported and extended Chomsky's view that the development of linguistic richness cannot be explained by *tabula rasa* theories of mind (e.g. Mehler *et al.* 1986; Jusczyk and Bertoncini 1988). Secondly, regardless of the particular language being learned, the process of acquisition by children appears to follow a relatively invariable developmental schedule (e.g. Slobin 1985), supporting the postulation of genetically specified mechanisms. Thirdly, severe disturbances of general cognitive abilities do not necessarily affect language acquisition (e.g. Curtis 1982; Bellugi *et al.* 1988), suggesting that the LAD, or equivalent mechanism, is modular to some extent.

In *The Modularity of Mind* (1983), Jerry Fodor brought together a growing body of evidence for genetically-specified perceptual or 'input' systems, not only for speech processing but for analysis of spatial relations, shape, colour, and other visual stimuli. Thus, in addition to evolved architecture for the language faculty, Fodor proposed innate, special-purpose mechanisms for processing a wide range of visual inputs. Fodor argued that these modules were 'hard-wired' – that is, they did not have to be built up out of other, simpler processes. Modular effects, in this view, are generated by fixed neural architecture and are automatic, mandatory, and informationally encapsulated. The principle of inform-ational encapsulation dictates that the outputs of modules cannot be altered by information from other parts of the cognitive system. For instance, when seated on a stationary train adjacent to a train in motion, you experience the sensation that the other train is static and *you* are moving. This kinaesthetic illusion is rapid and obligatory (automatic and mand-atory) and cannot be eliminated simply by reminding yourself that your own train has been delayed and stands motionless on the tracks. Modules make the same inferences about their proprietary inputs regardless of processes of learning and experience informing other aspects of mental activity.

The implications of modularity theory for accounts of cognitive evolution depend in part on how extensively modular the mind is envisaged to be. Fodor argued that modularity is only found at the margins of the mind, in its perceptual/input systems rather than in the heart of mental life where conscious, higher-level cognitive processes and the fixation of belief take place. Fodor's argument here was teleological: in the face of danger, for instance, it makes sense for perceptual inferences to be fast, mandatory, informationally encapsulated, etc. This is both a strength and a weakness of modular input systems, however. They deliver inferences fast, enabling swift responses to danger, but they are also liable to generate false positives and, thus, the wastage of resources on responses to non-dangerous signals *as if* they were dangerous. To compensate for this, Fodor postulated nonmodular, higher-level cognitive processes, capable of counteracting the more irrational inferences delivered by input systems, thereby (in theory) increasing the overall efficiency of the organism:

> If the perceptual mechanisms are indeed local, stupid, and extremely nervous, it is teleologically sensible to have the picture of the world that they present tempered, re-analyzed, and . . . above all *integrated* by slower, better informed, more conservative, and more holistic systems . . . Nature has contrived to have it both ways, to get the best out of fast dumb systems and slow contemplative ones, by simply refusing to choose between them (1983: 18).

Nevertheless, Fodor's argument is not without its drawbacks. Non-modularity in central processing (involved with reasoning, belief-fixation, decision-making, etc.) would not necessarily increase efficiency. Cognitive and behavioural evidence suggests that central processing is, in practice, highly error-prone and, of course, domain-general learning implies extremely slow and inefficient processes. Consider the complexity of teaching an undifferentiated neural network to recognize information as opposed to providing in advance a suitable programme for the task. More importantly (from an evolutionary perspective), even if we allow that domain-general, higher-level cognitive processes confer definite reproductive advantages, we are presented with the same problem confronting Piagetian perspectives (above) – how to model the specific processes by which such an advantageous computational system evolved. As Sperber points out in Chapter One, evolution proceeds in a short-sighted, piecemeal fashion – it does not produce massively complex designs out of the blue.

Sperber argues that one way to solve the problems posed by a Fodorian view of modularity-at-the-margins is to envisage the mind as thoroughly modular. Building on his earlier work with Deirdre Wilson, Sperber suggests that extensive modularity, coordinated by principles of *relevance* (Sperber and Wilson 1986), produces a phylogenetically plausible account of cognition. Sperber and Wilson originally focused primarily on utterance comprehension but, in Chapter One, Sperber applies the relevance model to central-processing tasks more generally.

Not all module-like effects, however, are interpreted within nativist epistemologies (see Elman, *et al.* 1996) and not all accounts of cognitive evolution envisage the mind as modular. For instance, Boyer in Chapter Two has little interest in postulating informationally-encapsulated cognitive modules, and focuses instead on evidence for intuitive ontological principles that, while normally operating on particular conceptual domains, are capable of being transferred between them. Such processes of transference, as we shall see, may be crucial to the development of religious concepts. Like Cosmides and Tooby (1994), Boyer envisages intuitive ontological principles as genetically specified. This allows a rich account of cognitive evolution without entertaining a specifically modular vision of the mind/brain.

Plotkin in Chapter Three is not greatly concerned about whether evolved cognitive architecture is modular or not – although it is, he argues, compartmentalized to a significant extent. Plotkin's main concern is to defend a nativist epistemology, in general terms, from the criticisms launched against it in Part Two of this volume. The case for a nativist stance, Plotkin argues, rests on three main arguments. First, human cognition is extremely complex and the emergence of complex mechanisms is in general a reliable indicator of the presence of specific evolutionary pressures. Secondly, the compartmentalization of human cognitive abilities suggests the presence of *specific* evolutionary pressures (as Sperber and Boyer also point out). Thirdly, Plotkin claims that experimental data (both psychological and ethological) overwhelmingly support nativist models of mind on the basis of the 'poverty of stimulus' argument. This argument, which has an impeccable pedigree in orthodox models of genetics, applies where the outputs of organisms are richer than the proximal inputs due to causes (e.g. genes) internal to the organisms. For instance, different anatomical features appear according to a predictable schedule in mammalian foetal development in a manner that cannot be caused solely by the proximal inputs to the unborn organism (delivered primarily through the umbilical cord). Likewise, Plotkin asserts, certain conceptual structures necessary for the acquisition of language and other cognitive abilities appear to develop in young children in a manner that is underdetermined by the proximal inputs.

According to Plotkin, the evolution of human intelligence must be understood as a 'two-way street' of causation between biology and culture. While maintaining, on the above grounds, that evolutionary forces have shaped the cognitive architecture that gives rise to culture, culture in turn has shaped human evolution by altering the environment within which natural selection operates. Plotkin illustrates this point with reference to the effects of long-term animal husbandry on the evolution of lactose tolerance in northern European populations.

Cognition and cultural transmission

As we have seen, the contributors to Part One of this volume argue that the evolution of the human brain under natural selection has resulted in a variety of specialized cognitive capacities which are established, in normal individuals and under normal conditions, according to a relatively fixed developmental schedule. It is proposed that these species-specific capacities limit the range of cultural variation by predisposing humans towards particular forms of sociality and concept-formation and by conferring a selective advantage on certain representations in the course of cultural transmission (all else being equal). Selectionist models play a particularly prominent role in Sperber's and Boyer's accounts of cultural recurrence.

Given certain evolved cognitive dispositions, Sperber suggests, humans are susceptible to particular types of representation. They are susceptible in the sense that they are more likely to remember and transmit certain representations than others. For instance, given the existence of innate mechanisms attuned to tonal variation, humans are more likely to remember and sing a song recently heard on the radio than they are to remember and recite the string of numbers that won the lottery last week. According to Sperber, the brain is thus a specialized computational device geared up for specific types of processing tasks. A typical analogue computer would require little memory to store a set of winning lottery numbers but require a lot of space to store the salient properties of a song. Having established what human minds are 'geared up' for, it should be possible to explain why some representations are widely selected, thus becoming part of culture, and others not.

In his Malinowski Memorial Lecture, Sperber (1985) first put forward the idea that the distribution of representations in society can be studied in much the same way as epidemiologists study the distribution of diseases. Some representations (like some diseases) are more contagious than others: fashions may spread suddenly and dramatically like epidemics; local traditions may be long-standing but not spread substantially beyond a definite region, just as diseases may become endemic within a given population; yet other representations may fall out of circulation or be confined to very small numbers of people, rather like rare diseases. The question is how we account for these and other patterns in the distribution of representations. For Sperber, the crucial process is one of *selection*.

One possibility is that representations are selected because they are logically implied by already existing cultural phenomena, have some sort of elective affinity with them, or serve the interests of power-holders. These possibilities (and others) have, of course, been extensively explored in social theory. Another possibility, presented by Sperber, is that innate mechanisms in the mind/brain render humans more likely to select some representations than others. For instance, according to Sperber, humans are especially susceptible to representations that can be organized taxonomically or which conform to established narrative structures. Moreover, Sperber suggests that humans are inclined to store and recall half-understood concepts, which are grounded in existing knowledge and assumptions but which depart radically from one's expectations in one or more specific respects.

Boyer's Chapter Two takes up and develops substantially Sperber's project, by specifying in considerable detail why certain representations might be more contagious than others as a result of certain properties of human cognition. Boyer's interest lies mainly in the contagious quality of what Sperber calls 'half-understood concepts': those representations that accord with existing assumptions in certain respects but violate them dramatically in certain others. A particularly obvious place to look for such concepts is religion, where adherents commonly postulate that there are beings without bodies (e.g. ghosts, gods, and other extranatural agencies), that there are planes of existence in which time is not durational (e.g. cyclical, 'frozen', partially parallel, etc.), that inanimate objects can behave like biological organisms (e.g. statues that weep, breath, bleed, etc.), and so on.

On the face of it, religious concepts appear to be highly variable and therefore unrelated to innate, universal structures of cognition. Boyer's contention, however, is that religious concepts violate intuitive ontological knowledge in a limited number of ways, and this is what makes them memorable or 'contagious'. Boyer's argument draws heavily on experimental evidence for the emergence of intuitive ontologies in the cognitive development of children according to a universal developmental schedule. The development of distinct ontological categories, such as 'person', 'animal', 'plant', and 'artefact' appears to be underdetermined by experience and for this reason partly caused by genetic factors. Moreover, the enrichment of intuitive ontological principles appears to follow an invariable pattern cross-culturally such that, for instance, certain principles of intuitive physics (e.g. objects move in continuous paths, unsupported objects fall downwards, etc.) invariably develop earlier than meta-representational conceptions (e.g. persons can entertain false beliefs, the thoughts of others can be inferred from their behaviour, etc.).

According to Boyer, religious representations run counter to intuitive ontological principles in two basic ways: first, by violating particular intuitive expectations (e.g. gods may exhibit all the characteristics of intentionality expectable on the basis of an innate 'theory of mind' mechanism and yet they may be endowed with additional counter-intuitive perceptual capabilities, such as the ability to 'see' people's desires and intentions directly without having to infer these things from behaviour); secondly, by transferring properties appropriate to objects in one onto-logical category onto another (e.g. artefacts that behave like persons, features of the landscape that are attributed organic properties, etc.). According to Boyer, concepts of extranatural agency are not random but entail specific violations and transfers of intuitive knowledge which can be predicted by his model. Concepts which are simply odd, as opposed to counter-intuitive, are much less widespread in religious culture. Boyer's point is that counter-intuitive representations involving violations or transfers between domains of intuitive knowledge enjoy a selective advantage in religious systems because they are especially easy to acquire, store, and communicate, given certain properties of the human mind-brain. Boyer supports his argument with a body of fresh experimental data designed to show that representations which are counter-intuitive in the ways identified in his model are easier to recall than other sorts of representation.

Boyer's and Sperber's epidemiological models bear comparison with 'co-evolution' selectionist theories of cultural transmission, of the sort developed by Richard Dawkins (1976; see also Durham 1991). As Boyer points out in Chapter Two, however, the co-evolutionists envisage cultural transmission as a process of *replicating* representations. When Sperber first set out the concept of an 'epidemiology of representations', he was at pains to emphasize that, whereas replication is normal in the trans-mission of viruses and mutation extremely rare, mutation is normal in the transmission of representations (1985: 75). This is because, as Boyer emphasizes, representations are not copied directly from one mind to another but, in Sperber's terminology, are spread through countless oscillations between mental and public, and public and mental, events or states. In the course of such oscillations, the forms of representations are constantly altered in subtle or not-so-subtle ways.

Moreover, according to Boyer's model, certain aspects of many religious representations do not have to be transmitted at all. To be sure, the specific ways in which such representations violate or transfer elements between domains of intuitive ontological knowledge need to be communicated (e.g. the notion that ghosts can pass through solid objects), but background intuitive assumptions applied to extranatural agents (e.g. that ghosts as quasi-persons have ordinary properties of intentionality), which Boyer regards as innate, are activated by default and therefore do not have to be explicitly articulated in order for the cultural representations to reproduce and spread. Although social anthropologists tend to assume that all ideas about the behaviour of ghosts in a particular culture must have been transmitted to each new generation, Boyer's point is that certain aspects of what people know about ghosts is based on intuitive assumptions about persons generally that develop automatically (rather than having to be explicitly taught). The problem, according to Boyer, stems from the fact that co-evolutionists, like most social anthropologists, assume that culture is acquired through a general learning mechanism, whereas the evidence from cognitive science suggests the presence of innate dispositions to 'package' knowledge in domain-specific ways.

As we have seen, Plotkin explicitly supports the nativist epistemology, adopted by Sperber and Boyer, but he extends their arguments about the impact of evolved cognitive architecture on cultural representations to the realm of social constructions more generally. For instance, he argues for the evolution, under natural selection, of cognitive devices that have conflict-reducing effects within small social groups. One such mechanism (or suite of mechanisms), which Plotkin glosses as 'social force', may have emerged from evolutionary pressures favouring a psychological disposition to accept group consensus. Any such disposition, however, presupposes that humans are capable of attributing thoughts, feelings, intentions, and beliefs to others. Recent evidence of a specialized, genetically prespecified cognitive device for 'mindreading' (i.e. a 'theory of mind' module), which shows varying degrees of impairment in such conditions as autism (see Whiten 1991), supports Plotkin's argument that some general aspects of human sociality are directly shaped by particular evolved cognitive capacities.

The challenge to neo-Darwinian evolutionary biology and cognitive science

Although fundamentally consistent with conventional assumptions and models in the biological sciences, almost every detail of the above account of the evolution of human intelligence is challenged in Part Two of this volume. Ingold observes in Chapter Four that neo-Darwinian evolutionary theory is premised on the notion that genes carry a set of plans or specifications for the development of organic form, even though biologists readily concede that these specifications can only be realized under particular developmental conditions. According to Ingold, this viewpoint is internally contradictory. If genes may be said to carry the information for building organic form then it must be possible to map consistently certain properties of DNA directly onto properties of form in a manner that is entirely independent of the process and context of development. Ingold's contention is that this will never be possible because organic form results from a wider set of circumstances of organic development, including genetic processes and environmental contexts. Thus, to describe any causal factor in the developmental process as a 'specification' or 'programme' for development is to misrepresent and potentially to misunderstand the actual situation. Instead, Ingold advocates a 'developmental systems' approach to genetics and evolution, which dispenses with such dichotomies as 'genes versus environment' and 'nature versus nurture', and argues that 'organic form . . . arises as an emergent property of the total system of relations set up by virtue of the presence of the organism in its environment' (p. 123).

In Ingold's view, the same faulty reasoning by which the operation of genes is conventionally held to be entailed in evolution is reproduced and compounded in cognitivist theories of cultural transmission. The error is reproduced insofar as the development of certain mental structures is thought to be 'specified' by the human genome; it is compounded where mental structures are described as having been actually pre-constructed by the genome, as Ingold argues is implied by certain passages in Sperber's writings. This profoundly affects both the terminology and conceptual frames of those approaches to transmission advanced in Part One. Assuming the existence of genetically specified processing devices in the mind/brain, these are seen as requiring to be 'filled up' by informational content. Thus, such processes as learning how to speak or recognize the effects of gravity are described by Sperber, Boyer, Plotkin, and others as forms of 'acquisition' ('acquiring' language, naive physics, etc.). The structures engaged in this sort of acquisition are meanwhile described as 'capacities'. As a result, Ingold argues that the matter of learning culture is misconstrued as a process of 'filling up modules' rather than of building and developing skills through varied experiences.

According to Ingold, one of the most crippling disadvantages of the cognitivist approach is that, having focused attention primarily on innate computational capacities, the realization of these capacities in practice appears to be comparatively simple and unproblematic. Expressing this in the Chomskean framework advocated by Plotkin, Ingold challenges the prioritizing of 'competence' over 'performance' as the area of greatest complexity and theoretical importance. As with the related dichotomies between genes and environment, nature and nurture, evolution and history, Ingold rejects the competence/performance distinction. But he points out that if we focus on what cognitivists take 'performance' to mean, it is clearly an extraordinarily complex process. For Ingold, it is also the appropriate starting point for any theory of how culture is constructed.

Through detailed consideration of what various kinds of cultural performances involve, Ingold suggests that these do not consist of the execution of pre-formed computational plans but resemble the unfolding of streams of consciousness. According to Ingold, planning and carrying out plans for acting in the world are rarely (if ever) separate mental operations, but are indissoluble elements of enactment itself.

Ingold's fundamental point is that in developmental systems of any type, no single element can be cast in an executive position, formulating plans which the rest of the system is required to implement. Just as Ingold criticizes evolutionary theory for presupposing that sets of instructions in the form of genes are passed down through the generations independently of developmental processes, he rejects the cognitivist approach to cultural transmission in which representations are assumed to be passed on independently of the same developmental processes. For Ingold, human knowledge is not reducible to sets of 'representations'. In what sense, asks Ingold, does a tune which I whistle as I walk down the street 'represent' anything (other than itself)? A tune, or for that matter an utterance, a gesture, or any of the other events that Sperber describes as 'representations' do not occur separately in public and mental modalities. They are, according to Ingold, manifestations of skill, expressed in developmental contexts. Borrowing a phrase from James Gibson (1979), Ingold suggests that we envisage learning, not as a process of transmitting things, but as a process of 'the education of attention', which is one of continuous sensitization and reorientation to the world through the labours of maturation.

If Ingold is correct, neo-Darwinian evolutionary theory, along with cognitive science which tends to caricature certain of its tenets, is a circular but powerful ideology. Toren meanwhile argues that *all* theories of the relationship between mind, evolution, and culture are necessarily ideological in important respects. Cognitive theories, she suggests, must be viewed in cultural and historical contexts. One object of such an exercise might be to distil from the contrasts in diverse cultural models of development and learning a more generalizable perspective on these topics.

Toren observes that the sorts of dichotomies (biology/culture, nature/nurture, competence/performance, etc.) which Ingold rejects on the grounds of circularity, are not entertained in the first place in Fijian models of child development. What Toren calls 'natural science models of mind' make certain assumptions that inhibit or even foreclose the possibility of understanding the ideas and practices of Fijians. In particular, the approaches of Sperber, Boyer, and Plotkin detach mental processes, as well as their own *models* of mental processes, from the historical and personal conditions in which both are generated, thereby overlooking the intersubjective and historically situated character of mental life and scientific accounts of it.

Toren argues that cognitivist perspectives envisage the mind primarily as an information-processing device which operates in a fundamentally similar manner in all individuals. In this way, the rational, logical, and relatively invariable aspects of mental life are treated as a distinct domain of investigation and analysis, the domain of cognitive science. The personal, variable, and affective dimensions of the human psyche are dealt with separately as the domain of those fields of psychology concerned with 'personality', life history, and emotional development. This is so, argues Toren, despite overwhelming evidence within the field of psychology itself that 'affect is a dimension of problem-solving and that emotion inevitably implicates cognition' (pp. 219–20).

Toren accounts for the separation of cognition and emotion in psychology in terms of the underlying assumptions of Western individualism. In Fiji, where such cultural constructs are traditionally lacking, personhood is construed relationally. Through a fine-grained description of the Fijian concept of *madua* (roughly 'shame'), its role in interpersonal struggles for 'effectiveness' in social relations, and in child development more generally, Toren follows Ingold in challenging the idea that culture is 'acquired', as if culture were somehow external to the mind-as-processor-of-culture. Toren describes children as 'constituting' (rather than 'acquiring') the categories in whose terms adults talk about the world, as 'making themselves' in inter-subjective relations with others over time through a developmental process of 'autopoiesis', that is the psychological correlate of physiological development.

Nuckolls' argument explicitly endorses and builds upon aspects of Toren's critique of Part One. Like Toren, Nuckolls suggests that the neglect of emotion and motivation in cognitive science seriously undermines its contribution to our understanding of mental life. But, whereas Toren believes that the models and methods of cognitive science are beyond repair, Nuckolls suggests that these models could be adapted successfully to accommodate both the dynamic unconscious, operating at an individual level, and cultural constraints on mental activity, operating at a collective level. What is needed, according to Nuckolls, is a synthesis of cognitivism, psychoanalysis, and social/cultural theory.

Unlike Ingold and Toren, Nuckolls agrees with the contributors to Part One that the naturalness of universal developmental schedules may derive from evolved neural architecture. Further, he endorses Sperber's and Boyer's project to construct an epidemiology of representations, and he agrees that the memorability of representations is a major part of what needs to be explained in this context. But, like the other contributors to Part Two, Nuckolls adopts a trenchantly critical stance on certain basic assumptions of cognitive science.

According to Nuckolls, cognitivism is premissed on a notion of mind denuded of its most encompassing and characteristic mechanisms. Following Toren, he traces this deficiency to a failure within cognitive science to reflect on the historical conditions of its own genesis. Cognitivism, he suggests, is ensnared by the ontological commitments of Enlightenment thinkers, who construed knowledge and rationality as emotionless and unconflicted. Thus, the major discovery by psychoanalysis of a cognitive unconscious formed through deep motivational conflict has largely passed unnoticed by cognitive scientists. It is true that most advocates of psychoanalysis, to their detriment, have tended to settle for evidence of an anecdotal kind but this is not sufficient to explain the neglect of such models in Part One. As Nuckolls points out, the presence of a cognitive unconscious has already been supported experimentally, for instance in studies of priming and transference effects predicted by psychoanalytic theory. Nuckolls argues for a version of psychoanalytic theory capable of expressing and testing its hypotheses with the same precision and rigour as experimental research in cognitive science.

Nuckolls builds his argument primarily with reference to Boyer's claims about the cognitive causes of counter-intuitive religious representations. While Boyer is able to specify certain constraints on the range of possible representations of extranatural agency, his theory does not explain why particular representations are selected from this range, and not others. Nuckolls cites ethnographic evidence from South India supporting his view that unconscious relational schemas, formed in childhood, deliver mutually unfulfillable desires that it is the task of cultural schemas to resolve. This they do by representing extranatural agents who condense precisely psychoanalytically-postulated forms of ambivalence generated unconsciously. In this view, the distribution of cultural representations is not simply an outcome of selectional processes constrained by the organization of intuitive ontological knowledge, but is more productively understood in terms of the interaction of cultural systems and conflicting unconscious motivations/schemas.

The debates outlined here unfold below in a particularly lively, at times even ferocious, fashion. If ever one required examples of the way emotion is implicated in conscious thought, as Toren and Nuckolls argue, this volume provides them. But, after all, no synthesis ever came about in the absence of oppositions and tensions, and few would deny that the production of theoretical knowledge in general is often a dialectical process.

References

Barkow, J., Cosmides, L. and Tooby, J. (eds) (1992), *The Adapted Mind: Evolutionary Psychology and the Generation of Culture*, New York: Oxford Universty Press.

Bechtel, W. and Abrahamsen, A. (1991), *Connectionism and the Mind: an Introduction to Parallel Processing in Networks*, Oxford: Blackwell.

Bellugi, U., Marks, S., Bihrle, A. M., and Sabo, H. (1988), 'Dissociation between language and cognitive functions in Williams Syndrome', in D. Bishop and K. Mogford (eds), *Language Development in Exceptional Circumstances*, Edinburgh: Churchill Livingstone.

Chase, W. and Simon, H. (1973), 'The mind's eye in chess', in W. Chase (ed.), *Visual Information Processing*, New York: Academic Press.

Clark, A. (1987), 'The kludge in the machine', *Mind and Language*, 2: 277–300.

Cosmides, L. and Tooby, J. (1994), 'Beyond intuition and instinct blindness: towards an evolutionarily rigorous cognitive science', *Cognition*, 50: 41–87.

Curtis, S. (1982), 'Developmental dissociation of language and cognition', in L.K. Obler and L. Menn (eds), *Exceptional Language and Linguistics*, New York: Academic Press.

Dawkins. R. (1976), *The Selfish Gene*, New York: Oxford University Press.

Dunbar. R.I.M. (1993), 'Coevolution of neocortical size, group size, and language in humans', *The Behavioural and Brain Sciences*, 16: 681–735.

Durham, W.H. (1991), *Coevolution, Genes, Cultures, and Human Diversity*, Stanford: Stanford University Press.

Edelman, G. (1992), *Bright Air, Brilliant Fire: on the Matter of the Mind*, London: Penguin.

Elman, J.L., Bates, E.A., Johnson, M.H., Karmiloff-Smith, A., Parisi, D. and Plunkett, K. (1996), *Rethinking Innateness: A Connectionist Perspective on Development*, Cambridge Mass.: MIT Press.

Fodor, J.A. (1983), *The Modularity of Mind*, Cambridge, Mass.: MIT Press.

Garcia, J. and Koelling, R. (1966), 'Relation of cue to consequence in avoidance learning', *Psychonomics Science*, 4: 123–4.

Gibson, J.J. (1979), *The Ecological Approach to Visual Perception*, Boston: Houghton Mifflin.

Hirschfeld, L.A. and Gelman, S.A. (eds) (1994), *Mapping the Mind: Domain Specificity in Cognition and Culture*, New York: Cambridge University Press.

Jusczyk, P.W. and Bertoncini, J. (1988), 'Viewing the development of speech perception as an innately guided learning process', *Language and Speech*, 31: 217–38.

Karmiloff-Smith, A. (1992) *Beyond Modularity: a Developmental Perspective on Cognitive Science*, Cambridge, Mass.: MIT Press.

Keil, F.C. (1989), *Concepts, Kinds, and Cognitive Development*, Cambridge, Mass.: MIT Press.

—— (1990) 'Constraints on constraints: surveying the epigenetic landscape', *Cognitive Science*, 14: 135–68.

Kellman, P.J. and Spelke, E.S. (1983), 'Perception of partly occluded objects in infancy', *Cognitive Psychology*, 15: 483–524.

Mehler, J., Lambertz, G., Jusczyk, P.W., and Amiel-Tison, C. (1986), 'Discrimination de la langue maternelle par le nouveau-né', *Comptes Rendus Académie des Sciences*, 303: 637–40.

Pinker, S. (1994), *The Language Instinct*, London: Allen Lane.

Sejnowski, T.J. and Rosenberg, C.R. (1987), 'Parallel networks that learn to pronounce English text', *Complex Systems*, 1: 145–68.

Slobin, D. (1985), *The Crosslinguistic Study of Language Acquisition*, Hillsdale, NJ: Erlbaum.

Spelke, E.S. (1988), 'Where perceiving ends and thinking begins: the apprehension of objects in infancy', in A. Yonas (ed.), *Perceptual Development in Infancy*, Hillsdale, NJ: Erlbaum.

—— (1990), 'Principles of object perception', *Cognitive Science*, 14: 29–56.

Sperber, D. (1985), 'Anthropology and psychology: towards an epidemiology of representations', *Man* (N.S.), 20: 73–89.

—— and Wilson, D. (1986), *Relevance: Communication and Cognition*, Cambridge, Mass.: Harvard University Press.

Whiten, A. (1991) (ed.), *Natural Theories of Mind: The Evolution, Development, and Simulation of Everyday Mindreading*, Oxford: Blackwell.

PART ONE

–1–

Mental Modularity and Cultural Diversity[1]

Dan Sperber

In *The Modularity of Mind*, published in 1983, Jerry Fodor attacked the then dominant view according to which there are no important discontinuities between perceptual processes and conceptual processes. Information flows freely, 'up' and 'down', between these two kinds of processes, and beliefs inform perception as much as they are informed by it. Against this view, Fodor argued that perceptual processes (and also linguistic decoding) are carried out by specialized, rather rigid mechanisms. Each of these 'modules' has its own proprietary data base, and does not draw on information produced by conceptual processes.

Although this was probably not intended and has not been much noticed, 'modularity of mind' was a paradoxical title, for, according to Fodor, modularity is to be found only at the periphery of the mind, in its input systems.[2] In its centre and bulk, Fodor's mind is decidedly non-modular. Conceptual processes – that is, thought proper – are presented as a big holistic lump lacking joints at which to carve. Controversies have focused on the thesis that perceptual and linguistic decoding processes are modular, much more than on the alleged nonmodularity of thought.

In this chapter, I have two aims. My first aim is to defend the view that thought processes might be modular too (what Fodor [1987: 27] calls 'modularity theory gone mad' – oh well!). Let me however echo Fodor and say that, 'when I speak of a cognitive system as modular, I shall . . . always mean "to some interesting extent"' (Fodor, 1983: 37). My second aim is to articulate a modular view of human thought with the naturalistic view of human culture that I have been developing under the label 'epidemiology of representations' (Sperber, 1985b). These aims are closely related: Cultural diversity has always been taken to show how plastic the human mind is, whereas the modularity of thought thesis seems to deny that plasticity. I want to show how, contrary to the received view, organisms endowed with truly modular minds might engender truly diverse cultures.

Dan Sperber

Two commonsense arguments against the modularity of thought

Abstractly and roughly at least, the distinction between perceptual and conceptual processes is clear: Perceptual processes have, as input, information provided by sensory receptors and, as output, a conceptual representation categorizing the object perceived. Conceptual processes have conceptual representations both as input and as output. Thus seeing a cloud and thinking 'here is a cloud' is a perceptual process. Inferring from this perception 'it might rain' is a conceptual process.

The rough idea of modularity is also clear: A cognitive module is a genetically specified computational device in the mind/brain (henceforth: The mind) that works pretty much on its own on inputs pertaining to some specific cognitive domain and provided by other parts of the nervous systems (e.g., sensory receptors or other modules). Given such notions, the view that perceptual processes might be modular is indeed quite plausible, as argued by Fodor. On the other hand, there are two main commonsense arguments (and several more technical ones) that lead one to expect conceptual thought processes not to be modular.

The first commonsense argument against the modularity of thought has to do with integration of information. The conceptual level is the level at which information from different input modules, each presumably linked to some sensory modality, gets integrated into a modality-independent medium: a dog can be seen, heard, smelled, touched, and talked about. The percepts are different, the concept is the same. As Fodor points out,

> the general form of the argument goes back at least to Aristotle: The representations that input systems deliver have to interface somewhere, and the computational mechanisms that effect the interface must *ipso facto* have access to information from more than one cognitive domain (Fodor, 1983: 101–2).

The second commonsense argument against the modularity of thought has to do with cultural diversity and novelty. An adult human's conceptual processes range over an indefinite variety of domains, including party politics, baseball history, motorcycle maintenance, Zen Buddhism, French cuisine, Italian opera, chess playing, stamp collecting, and Fodor's chosen example, modern science. The appearance of many of these domains in human cognition is very recent and not relevantly correlated with changes in the human genome. Many of these domains vary dramatically in content from one culture to another, or are not found at all in many cultures. In such conditions, it would be absurd to assume that there is an *ad hoc* genetically specified preparedness for these culturally developed conceptual domains.

These two commonsense arguments are so compelling that Fodor's more technical considerations (having to do with 'isotropy', illusions, rationality, etc.) look like mere nails in the coffin of a dead idea. My goal will be to shake the commonsense picture and to suggest that the challenge of articulating modularity, conceptual integration, and cultural diversity may be met and will turn out to be a source of psychological and anthropological insights.

Notice, to begin with, that both the informational integration argument and the cultural diversity argument are quite compatible with partial modularity at the conceptual level.

True, it would be functionally self-defeating to reproduce at the conceptual level the same domain partition found at the perceptual level, and have a different conceptual module treat separately the output of each perceptual module. No integration whatsoever would take place, and the dog seen and the dog heard could never be one and the very same mastiff Goliath. But who says conceptual domains have to match perceptual domains? Why not envisage, at the conceptual level, a wholly different, more or less orthogonal domain partition, with each domain-specific conceptual mechanism getting its inputs from several input mechanisms? For instance, all the conceptual outputs of perceptual modules that contain the concept MASTIFF (and that are therefore capable of recognizing the presence of a mastiff) might be fed into a specialized module (say a domain-specific inferential device handling living-kind concepts) which takes care (*inter alia*) of Goliath *qua* mastiff. Similarly, all the conceptual outputs of input modules which contain the concept THREE might be fed into a specialized module which handles inference about numbers, and so forth. In this way, information from different input devices might get genuinely integrated, though not into a single, but into several conceptual systems.

Of course if you have, say, a prudential rule that tells you to run away when you encounter more than two bellicose dogs, you would not really be satisfied to be informed by the living-kinds module that the category BELLICOSE DOG is instantiated in your environment, and by the numerical module that there are more than two of something. Some further, at least partial, integration had better take place. It might even be argued – though that is by no means obvious – that a plausible model of human cognition should allow for full integration of all conceptual information at some level. Either way, partial or full integration might take place further up the line, among the outputs of conceptual rather than of perceptual modules. Conceptual integration is not incompatible with at least some conceptual modularity.

Similarly, the conceptual diversity argument implies that some conceptual domains (expertise in postage stamps for instance) could not be modular. It certainly does not imply that none of them could be. Thus, in spite of superficial variations, living-kind classification exhibits strong commonalities across cultures (see Berlin, 1978) in a manner that does suggest the presence of a domain-specific cognitive module (see Atran, 1987, 1990).

The thesis that some central thought processes might be modular gets support from a wealth of recent work (well illustrated in Hirschfeld and Gelman 1994) tending to show that many basic conceptual thought processes, found in every culture and in every fully developed human, are governed by domain-specific competences. For instance, it is argued that people's ordinary understanding of the movements of an inert solid object, of the appearance of an organism, or of the actions of a person are based on three distinct mental mechanisms, a naive physics, a naive biology, and a naive psychology (see for instance Atran 1987, 1994; Carey, 1985; Keil 1989, 1994; Leslie 1987, 1988, 1994; Spelke 1988). It is argued moreover that these mechanisms, at least in rudimentary form, are part of the equipment that makes acquisition of knowledge possible, rather than being acquired competences.

Accepting as a possibility some degree of modularity in conceptual systems is innocuous enough. Jerry Fodor himself recently considered favourably the view that 'intentional folk psychology is, essentially, an innate, *modularized* database' (Fodor,1992: 284 – italics added) without suggesting that he was thereby departing from his former views on modularity. But what about the possibility of massive modularity at the conceptual level? Do the two commonsense arguments, integration and diversity, really rule it out?

Modularity and evolution

If modularity is a genuine natural phenomenon, an aspect of the organisation of the brain, then what it consists of is a matter of discovery, not stipulation. Fodor himself discusses a number of characteristic and diagnostic features of modularity. Modules, he argues, are 'domain-specific, innately specified, hardwired, autonomous' (1983: 36). Their operations are mandatory (p. 52) and fast (p. 61); they are 'informationally encapsulated' (p. 64), that is, the only background information available to them is that found in their proprietary data base. Modules are 'associated with fixed neural architecture' (p. 98). Fodor discusses still other features that are not essential to the present discussion.

There is one feature of modularity that is implied by Fodor's description, but that he does not mention or discuss. If, as Fodor argues, a module is innately specified, hardwired, and autonomous, then it follows that a cognitive module is an evolved mechanism with a distinct phylogenetic history. This is a characteristic, but hardly a diagnostic feature, because we know close to nothing about the actual evolution of cognitive modules. But I have been convinced by Leda Cosmides and John Tooby (see Cosmides 1989, Cosmides and Tooby 1987, 1994; Tooby and Cosmides 1989, 1992)[3] that we know enough about evolution on the one hand and cognition on the other to come up with well-motivated (though, of course, tentative) assumptions as to when to expect modularity, what properties to expect of modules, and even what modules to expect. This section of the chapter owes much to their ideas.

Fodor himself does mention evolutionary considerations, but only in passing. He maintains that, phylogenetically, modular input systems should have preceded nonmodular central systems:

> Cognitive evolution would thus have been in the direction of gradually freeing certain sorts of problem-solving systems from the constraints under which input analysers labour – hence of producing, as a relatively late achievement, the comparatively domain-free inferential capacities which apparently mediate the higher flights of cognition (Fodor 1983: 43).

Let us spell out some of the implications of Fodor's evolutionary suggestion. At an early stage of cognitive evolution we should find modular sensory input analysers directly connected to modular motor controllers. There is no level yet where information from several perceptual processes would be integrated by a conceptual process. Then there emerges a conceptual device, that is, an inferential device that is not itself directly linked to sensory receptors. This conceptual device accepts input from two or more perceptual devices, constructs new representations warranted by these inputs, and transmits information to motor-control mechanisms.

Initially, of course, this conceptual device is just another module: It is specialized, innately wired, fast, automatic, and so forth. Then, so the story should go, it grows and becomes less specialized – possibly it merges with other similar conceptual devices – to the point where it is a single big conceptual system, able to process all the outputs of all the perceptual modules, and able to manage all the conceptual information available to the organism. This true central system cannot, in performing a given cognitive task, activate all the data accessible to it, or exploit all of its many procedures. Automaticity and speed are no longer possible. Indeed, if the central system automatically did what it is capable of doing, this would trigger a computational explosion with no end in sight.

An evolutionary account of the emergence of a conceptual module in a mind that had known only perceptual processes is simple enough to imagine. Its demodularization would be much harder to explain.

A toy example might go like this: Organisms of a certain species, call them 'protorgs', are threatened by a danger of a certain kind. This danger (the approach of elephants that might trample the protorgs, as it might be) is signalled by the co-occurrence of a noise N and soil vibrations V. Protorgs have an acoustic perception module that detects instances of N and a vibration-perception module that detects instances of V. The detection either of N by one perceptual module or of V by the other activates an appropriate flight procedure. Fine, except that when N occurs alone, or when V occurs alone, it so happens that there is no danger. So protorgs end up with a lot of 'false positives', uselessly running away, and thus wasting energy and resources.

Some descendants of the protorgs, call them 'orgs', have evolved another mental device: A conceptual inference mechanism. The perceptual modules no longer directly activate the flight procedure. Rather their relevant outputs, that is, the identification of noise N and that of vibrations V, go to the new device. This conceptual mechanism acts essentially as an AND-gate: When, and only when both N and V have been perceptually identified, does the conceptual mechanism get into a state that can be said to represent the presence of danger, and it is this state that activates the appropriate flight procedure.

Orgs, so the story goes, competed successfully with protorgs for food resources, and that is why you won't find protorgs around. The orgs' conceptual mechanism, though not an input module, is nevertheless a clear case of a module: It is a domain-specific problem-solver; it is fast, informationally encapsulated, associated with fixed neural architecture, and so forth. Of course, it is a tiny module, but nothing stops us from imagining it becoming larger: Instead of accepting just two bits of information from two simple perceptual modules, the conceptual module could come to handle more from more sources, and to control more than a single motor procedure, but still be domain-specific, automatic, fast, and so on.

At this juncture, we have two diverging evolutionary scenarios on offer. According to the scenario suggested by Fodor, the conceptual module should evolve towards less domain-specificity, less informational encapsulation, less speed, and so on. In other words, it would become less and less modular, possibly merging with other demodularized devices, and ending up like the kind of central system with which Fodor believes we are endowed ('Quineian', 'isotropic', etc.). There are two gaps in this scenario. The first gap has to do with mental mechanisms and is highlighted by Fodor himself in his 'First Law of the Nonexistence of Cognitive Science'. This law says in substance that the mechanisms of nonmodular thought processes are too complex to be understood. So, just accept that there are such mechanisms and don't ask how they work!

The second gap in Fodor's scenario has to do with the evolutionary process itself that is supposed to bring about the development of such a mysterious mechanism. No doubt, it might be advantageous to trade a few domain-specific inferential micromodules for an advanced all-purpose macro-intelligence, if there is any such thing. For instance, super-orgs endowed with general intelligence might develop technologies to eradicate the danger once and for all instead of having to flee again and again. But evolution does not offer such starkly contrasted choices. The available alternatives at any one time are all small departures from the existing state. Selection, the main force driving evolution, is near-sighted (whereas the other forces, genetic drift, etc., are blind). An immediately advantageous alternative is likely to be selected from the narrow available range, and this may bar the path to highly advantageous long-term outcomes. A demodularization scenario is implausible for this very reason.

Suppose indeed that the conceptual danger analyser is modified in some mutant orgs, not in the direction of performing better at its special task, but in that of less domain-specificity. The modified conceptual device processes not just information relevant to the orgs' immediate chances of escape, but also information about innocuous features of the dangerous situation, and about a variety of innocuous situations exhibiting these further features; the device draws inferences not just of an urgent practical kind, but also of a more theoretical character. When danger is detected, the new, less modular system does not automatically trigger flight behaviour, and when it does, it does so more slowly – automaticity and speed go with modularity – but it has interesting thoughts that are filed in memory for the future . . . if there is any future for mutant orgs endowed with this partly demodularized device.

Of course, speed and automaticity are particularly important for danger analysers, and less so for other plausible modules, for instance modules governing the choice of sexual partners. However, the general point remains: Evolved cognitive modules are likely to be answers to specific, usually environmental problems. Loosening the domain of a module will bring about not greater flexibility, but greater slack in the organism's response to the problem. To the limited extent that evolution goes toward improving a species' biological endowments, then we should generally expect improvements in the manner in which existing modules perform their task, emergence of new modules to handle other problems, but not demodularization. True, it is possible to conceive of situations in which the marginal demodularization of a conceptual device might be advantageous, or at least not detrimental, in spite of the loss of speed and reliability involved. Imagine, for instance, that the danger the conceptual module was initially selected to analyse has vanished from the environment; then the module is not adapted any more and a despecialization would do no harm. On the other hand why should it do any good? Such odd possibilities fall quite short of suggesting a positive account of the manner in which, to repeat Fodor's words, 'cognitive evolution would . . . have been in the direction of gradually freeing certain sorts of problem-solving systems from the constraints under which input analysers labour'. It is not that this claim could not be right, but it is poorly supported. In fact the only motivation for it seems to be the wish to integrate the belief that human thought processes are nonmodular in some evolutionary perspective, however vague. Better officialize the explanatory gap with a 'Second Law of the Nonexistence of Cognitive Science', according to which the forces that have driven cognitive evolution can never be identified.[4] Just accept that cognitive evolution occurred (and resulted in the demodularization of thought) and don't ask how.

Instead of starting from an avowedly enigmatic view of Homo Sapiens's thought processes and concluding that their past evolution is an unfathomable mystery, one might start from evolutionary considerations plausible in their own right and wonder what kind of cognitive organization these might lead one to expect in a species which we know relies heavily on its cognitive abilities for its survival. This yields our second scenario.

As already suggested, it is reasonable to expect conceptual modules to gain in complexity, fine-grainedness, and inferential sophistication in the performance of their function. As with any biological device, the function of a module may vary over time, but there is no reason to expect new functions to be systematically more general than old ones. It is reasonable, on the other hand, to expect new conceptual modules to appear in response to different kinds of problem or opportunity. Thus more and more modules should accumulate.

Because each cognitive module is the result of a different phylogenetic history, there is no reason to expect all cognitive modules to be built on the same general pattern and elegantly interconnected. Though most if not all conceptual modules are inferential devices, the inferential procedures that they use may be quite diverse. Therefore, from a modular point of view, it is unreasonable to ask what is the general form of human inference (logical rules, pragmatic schemas, mental models, etc.) as is generally done in the literature on human reasoning. (See Manktelow and Over 1990 for a recent review.)

The 'domains' of modules may vary in character and in size: there is no reason to expect each domain-specific module to handle a domain of comparable size. In particular there is no reason to exclude micromodules the domain of which is the size of a concept rather than that of a semantic field. In fact, I will argue that many human concepts are individually modular. Because conceptual modules are likely to be many, their interconnections and their connections with perceptual and motor-control modules may be quite diverse too. As argued by Andy Clark (1987, 1990), we had better think of the mind as *kludge*, with sundry bits and components added at different times, and interconnected in ways that would make an engineer cringe.

Modularity and conceptual integration

The input to the first conceptual modules to have appeared in cognitive evolution must have come from the perceptual modules. However, once some conceptual modules were in place, their output could serve as input to other conceptual modules.

Suppose the orgs can communicate among themselves by means of a small repertoire of vocal signals. Suppose further that the optimal interpretation of some of these signals is sensitive to contextual factors. For instance, an ambiguous danger signal indicates the presence of a snake when emitted by an org on a tree, and approaching elephants when emitted by an org on the ground. Identifying the signals and the relevant contextual information is done by perceptual modules. The relevant output of these perceptual modules is processed by an *ad hoc* conceptual module that interprets the ambiguous signals. Now, it would be a significant improvement if the conceptual module specialized in inferring the approach of elephants would accept as input not only perceptual information on specific noises and soil vibrations but also interpretations of the relevant signals emitted by other orgs. If so, this danger-inferring conceptual module would receive input not just from perceptual modules but also from another conceptual module, the context-sensitive signal interpreter.

In the human case, it is generally taken for granted that domain-specific abilities can handle not just primary information belonging to their domain and provided by perception but also verbally or pictorially communicated information. Thus experiments on the development of zoological knowledge use as material, not actual animals, but pictures or verbal descriptions. This methodology would deserve discussion, but it does not seem to raise serious problems. This in itself is quite remarkable.

Then too, some conceptual modules might get all of their input from other conceptual modules. Imagine for instance that an org emits a danger signal only when two conditions are fulfilled: It must have inferred the presence of a danger on the one hand, and that of friendly orgs at risk on the other hand. Both inferences are performed by conceptual modules. If so, then the conceptual module that decides whether or not to emit the danger signal gets all of its input from other conceptual modules, and none from perceptual ones. We are now envisaging a complex network of conceptual modules: some conceptual modules get all of their input from perceptual modules, other modules get at least some of their input from conceptual modules, and so forth. Every piece of information may get combined with many others across or within levels and in various ways (though overall conceptual integration seems excluded). What would be the behaviour of an organism endowed with such complex modular thought processes? Surely, we don't know. Would it behave in a flexible manner as humans do? Its responses could at least be extremely fine-grained. Is there more to flexibility than this fine-grainedness? 'Flexibility' is a metaphor without a clear literal interpretation, and therefore it is hard to tell. Still, when we think of flexibility in the human case, we particularly have in mind the ability to learn from experience. Can a fully modular system learn? Imprinting is a very simple form of modular learning. What, for instance, do orgs know about one another? If orgs are non-learning animals, they might be merely endowed with a conspecific detector and detectors for some properties of other orgs such as sex or age, but they might otherwise be unable to detect any single individual as such – not even, say, their own mothers. Or, if they are very primitive learners, they might have a mother-detector module the workings of which will be fixed once and for all by the new-born org's first perception of a large moving creature in its immediate vicinity (hopefully its real mum), and of the resultant imprinting of the relevant information. The module then becomes a detector for the particular individual who caused the imprinting.

More generally, I wish to introduce here a technical notion, that of initialization, borrowed from computer vocabulary. A cognitive module may, just like a computer program, be incomplete in the sense that specific pieces of information must be fixed before it can function normally. An email program for instance may ask you to fix a few parameters (e.g. baud rate or parity) and to fill empty slots (e.g. phone numbers to call or password). It is only after having been so initialized that your program can work. Similarly, first-language learning, according to Noam Chomsky (1986) (whose work was seminal in the development of a modularist approach to the human mind – see Hirschfeld and Gelman 1984, Introduction), involves in particular the fixing of several grammatical parameters common to all languages of the values these parameters take in the language to be learnt, and the filling in of a lexicon. To initialize a cognitive module is thus a matter of fixing parameter values and of filling empty slots. The initialization of the mother-detector described in the preceding paragraph involves just filling its single empty slot with the perceptual representation of a single individual.

If they are slightly more sophisticated learners, orgs may have the capacity to construct several detectors for different individual conspecifics. They might have a template module quite similar to a mother-detector, except that it can be 'initialized' several times, each time projecting a differently initialized copy of itself that is specialized for the identification of a different individual. Would the initialized copies of the template module be modules too? I don't see why not. The only major difference is that these numerous projected modules seem less likely to be hard-wired than a single mother-detector module. Otherwise, both kinds of module get initialized and operate in exactly the same manner. Of our more sophisticated orgs, we would want to say, then, that they had a modular domain-specific ability to mentally represent conspecific individuals, an ability resulting in the generation of micromodules for each represented individual.

Consider in this light the human domain-specific ability to categorize living kinds. One possibility is that there is an initial template module for living-kind concepts that gets initialized many times, producing each time a new micromodule corresponding to one living-kind concept (the DOG module, the CAT module, the GOLDFISH module, etc.). Thinking of such concepts as modules may take some getting-used-to, I admit. Let me help: Concepts are domain-specific (obviously), they have a proprietary data-basis (the encyclopaedic information filed under the concept), and they are autonomous computational devices. (They work, I will argue, on representations in which the right concept occurs, just as digestive enzymes work on food in which the right molecule occurs.) When, on top of all that, concepts are partly genetically specified (via some domain-specific conceptual template), they are modular at least to some interesting extent, no?

The template–copy relationship might sometimes involve more levels. A general living-kind-categorization meta-template could project, not directly concepts, but other, more specific templates for different domains of living kinds. For instance, a fundamental parameter to be fixed might concern the contrast between self-propelled and non-self-propelled objects (Premack, 1990), yielding two templates, one for zoological concepts and another one for botanical concepts.

Another possibility still is that the initial meta-template has three types of feature: (1) fixed features that characterize living kinds in general – for instance it might be an unalterable part of any living-kind concept that the kind is taken to have an underlying essence (Atran 1987; Gelman and Coley 1991; Gelman and Markman 1986, 1987; Keil 1989; Medin and Ortony 1989); (2) parameters with default values that can be altered in copies of the template – for instance, 'self-propelled' and 'non-human' might be revisable features of the initial template; (3) empty slots for information about individual kinds. If so, then, the default-value template could serve as such for non-human animal concepts. To use the template for plant concepts, or to include humans in a taxonomy of animals would involve changing a default value of the initial template.

How is the flow of information among modules actually governed? Is there a regulating device? Is it a pandemonium? A market economy? Many types of model can be entertained. Here is a simple possibility.

The output of perceptual and conceptual modules is in the form of conceptual representations. Perceptual modules categorize distal stimuli (things seen, for instance) and must each have therefore the conceptual repertoire needed for the output categorizations of which they are capable. Conceptual modules may infer new output categorizations from the input conceptual representations they process; they must have an input and an output conceptual repertoire to do so. Let us assume that conceptual modules accept as input any conceptual representation in which a concept belonging to their input repertoire occurs. In particular single-concept micromodules process all and only representations where their very own concept occurs. These micromodules generate transformations of the input representation by replacing the concept with some inferentially warranted expansion of it. They are otherwise blind to the other conceptual properties of the representations they process (in the manner of the 'calculate' procedure in some word-processors, which scans the text but 'sees' only numbers and mathematical signs). Generally, the presence of specific concepts in a representation determines what modules will be activated and what inferential processes will take place (see Sperber and Wilson 1986, chapter 2).

A key feature of modularity in Fodor's description is informational encapsulation: A full-fledged module uses a limited database and is not able to take advantage of information relevant to its task if that information is in some other database. Central processes on the other hand are not so constrained. They are characterized, on the contrary, by free flow of information. Thus beliefs about Camembert cheese might play a role in forming conclusions about quarks, even though they hardly belong to the same conceptual domain. This is a fact, and I wouldn't dream of denying it. What does it imply regarding the modularity of conceptual processes? It implies that one particular modular picture cannot be right: Imagine a single layer of a few large mutually unconnected modules; then information treated by one module won't find its way to another. If, on the other hand, the output of one conceptual module can serve as input to another one, each module can be informationally encapsulated while chains of inference can take a conceptual premise from one module to the next and therefore integrate the contribution of each in some final conclusion. A holistic effect need not be the outcome of a holistic procedure.

Once a certain level of complexity in modular thought is reached, modules can emerge whose function it is to handle problems raised, not externally by the environment, but internally by the workings of the mind itself. One problem that a rich modular system of the kind we are envisaging would encounter as surely as Fodor's nonmodular central processes is the risk of computational explosion. Assume that a device would have emerged, the function of which is to put up on the board, so to speak, some limited information for actual processing. Call this device 'attention'. Think of it as a temporary buffer. Only representations stored in that buffer are processed (by the modules whose input conditions they satisfy), and they are processed only as long as they stay in the buffer. There is, so to speak, competition among representations for attention. The competition tends to work out so as to maximize cognitive efficiency – that is, it tends to select for a place in the buffer, and thus for inferential processing, the most relevant information available at the time. There is a much longer story to be told: Read *Relevance* (Sperber and Wilson 1986).

Attention is of course not domain-specific. On the other hand it is a clear adaptation to an internal processing problem: the problem encountered by any cognitive system able to identify perceptually and to hold in memory much more information than it can simultaneously process conceptually. Such a system must be endowed with a means of selecting the information to be conceptually processed. Relevance-guided attention is such a means. Whether or not it should be called a module, does not really matter: attention so conceived fits snugly into a modular picture of thought.

I don't expect these speculations to be convincing – I am only half convinced myself, though I will be a bit more by the end of this chapter – but I hope they are intelligible. If so, this means that one can imagine a richly modular conceptual system that integrates information in so many partial ways that it is not obvious any more that we, human beings, genuinely integrate it in any fuller way. The argument against the modularity of thought based on the alleged impossibility of modular integration should lose at least its immediate commonsense appeal.

Actual and proper domains of modules

Modules are domain-specific, and many – possibly most – domains of modern human thought are too novel and too variable to be the specific domain of a genetically specified module. This second commonsense argument against the modularity of thought is reinforced by adaptationist considerations: In many domains, cultural expertise is hard to see as a biological adaptation. This is true not just of new domains such as chess, but also of old domains such as music. Expertise in these domains is unlikely therefore to be based on an *ad hoc* evolved mechanism. Of course, one can always try to concoct some story showing that, say, musical competence is a biological adaptation. However, merely assuming the adaptive character of a trait without a plausible demonstration is an all too typical misuse of the evolutionary approach.

Let me try an altogether different line. An adaptation is, generally, an adaptation to given environmental conditions. If you look at an adaptive feature just by itself, inside the organism, and forget altogether what you know about the environment and its history, you cannot tell what its function is, what it is an adaptation to. The function of a giraffe's long neck is to help it eat from trees, but in another environment – make it on another planet to free your imagination – the function of an identical body part on an identical organism could be to allow the animal to see further, or to avoid breathing foul air near the ground, or to fool giant predators into believing that its flesh was poisonous.

A very similar point – or, arguably, a special application of the very same point – has been at the centre of major recent debates in the philosophy of language and mind between 'individualists' and 'externalists'. Individualists hold that the content of a concept is in the head of the thinker, or, in other terms, that a conceptual content is an intrinsic property of the thinker's brain state. Externalists maintain – rightly, I believe – that the same brain state that realizes a given concept might realize a different concept in another environment, just as internally identical biological features might have different functions in different environments.[5]

The content of a concept is not an intrinsic but a relational property[6] of the neural realizer of that concept, and is contingent upon the environment and the history (including the phylogenetic prehistory) of that neural object. This extends straightforwardly to the case of domain-specific modules. A domain is semantically defined, that is, by a concept under which objects in the domain are supposed to fall. The domain of a module is therefore not a property of its internal structure (whether described in neurological or in computational terms).

There is no way a specialized cognitive module might pick its domain just in virtue of its internal structure, or even in virtue of its connections to other cognitive modules. All that the internal structure provides is, to borrow an apt phrase from Frank Keil (1994), a mode of construal, a disposition to organize information in a certain manner and to perform computations of a certain form. A cognitive module also has structural relations to other mental devices with which it interacts. This determines in particular its input conditions: through which other devices the information must come, and how it must be categorized by these other devices. But, as long as one remains within the mind and ignores the connections of perceptual modules with the environment, knowledge of the brain-internal connections of a specialized cognitive module does not determine its domain.

The fact that the mode of construal afforded by a mental module might fit many domains does not make the module any less domain-specific, just as the fact that my key might fit many locks does not make it any less the key to my door. The mode of construal and the domain, just as my key and my lock, have a long common history. How, then, do interactions with the environment over time determine the domain of a cognitive module? To answer this question, we had better distinguish between the actual and the proper domain of a module.

The actual domain of a conceptual module is all the information in the organism's environment that may (once processed by perceptual modules, and possibly by other conceptual modules) satisfy the module's input conditions. Its proper domain is all the information that it is the module's biological function to process. Very roughly, the function of a biological device is a class of effects of that device that contributes to making the device a permanent feature of a viable species. The function of a module is to process a specific range of information in a specific manner. That processing contributes to the reproductive success of the organism. The range of information that it is the function of a module to process constitutes its proper domain. What a module actually processes is information found in its actual domain, whether it also belongs to its proper domain or not. Back to the orgs. The characteristic danger that initially threatened them was being trampled by elephants. Thanks to a module, the orgs reacted selectively to various signs normally produced, in their environment, by approaching elephants.

Of course, approaching elephants were sometimes missed, and other, unrelated and innocuous events did sometimes activate the module. But even though the module failed to pick out all and only approaching elephants, we describe its function as having been to do just that (rather than doing what it actually did). Why? Because it is its relative success at that task that explains its having been a permanent feature of a a viable species. Even though they were not exactly coextensive, the actual domain of the module overlapped well enough with the approaching-elephants domain. Only the latter, however, was the proper domain of the module.

Many generations later, elephants had vanished from the orgs' habitat, while hippopotamuses had multiplied, and now *they* trampled absent-minded orgs. The same module that had reacted to most approaching elephants and a few sundry events now reacted to most approaching hippos and a few sundry events. Had the module's proper domain become that of approaching hippos? Yes, and for the same reasons as before: Its relative success at reacting to approaching hippos explains why this module remained a permanent feature of a viable species.[7]

Today, however, hippopotamuses too have vanished and there is a railway passing through the orgs' territory. Because orgs don't go near the rails, trains are no danger. However the same module that had reacted selectively to approaching elephants and then to approaching hippos now reacts to approaching trains (and produces a useless panic in the orgs). The actual domain of the module includes mostly approaching trains. Has its proper domain therefore become that of approaching trains? The answer should be 'no' this time: Reacting to trains is what it does, but it is not its function. The module's reacting to trains does not explain its remaining a permanent feature of the species. In fact, if the module and the species survive, it is in spite of this marginally harmful effect.[8]

Still, an animal psychologist studying the orgs today might well come to the conclusion that they have a domain-specific ability to react to trains. She might wonder how they have developed such an ability given that trains have been introduced in the area too recently to allow the emergence of a specific biological adaptation (the adaptive value of which would be mysterious anyhow). The truth, of course, is that the earlier proper domains of the module, approaching elephants and then hippos, are now empty, that its actual domain is, by accident, roughly coextensive with the set of approaching trains, and that the explanation of this accident is the fact that the input conditions of the module, which had been positively selected in a different environment, happen to be satisfied by trains and hardly anything else in the orgs' present environment.

Enough of toy examples. In the real world, you are not likely to get elephants neatly replaced by hippos and hippos by trains, and to have each kind in turn satisfying the input conditions of some specialized module. Natural environments, and therefore cognitive functions, are relatively stable. Small shifts of cognitive function are more likely to occur than radical changes. When major changes occur in the environment, for instance as the result of a natural cataclysm, some cognitive functions are just likely to be lost: If elephants go, so does the function of your erstwhile elephant-detector. If a module loses its function, or equivalently if its proper domain becomes empty, then it is unlikely that its actual domain will be neatly filled by objects all falling under a single category, such as passing trains. More probably, the range of stimuli causing the module to react will end up being such an awful medley as to discourage any temptation to describe the actual domain of the module in terms of a specific category. Actual domains are usually not conceptual domains.

Cultural domains and the epidemiology of representations

Most animals get only highly predictable kinds of information from their conspecifics, and not much of it at that. They depend therefore on the rest of the environment for their scant intellectual kicks. Humans are special. They are naturally massive producers, transmitters, and consumers of information. They get a considerable amount and variety of information from fellow humans, and they even produce and store some for their own private consumption. As a result, I will argue, the actual domain of human cognitive modules is likely to have become much larger than their proper domain. Moreover these actual domains, far from being uncategorizable chaos, are likely to be partly organized and categorized by humans themselves. So much so, I will argue, that we should distinguish the cultural domains of modules from both their proper and actual domains. Just a quick illustration before I give a more systematic sketch and a couple of more serious examples. Here is the infant in its cradle, endowed with a domain-specific, modular, naive physics. The proper domain of that module is a range of physical events that typically occur in nature, and the understanding of which will be crucial to the organism's survival. Presumably, other primates are endowed with a similar module. The naive physics module of the infant chimp (and of the infant Pleistocene Homo not-yet-sapiens) reacts to the odd fruit or twig falling, to the banana peel being thrown away, to occasional effects of the infant's own movement, and it may be challenged by the irregular fall of a leaf. Our human infant's module, on the other hand, is stimulated not just by physical events happening incidentally, but also by an 'activity centre' fixed to the side of its cradle, a musical merry-go- nced by elder siblings, moving picture ty of educational toys devised to st sical processes. What makes the human case special? Humans their own environment at a rhythm that natural selection cannot follow, so that many genetically specified traits of the human organism are likely to be adaptations to features of the environment that have ceased to exist or have greatly changed. This may be true not just of adaptations to the non-human environment, but also of adaptations to earlier stages of the hominid social environment.

In particular, the actual domain of any human cognitive module is unlikely to be even approximately coextensive with its proper domain. The actual domain of any human cognitive module is sure, on the contrary, to include a large amount of cultural information that meets its input conditions. This results neither from accident nor from design. It results from a process of social distribution of information.

Humans not only construct individually mental representations of information, but they also produce information for one another in the form of public representations (e.g. utterances, written texts, pictures), or in the form of other informative behaviours and artefacts. Most communicated information, though, is communicated to one person or a few people on a particular occasion, and that is the end of it. Sometimes, however, addressees of a first act of communication communicate the information received to other addressees who communicate it in turn to others, and so on. This process of repeated transmission may go on to the point where we have a chain of mental and public representations both causally linked and similar in content – similar in content because of their causal links – instantiated throughout a human population. Traditions and rumours spread in this particular manner. Other types of representation may be distributed by causal chains of a different form (e.g. through imitation with or without instruction, or through broadcast communication). All such causally linked, widely distributed represent- ations are what we have in mind when we speak of culture.

I have argued (Sperber 1985b, 1990a) that to explain culture is to explain why some representations become widely distributed: a natural- istic science of culture should be an epidemiology of representations. It should explain why some representations are more successful – more 'contagious' – than others.

In this epidemiological perspective, all the information that humans introduce into their common environment can be seen as competing[9] for private and public space and time, that is, for attention, internal memory, transmission, and external storage. Many factors affect the chances of some information being successful and reaching a wide and lasting level of distribution, of being stabilized in a culture. Some of these factors are psychological, others are ecological. Most of these factors are relatively local, others are quite general. The most general psychological factor affecting the distribution of information is its compatibility and fit with human cognitive organization.

In particular, relevant information the relevance of which is relatively independent from the immediate context is, *ceteris paribus*, more likely to reach a cultural level of distribution: relevance provides the motivation both for storing and for transmitting the information, and independence from an immediate context means that relevance will be maintained in spite of changes of local circumstances – that is, it will be maintained on a social scale. Relevance is, however, always relative to a context; independence from the immediate context means relevance in a wider context of stable beliefs and expectations. On a modular view of con- ceptual processes, these beliefs, which are stable across a population, are those which play a central role in the modular organization and processing of knowledge. Thus information that either enriches or contradicts these basic modular beliefs stands a greater chance of cultural success.

I have argued (Sperber 1975, 1980,1985b) that beliefs that violate head-on module-based expectations (e.g. beliefs in supernatural beings capable of action at a distance, ubiquity, metamorphosis, etc.) thereby gain a salience and relevance that contribute to their cultural robustness. Pascal Boyer (1990) has rightly stressed that these violations of intuitive expectations in the description of supernatural beings are in fact few and take place against a background of satisfied modular expectations. Kelly and Keil (1985) have shown that cultural exploitation of representations of metamorphoses are closely constrained by domain-based conceptual structure. Generally speaking, we should expect many culturally successful representations to be squarely grounded in a conceptual module and at the same time to differ enough from the information found in the module's proper domain to command attention.

A cognitive module stimulates in every culture the production and distribution of a wide array of information that meets its input conditions. This information, being artifactually produced or organized by the people themselves, is from the start conceptualized and therefore belongs to conceptual domains that I propose to call the module's cultural domain(s). In other terms, cultural transmission causes, in the actual domain of any cognitive module, a proliferation of parasitic information that mimics the module's proper domain. Let me first illustrate this epidemiological approach with speculations on a non-conceptual case, that of music. This is intended to be an example of a way of thinking suggested by the epidemiological approach rather than a serious scientific hypothesis, which I would not have the competence to develop.

Imagine that the ability and propensity to pay attention to, and analyse, certain complex sound patterns became a factor of reproductive success for a long enough period in human prehistory. The sound patterns would have been discriminable by pitch variation and rhythm. What sounds would have exhibited such patterns? The possibility that springs to mind is human vocal communicative sounds. It need not be the sounds of Homo sapiens speech, though. One may imagine a human ancestor with much poorer articulatory abilities and relying more than modern humans do on rhythm and pitch for the production of vocal signals. In such conditions, a specialized cognitive module might well have evolved.

This module would have had to combine the necessary discriminative ability with a motivational force to cause individuals to attend to the relevant sound patterns. The motivation would have to be on the hedonistic side: pleasure and hopeful expectation rather than pain and fear. Suppose that the relevant sound pattern co-occurred with noise from which it was hard to discriminate. The human ancestor's vocal abilities may have been quite poor, and the intended sound pattern may have been embedded in a stream of parasitic sounds (a bit like when you speak with a sore throat, a cold, and food in your mouth). Then the motivational component of the module should have been tuned so that detecting a low level of the property suffices to procure a significant reward.

The proper domain of the module we are imagining is the acoustic properties of early human vocal communications. It could be that this proper domain is now empty: another adaptation, the improved modern human vocal tract, may have rendered it obsolete. Or it may be that the relevant acoustic properties still play a role in modern human speech (in tonal languages in particular) so that the module is still functional. The sounds that the module analyses thereby causing pleasure to the organism of which it is a part – that is, the sounds meeting the module's input conditions – are not often found in nature (with the obvious exception of bird songs). However, such sounds can be artificially produced. And they have been, providing this module with a particularly rich cultural domain, music. The relevant acoustic pattern of music is much more detectable and delectable than that of any sound in the module's proper domain. The reward mechanism, which was naturally tuned for a hard-to-discriminate input, is now being stimulated to a degree that makes the whole experience utterly addictive.

The idea is, then, that humans have created a cultural domain, music, which is parasitic on a cognitive module whose proper domain pre-existed music and had nothing to do with it. The existence of this cognitive module has favoured the spreading, stabilization, and progressive diversification and growth of a repertoire meeting its input conditions. First, pleasing sounds were serendipitously discovered; then sound patterns were deliberately produced and became music proper. These bits of culture compete for mental and public space and time, and ultimately for the chance to stimulate the module in question in as many individuals as possible for as long as possible. In this competition, some pieces of music do well, at least for a time, whereas others are eliminated, and thus music, and musical competence, evolve.

In the case of music, the cultural domain of the module is much more developed and salient than its proper domain, assuming that it still has a proper domain. So much so that it is the existence of the cultural domain and the domain-specificity of the competences it manifestly evokes that justify looking, in the present or in the past, for a proper domain that is not immediately manifest.

In other cases, the existence of a proper domain is at least as immediately manifest as that of a cultural one. Consider zoological knowledge. The existence of a domain-specific competence in the matter is not hard to admit, if the general idea of domain-specificity is accepted at all. One way to think of it, as I have suggested, is to suppose that humans have a modular template for constructing concepts of animals. The biological function of this module is to provide humans with ways of categorizing animals they may encounter in their environment and of organizing the information they may gather about them. The proper domain of this modular ability is the living local fauna. What happens, however, is that you end up, thanks to cultural input, constructing many concepts for animal species with which you will never interact. If you are a twentieth-century Westerner, you may, for instance, have a cultural sub-domain of dinosaurs. You may even be a dinosaur expert. In another culture you might have been a dragon expert.

This invasion of the actual domain of a conceptual module by cultural information occurs irrespective of the size of the module. Consider a micromodule such as the concept of a particular animal, say the rat. Again, you are likely to have fixed, in the database of that module, culturally transmitted information about rats, whether of a folkloristic or of a scientific character, that goes well beyond the proper domain of that micromodule, that is, well beyond information derivable from, and relevant to, interactions with rats. Of course, this cultural information about rats may be of use for your interactions with other human beings, by providing for instance a database exploitable in metaphorical communication.

On the macro-modular side of things, accept for the sake of this discussion that the modular template on which zoological concepts are constructed is itself an initialized version (maybe the default version) of a more abstract living-kinds meta-template. That meta-template is initialized in other ways for other domains (e.g. botany), projecting several domain-specific templates, as I have suggested above. What determines a new initialization is the presence of information that (1) meets the general input conditions specified in the meta-template, but (2) does not meet the more specific conditions found in the already initialized templates. That information need not be in the proper domain of the meta-template module. In other words the meta-template might get initialized in a manner that fits no proper domain at all but only a cultural domain. A cultural domain that springs to mind in this context is that of representations of supernatural beings (see Boyer 1990, 1993, 1994). But there may also be less apparent cases.

Consider in this light the problem raised by Hirschfeld (1988, 1993, 1994). Children, he shows, are disposed to categorize humans into 'racial' groups. Moreover, they draw inferences from these categorizations, as if different racial groups had different 'essences', or 'natures', comparable to the different natures attributed to different animal species. Do children possess a competence the function of which is to develop such categorizations? In other terms, are humans naturally disposed to racism? Avoiding such an unappealing conclusion, it has been suggested (Atran 1990; Boyer 1990) that children transfer to the social sphere a competence that they have first developed for natural living kinds, and that they do so in order to make sense of the systematic differences in human appearance (e.g. skin colour) that they may have observed. However, Hirschfeld's experimental evidence shows that racial categorization develops without initially drawing on perceptually relevant input. This seems to suggest that there is after all a domain-specific competence for racial classification.

What the epidemiological approach suggests is that racial classification might result from a domain-specific but not innate template derived from the living-kinds meta-template, through an initialization process triggered by a cultural input. Indeed, recent experiments suggest that, in certain conditions, the mere encounter with a nominal label used to designate a living thing is enough to tilt the child's categorization of that thing toward an essentialist construal (Markman and Hutchinson 1984; Markman 1990; Davidson and Gelman 1990; Gelman and Coley 1991). It is quite possible then that being presented with nominal labels for otherwise undefined and undescribed humans is enough (given an appropriate context) to activate the initialization of the ad hoc template. If so, then perception of physical differences among humans is indeed not the triggering factor of racial classification.

There is, as Hirschfeld suggested, a genetically specified competence that determines racial classification without importing its models from another concrete domain. However, the underlying competence need not have racial classification as its proper domain. Racial classification may be a mere cultural domain, based on an underlying competence that does not have any proper domain. The initialization of an *ad hoc* template for racial classification could well be the effect of parasitic, cultural input information on the higher-level learning module the function of which is to generate *ad hoc* templates for genuine living-kind domains such as zoology and botany. If this hypothesis is correct – mind you, I am not claiming that it is, merely that it may be – then no racist disposition has been selected for (Sober 1984) in humans. The dispositions that have been selected for, however, make humans all too easily susceptible to racism given minimal, innocuous-looking cultural input. The relationship between the proper and the cultural domains of the same module is not one of transfer. The module itself does not have a preference between the two kinds of domains, and indeed is blind to a distinction that is grounded in ecology and history.

Even when an evolutionary and epidemiological perspective is adopted, the distinction between the proper and the cultural domain of a module is not always easy to draw. Proper and cultural domains may overlap. Moreover, because cultural domains are things of this world, it can be a function of a module to handle a cultural domain, which *ipso facto* becomes a proper domain.

Note that the very existence of a cultural domain is an effect of the existence of a module. Therefore, initially at least, a module cannot be an adaptation to its own cultural domain. It must have been selected because of a pre-existing proper domain. In principle, it might become a function of the module to handle its own cultural domain. This would be so when the ability of the module to handle its cultural domain contributed to its remaining a permanent feature of a viable species. The only clear case of an adaptation of a module to its own effects is that of the linguistic faculty. The linguistic faculty in its initial form cannot have been an adaptation to a public language that could not exist without it. On the other hand it seems hard to doubt that language has become the proper domain of the language faculty.[10]

If there are modular abilities to engage in specific forms of social interaction (as claimed by Cosmides 1989), then, as in the case of the language faculty, the cultural domains of these abilities should at least overlap with their proper one. Another interesting issue in this context is the relationship between numerosity – the proper domain of a cognitive module – and numeracy, an obviously cultural domain dependent on language (see Gelman and Gallistel 1978; Gallistel and Gelman 1992; Dehaene 1992). In general, however, there is no reason to expect the production and maintenance of cultural domains to be a biological function of all, or even most, human cognitive modules. If this approach is correct, it has important implications for the study of domain-specificity in human cognition. In particular it evaporates, I believe, the cultural diversity argument against the modularity of thought. For even if thought were wholly modular, we should nevertheless find many cultural domains, varying from culture to culture, and whose contents are such that it would be preposterous to assume that they are the proper domain of an evolved module. The cultural idiosyncrasy and lack of relevance to biological fitness of a cognitive domain leaves entirely open the possibility that it might be a domain of a genetically specified module: its cultural domain.

Metarepresentational abilities and cultural explosion

If you are still not satisfied that human thought could be modular through and through, if you feel that there is more integration taking place than I have allowed for so far, if you can think of domains of thought that don't fit with any plausible module, well then we agree. It is not just that beliefs about Camembert cheese might play a role in forming conclusions about quarks; it is that we have no trouble at all entertaining and understanding a conceptual representation in which Camembert and quarks occur simultaneously. You have just proved the point by understanding the previous sentence.

Anyhow, with or without Camembert, beliefs about quarks are hard to fit into a modular picture. Surely, they don't belong to the actual domain of naive physics; similarly, beliefs about chromosomes don't belong to the actual domain of naive biology, beliefs about lycanthropy don't belong to the actual domain of folk zoology, beliefs about the Holy Trinity or about cellular automata seem wholly removed from any module.

Is this to say that there is a whole range of extra-modular beliefs, of which many religious or scientific beliefs would be prime examples? Not really. We have not yet exhausted the resources of the modular approach. Humans have the ability to form mental representations of mental representations: in other words, they have a meta-representational ability. This ability is so particular, in terms of both its domain and of its computational requirements, that anybody willing to contemplate the modularity of thought thesis will be willing to see it as modular. Even Fodor does (Fodor 1992). The meta-representational module[11] is a special conceptual module, however – a second-order one, so to speak. Whereas other conceptual modules process concepts and representations of things, typically of things perceived, the meta-representational module processes concepts of concepts and representations of representations.

The actual domain of the meta-representational module is clear enough: It is the set of all representations of which the organism is capable of inferring or otherwise apprehending the existence and content. But what could be the proper domain of that module? Much current work (e.g. Astington, *et al.* 1989) assumes that the function of the ability to form and process meta-representations is to provide humans with a naive psychology. In other terms, the module is a 'theory of mind module' (Leslie, 1994), and its proper domain is made of the beliefs, desires, and intentions that cause human behaviour. This is indeed highly plausible. The ability to understand and categorize behaviour, not as mere bodily movements but in terms of underlying mental states, is an essential adaptation for organisms that must cooperate and compete with one another in a great variety of ways.

Once you have mental states in your ontology, and the ability to attribute mental states to others, there is but a short step, or no step at all, to your having desires about these mental states – desiring that she should believe this, desiring that he should desire that – and to forming intentions to alter the mental states of others. Human communication is both a way to satisfy such meta-representational desires and an exploitation of the meta-representational abilities of one's audience. As suggested by Grice (1957) and developed by Deirdre Wilson and myself (1986), a communicator, by means of her communicative behaviour, is deliberately and overtly helping her addressee to infer the content of the mental representation she wants him to adopt (Sperber and Wilson 1986).

Communication is, of course, radically facilitated by the emergence of a public language. A public language is rooted in another module, the language faculty. We claim, however, that the very development of a public language is not the cause but an effect of the development of communication made possible by the meta-representational module.

As a result of the development of communication, and particularly of linguistic communication, the actual domain of the meta-representational module is teeming with representations made manifest by communicative behaviours: intentions of communicators and contents communicated. Most representations about which there is some interesting epidemiological story to be told are communicated in this manner and therefore enter people's minds via the meta-representational module.

As already suggested, communicated contents, although they enter via the metarepresentational module, may find their way to the relevant modules: what you are told about cats is integrated with what you see of cats, in virtue of the fact that the representation communicated contains the concept CAT. But now you have the information in two modes: as a representation of cats, handled by a first-order conceptual module, and as representation of a representation of cats, handled by the second-order meta-representational module. That module knows nothing about cats but it may know something about semantic relationships among representations; it may have some ability to evaluate the validity of an inference, the evidential value of some information, the relative plausibility of two contradictory beliefs and so forth. It may also evaluate a belief, not on the basis of its content, but on the basis of the reliability of its source. The meta-representational module may therefore form or accept beliefs about cats for reasons that have nothing to do with the kind of intuitive knowledge that the CAT module (or whatever first-order module handles cats) delivers.

An organism endowed with perceptual and first-order conceptual modules has beliefs delivered by these modules, but has no beliefs about beliefs, either its own or those of others, and no reflexive attitude to them. The vocabulary of its beliefs is limited to the output vocabulary of its modules, and it cannot conceive or adopt a new concept nor criticize or reject old ones. An organism also endowed with a meta-representational module can represent concepts and beliefs *qua* concepts and beliefs, evaluate them critically, and accept them or reject them on meta-representational grounds. It may form representations of concepts and of beliefs pertaining to any conceptual domain, of a kind that the modules specialized in those domains might be unable to form on their own, or even to incorporate. In doing so, however, the better-endowed organism is merely using its meta-representational module within the module's own domain, that is, representations.

Humans, with their outstanding meta-representational abilities, may thus have beliefs pertaining to the same conceptual domain rooted in two quite different modules: the first-order module specialized in that conceptual domain, or the second-order meta-representational module, specialized in representations. These are, however, two different kinds of belief: 'intuitive beliefs' rooted in first-order modules, and 'reflective beliefs' rooted in the meta-representational module (see Sperber 1985a Ch 2, 1985b, 1990a). Reflective beliefs may contain concepts (e.g. 'quarks', 'Trinity') that do not belong in the repertoire of any module, and that are therefore available to humans only reflectively, via the beliefs or theories in which they are embedded. The beliefs and concepts that vary most from culture to culture (and that often seem unintelligible or irrational from another culture's perspective) are typically reflective beliefs and the concepts they introduce.

Reflective beliefs can be counterintuitive. (More exactly, they can be counterintuitive with respect to our intuitions about their subject-matter, while at the same time our meta-representational reasons for accepting them are intuitively compelling.) This is relevant to the most interesting of Fodor's technical arguments against the modularity of central processes. The informational encapsulation and mandatory character of perceptual modules is evidenced, Fodor points out, by the persistence of perceptual illusions, even when we are apprised of their illusory character. There is, he argues, nothing equivalent at the conceptual level. True, perceptual illusions have the feel, the vividness of perceptual experiences, that you won't find at the conceptual level. But what you do find is that we may give up a belief and still feel its intuitive force, and feel also the counterintuitive character of the belief we adopt in its stead.

You may believe with total faith in the Holy Trinity, and yet be aware of the intuitive force of the idea that a father and son cannot be one and the same. You may understand why black holes cannot be seen, and yet feel the intuitive force of the idea that a big, solid, indeed dense object cannot but be visible. The case of naive versus modern physics provides many other blatant examples.[12] What happens, I suggest, is that the naive physics module remains largely unpenetrated by the ideas of modern physics, and keeps delivering the same intuitions, even when they are not believed any more (or at least not reflectively believed).

More generally the recognition of the meta-representational module, of the duality of beliefs that it makes possible, and of the gateway it provides for cultural contagion, plugs a major gap in the modular picture of mind I have been trying to outline. The mind is here pictured as involving three tiers: a single thick layer of input modules, just as Fodor says, then a complex network of first-order conceptual modules of all kinds, and then a second-order meta-representational module. Originally, this meta-representational module is not very different from the other conceptual modules, but it allows the development of communication and triggers a cultural explosion of such magnitude that its actual domain is blown up and ends up hosting a multitude of cultural representations belonging to several cultural domains. This is how you can have a truly modular mind playing a major causal role in the generation of true cultural diversity.

Meta-representation module is crucial to understanding modular theory & its criticisms

Notes

1. An earlier version of this chapter came out in L.A. Hirschfeld and S.A. Gelman (eds), *Mapping the Mind: Domain specificity in cognition and culture*, New York: Cambridge University Press, 1994, under the title 'The modularity of thought and the epidemiology of represent-ations'. The present version first appeared in Dan Sperber, *Explaining Culture: A Naturalistic Approach*, Oxford: Blackwell, 1996.
2. Fodor also mentions the possibility that output, i.e. motor systems might be modular too. I assume that it is so, but will not discuss the issue here.
3. See also Rozin 1976; Symons 1979; Rozin and Schull 1988; Barkow 1989; Brown 1991; Barkow *et al.* (eds) 1992.
4. The point cannot just be that the forces that have driven cognitive evolution cannot be identified for certain; that much is trivially true. The claim must be that these forces cannot be even tentatively and

reasonably identified, unlike the forces that have driven the evolution of, say, organs of locomotion. See Piatelli-Palmarini 1989 and Stich 1990 for clever but unconvincing arguments in favour of this Second Law.

5. Putnam 1975 and Burge 1979 offered the initial arguments for externalism. (I myself am convinced by Putnam's but not by Burge's.) For a sophisticated discussion, see Recanati 1993.

6. Arguably, content is a biological function in an extended sense – see Dennett 1987; Dretske 1988; Millikan 1984; Papineau 1987. My views have been influenced by Millikan's.

7. There are of course conceptual problems here (see Dennett 1987; Fodor 1988). It could be argued for instance that the module's proper domain was neither elephants nor hippos, but something else, say, 'approaching big animals that might trample orgs'. If so, we would want to say that its proper domain had not changed with the passing of the elephants and the coming of the hippos. I side with Dennett in doubting that much of substance hinges on which of these descriptions we choose: the overall explanation remains exactly the same.

8. That is why it would be a mistake to say that the function of a device is to react to whatever might satisfy its input conditions and to equate its actual and proper domains. Though there may be doubt about the correct assignment of the proper domain of some device (see the preceding note), the distinction between actual and proper domains is as solid as that between effect and function.

9. Here, as in talk of representations competing for attention, the term 'competition' is only a vivid metaphor. Of course, no intention or disposition to compete is implied. What is meant is that, out of all the representations present in a human group at a given time, some, at one extreme, will spread and last while, at the opposite extreme, others will occur only very briefly and very locally. This is not a random process, and it is asssumed that properties of the information itself play a causal role in determining its wide or narrow distribution.

10. See Pinker and Bloom (1990) and my contribution to the discussion of their paper (Sperber 1990b).

11. The capacity to form and process meta-representations could be instantiated not in a single module but in several distinct modules, each, say, meta-representing a different domain or type of representation. For lack of compelling arguments, I will ignore this genuine possibility.

12. And a wealth of subtler examples have been analysed in a proper cognitive perspective by Atran (1990).

References

Astington, J.W., Harris, P. and Olson, D. (1989), *Developing Theories of Mind*, Cambridge: Cambridge University Press.

Atran, S. (1987), 'Constraints on the ordinary semantics of living kinds', *Mind and Language*, 2: 27–63.

—— (1990), *Cognitive Foundations of Natural History: Towards an Anthropology of Science*, Cambridge: Cambridge University Press.

—— (1994), 'Core domains versus scientific theories' in L.A. Hirschfeld and S.A. Gelman (eds), *Mapping the Mind: Domain specificity in cognition and culture*, New York: Cambridge University Press.

Barkow, J. (1989), *Darwin, Sex and Status: Biological Approaches to Mind and Culture*, Toronto: University of Toronto Press.

——, Cosmides, L. and Tooby, J. (eds) (1992), *The Adapted Mind: Evolutionary Psychology and the Generation of Culture*, New York: Oxford University Press.

Berlin, B. (1978), 'Ethnobiological classification', in E. Rosch and B. Lloyd (eds), *Cognition and Categorization*, Hillsdale: Lawrence Erlbaum Associates.

Boyer, P. (1990), *Tradition as Truth and Communication*, Cambridge: Cambridge University Press.

——(1994), *The Naturalness of Religious Ideas: A Cognitive Theory of Religion*, Berkeley: University of California Press.

—— (1994), 'Cognitive constraints on cultural representations: natural ontologies and religious ideas', in L.A. Hirschfeld and S.A. Gelman (eds), *Mapping the Mind: Domain Specificity in Cognition and Culture*, New York: Cambridge University Press.

Brown, A. (1991), *Human Universals*, New York: McGraw-Hill.

Burge, T. (1979), 'Individualism and the mental', *Midwest Studies in Philosophy*, 5: 73–122.

Carey, S. (1985), *Conceptual Change in Childhood*, Cambridge, Mass.: MIT Press.

Chomsky, N. (1986), *Knowledge of Language: Its Nature, Origin, and Use*, New York: Praeger.

Clark, A. (1987), 'The kludge in the machine', *Mind and Language* 2: 277–300.

—— (1990), *Microcognition: Philosophy, Cognitive Science, and Parallel Distributed Processing*, Cambridge, Mass.: MIT Press.

Cosmides, L. (1989), 'The logic of social exchange: Has natural selection shaped how humans reason? Studies with the Wason selection task', *Cognition*, 31: 187–276.

——— and Tooby, J. (1987), 'From evolution to behavior: evolutionary psychology as the missing link', in J. Dupré (ed.) *The Latest on the Best: Essays on Evolution and Optimality*, Cambridge, Mass.: MIT Press.

——— and Tooby, J. (1994), 'Origins of domain-specificity: the evolution of functional selection', in L.A. Hirschfeld and S.A. Gelman (eds), *Mapping the Mind: Domain Specificity in Cognition and Culture*, New York: Cambridge University Press.

Davidson, N.S. and Gelman, S. (1990), 'Induction from novel categories: the role of language and conceptual structure', *Cognitive Development*, 5: 121–52.

Dehaene, S. (1992), 'Varieties of numerical abilities', *Cognition*, 44: 1–42.

Dennett, D. (1987), *The Intentional Stance*, Cambridge, Mass.: MIT Press.

Dretske, F. (1988), *Explaining Behavior*, Cambridge, Mass.: MIT Press.

Fodor, J. (1983), *The Modularity of Mind*, Cambridge, Mass.: MIT Press.

——— (1987), 'Modules, frames, fridgeons, sleeping dogs, and the music of the spheres', in J. Garfield (ed.) *Modularity in Knowledge Representation and Natural-Language Understanding*, Cambridge, Mass.: MIT Press.

——— (1988), *Psychosemantics*, Cambridge, Mass.: MIT Press.

——— (1992), 'A theory of the child's theory of mind', *Cognition*, 44: 283–96.

Gallistel, C.R. and Gelman, R. (1992), 'Preverbal and verbal counting and computation', *Cognition*, 44: 43–74.

Gelman, R. and Gallistel, C.R. (1978), *The Child's Understanding of Number*, Cambridge, Mass.: Harvard University Press.

Gelman, S and Coley, J.D. (1991), 'The Acquisition of natural kind terms', in S. Gelman and J. Byrnes (eds), *Perspectives on Language and Thought*, New York: Cambridge University Press.

Gelman, S. and Markman, E. (1986), 'Categories and induction in young children', in *Cognition*, 23: 183–209.

——— (1987), 'Young children's inductions from natural kinds: the role of categories and appearances', *Child Development*, 58: 1532–41.

Grice, H.P. (1957), 'Meaning', *Philosophical Review*, 66: 377–88.

Hirschfeld, L.A. (1984), 'Kinship and cognition', *Current Anthropology*, 27: 235.

——— (1988) 'On acquiring social categories: cognitive development and anthropological wisdom', *Man* (N.S.), 23: 611–38.

——— (1993), 'Discovering social difference: the role of appearance in the development of racial awareness', *Cognitive psychology*, 25: 317–50.

Dan Sperber

—— (1994), 'The acquisition of social categories', in L.A. Hirschfeld and S.A. Gelman (eds), *Mapping the Mind: Domain Specificity in Cognition and Culture*, New York: Cambridge University Press.

Keil, F.C. (1989), *Concepts, Kinds, and Cognitive Development*, Cambridge, Mass.: MIT Press.

—— (1994), 'The birth and nurturance of concepts by domains: the origins of concepts of living things', in L.A. Hirschfeld and S.A. Gelman (eds), *Mapping the Mind: Domain Specificity in Cognition and Culture*, New York: Cambridge University Press.

Kelly, M. and Keil, F.C. (1985), 'The more things change . . .: metamorphoses and conceptual development', *Cognitive Science*, 9: 403–16.

Leslie, A. (1987), 'Pretense and representation: the origins of "theory of mind"', *Psychological Review*, 94: 412–26.

—— (1988), 'The necessity of illusion: perception and thought in infancy', in L. Weiskrantz (ed.), *Thought Without Language*, Oxford: Clarendon Press.

Leslie, A. (1994), 'ToMM, ToBY, and Agency: core architecture and domain specificity', in L.A. Hirschfeld and S.A. Gelman (eds), *Mapping the Mind: Domain Specificity in Cognition and Culture*, New York: Cambridge University Press.

Manktelow, K. and Over, D. (1990), *Inference and Understanding: A Philosophical and Psychological Perspective*, London: Routledge.

Markman E.M. (1990), 'The whole-object, taxonomic, and mutual exclusivity assumptions as initial constraints on word meanings', in S. Gelman and J. Byrnes (eds), *Perspectives on Language and Thought*, New York: Cambridge University Press.

—— and Hutchinson, J.E. (1984), 'Children's sensitivity to constraints on word meaning: taxonomic versus thematic relations', *Cognitive Psychology*, 16: 1–27.

Medin, D. and Ortony, A. (1989), 'Psychological essentialism', in S. Vosniadou and A. Ortony (eds), *Similarity and Analogical Reasoning*, Cambridge: Cambridge University Press.

Millikan, R.G. (1984), *Language, Thought, and Other Biological Categories*, Cambridge, Mass.: MIT Press.

Papineau, D. (1987), *Reality and Representation*, Oxford: Blackwell

Piatelli-Palmarini, M. (1989), 'Evolution, selection and cognition: from "learning" to parameter setting in biology and the study of language', *Cognition*, 31: 1–44.

Pinker, S. and Bloom, P. (1990), 'Natural language and natural selection', *Behavioral and Brain Sciences*, 12: 707–84.

Premack, D. (1990), 'The infant's theory of self-propelled objects', *Cognition*, 36: 1–16.

Putnam, H. (1975), 'The meaning of "meaning"', *Mind, Language and Reality: Philosophical papers, volume II*, Cambridge: Cambridge University Press.

Recanati, F. (1993), *Direct Reference, Meaning and Thought*, Oxford: Blackwell.

Rozin, P. (1976), 'The evolution of intelligence and access to the cognitive unconscious', in J.M. Sprague and A.N. Epstein (eds), *Progress in Psychobiology and Physiological Psychology*, New York: Academic Press.

Rozin, P. and Schull, J. (1988), 'The adaptive-evolutionary point of view in experimental psychology', in R. Atkinson, R. Herrnstein, G. Lindzey and R. Luce (eds), *Steven's Handbook of Experimental Psychology*, NY: John Wiley & Sons.

Sober, E. (1984), *The Nature of Selection*, Cambridge, Mass.: MIT Press.

Spelke, E.S. (1988), 'The origins of physical knowledge', in L. Weiskrantz (ed.) *Thought Without Language*, Oxford: Clarendon Press.

Sperber, D. (1975), *Rethinking Symbolism*, Cambridge: Cambridge University Press.

—— (1980), 'Is symbolic thought prerational?', in M. Foster and S. Brandes (eds), *Symbol as Sense*, New York: Academic Press.

—— (1985a), *On Anthropological Knowledge*, Cambridge: Cambridge University Press.

—— (1985b), 'Anthropology and psychology: towards an epidemiology of representations', in *Man* (N.S.), 20: 73–89 (Reprinted in D. Sperber, (1996), *Explaining Culture: A Naturalistic Approach*, Oxford: Blackwell).

—— (1990a), 'The epidemiology of beliefs', in C. Fraser and G. Gaskell (eds), *The Social Psychological Study of Widespread Beliefs*, Oxford: Clarendon Press (Reprinted in D. Sperber (1996), *Explaining Culture: A Naturalistic Approach*, Oxford: Blackwell).

—— (1990b), 'The evolution of the language faculty: a paradox and its solution', *Behavioral and Brain Sciences*, 13: 756–8.

—— and Wilson, D. (1986), *Relevance: Communication and Cognition*, Cambridge, Mass.: Harvard University Press.

Stich, S. (1990), *The Fragmentation of Reason*, Cambridge Mass.: MIT Press.

Symons, D. (1979), *The evolution of human sexuality*, New York: Oxford University Press.

Tooby, J. and Cosmides, L. (1989), 'Evolutionary psychology and the generation of culture, Part I: theoretical considerations', *Ethology and Sociobiology*, 10, 29–49.

Tooby, J. and Cosmides, L. (1992), 'The psychological foundations of culture', in J. Barkow, L. Cosmides and J. Tooby (eds), *The Adapted Mind: Evolutionary Psychology and the Generation of Culture*, New York: Oxford University Press.

Wittgenstein, L. (1953), *Philosophical Investigations*, Oxford: Blackwell.

2

Cultural Inheritance Tracks and Cognitive Predispositions: The Example of Religious Concepts
Pascal Boyer

Cognitive dispositions that result from the evolutionary history of the species account for certain general or recurrent properties of cultural representations. This claim should not be too contentious. It all hinges, after all, on what one means by 'certain general or recurrent properties'. In my view, one can make a good case for the notion that these properties extend to domains that may seem 'culturally constructed' and therefore highly variable. This could be argued in purely theoretical terms. However, theoretical debates about the value or even possibility of a naturalistic approach to culture are often too abstract to appear of much relevance to anthropologists engaged in empirical work. They may see the point of the debate and even feel that one side has a simpler or more coherent view of culture, but find it quite difficult to see how this would change anything in what they study or how they study it. This is why I consider here a limited domain, that of recurrent features of religious concepts, and focus on empirical evidence, both anthropological and psychological.

The main line of argument here is that human minds are predisposed to build particular types of conceptual structure from the earliest stages of conceptual development. These conceptual structures in turn constrain the inferences produced on the basis of experiential and cultural input. In this way, evolved predispositions impose constraints on the range of cultural representations likely to be acquired, stored and transmitted, and therefore likely to be found in diverse cultural environments. (See Boyer 1994a for a general presentation.)

'Religion' in the ordinary sense combines (among other things) at least four different domains of representation, to do with (1) the existence and specific powers of supernatural entities, (2) sets of moral rules, (3) notions of group identity ('our' religion is not 'theirs'), and sometimes (4) particular types of experience and associated emotional states. Although these different domains are connected in an individual's religious beliefs, they are not necessarily transmitted and acquired as an integral conceptual package. In the following pages I only deal with religious ontological concepts. The aim is to explain why religious ontologies tend to display a limited number of recurrent types – in other words, why there is a limited 'catalogue' of concepts.

Religious ontological assumptions: a concept-based model

The domain of religious ontological concepts is not a free-for-all where any odd conceptual association is as good as any other. That much is familiar to most anthropologists. The point of the model summarized here (see Boyer 1994b for more details) is to explain why. The starting-point is that the concepts we call 'cultural', because we find roughly similar versions of them in the minds of different members of a group, are concepts that can be acquired, stored and communicated more easily than others. What makes them so? The answer is likely to be different for different cultural domains. As far as religious concepts are concerned, a long tradition suggests that such concepts include an obvious and salient departure from common, everyday understandings. As E. Gellner once put it, an ideology needs to provide a 'cognitive shock' to be successful (Gellner 1979). But a 'shock' relative to what? In the present model, religious concepts are departures or deviations, not from everyday concepts, rational understandings or familiar notions, but from a very specific and very limited source of information. Religious concepts include violations of intuitive ontology.

Intuitive ontology is distinct from conceptual information included in 'basic-level' categories like telephone or snake, in two ways. First, it only includes information about very broad categories of objects found in the world (persons, artefacts, animals, plants, etc.) as well as causal properties of objects belonging to these categories. Second, it delivers intuitive expectations, about likely states and processes, based on principles that are not accessible to conscious inspection and that emerge very early in the course of conceptual development. (All this will be fleshed out further on.)

For religious concepts to be successful, in this view, two conditions must obtain. First, they must attract more attention than other representations (salience constraint). Second, they must allow inferences about the objects or agents described (inferential constraint). Both constraints are satisfied by a particular use of information delivered by intuitive ontology.

The salience constraint is satisfied by the fact that the central assumptions of most religious systems, in otherwise diverse environments, constitute direct violations of intuitive expectations (Boyer 1994b). Consider some widespread forms of religious ontology. Spirits and ghosts are commonly represented as intentional agents whose physical properties go against the ordinary physical qualities of embodied agents. They go through physical obstacles, move instantaneously, etc. Gods have non-standard physical and biological qualities. For instance, they are immortal, they feed on the smell of sacrificed foods, etc. Also, religious systems the world over include counter-intuitive assumptions about particular artefacts, statues for instance, which are endowed with intentional psychological processes. They can perceive states of affairs, form beliefs, have intentions, etc.

Such counter-intuitive representations consist of either breaches or transfers of expectations. In the first case, expectations that are activated for a particular ontological category are violated. For instance, gods may be represented as intentional agents with counter-intuitive cognitive processes, e.g. they may perceive the future as well as the present. In the case of transfer, expectations are activated for an ontological category that does not usually activate them. For instance, an artefact is said to have cognitive powers, a mountain to have a physiology or a tree to have thoughts. (See illustrations below.)

To say that some religious assumptions are counter-intuitive does not mean that they are perceived as unfamiliar. Some religious assumptions can become part of a cultural 'routine'; this is orthogonal to the question whether they violate tacit, intuitive expectations. Also, one must not take this as suggesting that the counter-intuitive entities and situations described by religious concepts are not taken as real by most people who hold them. On the contrary, it is precisely insofar as a certain situation violates intuitive principles and is taken as real that it may become particularly salient; it is the conjunction of these two assumptions that gives such representations their attention-grabbing potential.

The inference constraint is satisfied by the fact that counter-intuitive elements do not exhaust the representation of religious entities and agencies. They are supplemented by all non-violated assumptions for the category, which are activated by default. Consider ghosts or spirits, for instance. They are construed as physically counter-intuitive. At the same time, however, people routinely produce a large number of inferences about what the ghosts or spirits know or want, which are based on a straightforward extension of 'theory of mind'-expectations to the spirits. Indeed, most inferences people produce about religious agencies are straightforward consequences of activating those intuitive principles that are not violated in the representation of those supernatural entities. These background assumptions are generally tacit and provide the inferential potential without which cultural representations are very unlikely to be transmitted.

The claim, then, is not that religious ontological representations consist in any odd combination of 'something strange' and 'something banal'. The hypothesis is more specific and concerns the connection between the assumptions underlying religious categories and early developed ontological categories and principles. Counter-intuitive assumptions, which provide the attention-grabbing quality of religious representations, are counter-intuitive only in the sense that they violate expectations from intuitive ontology. The idea of spirits being in several places at once would not be counter-intuitive, if there was not a stable expectation that agents are solid objects and that solid objects occupy a unique point in space. In the same way, the notion of statues that listen to one's prayers is attention-grabbing only against a background of expectations about artefacts, including the assumption that they do not have mental capacities. The various inferences that complete the representations result from the activation of intuitive ontological principles.

All this points to limits on the variability of religious ontological assumptions. Intuitive ontology comprises only a small number of domain-specific principles applied to a small number of categories, and religious categories constitute a limited departure from intuitive principles. It follows that there should be a small number of culturally viable religious ontologies, a limited 'catalogue' of potential religious concepts.

For this to be more than speculation we need:

1. independent psychological evidence that ontological categories with associated intuitive theories are indeed entrenched and early-developed, as well as plausibly universal, and that they constitute a limited source of information;[1]
2. anthropological evidence that combinations of explicit counter-intuitive and background intuitive assumptions are indeed found in religious concepts;
3. experimental evidence to the effect that such conceptual structures actually result in better transmission.

Developmental evidence for intuitive ontology

Intuitive ontology is not just a catalogue of objects in the world, but also a set of quasi-theoretical assumptions about their underlying properties and of definite expectations about their observable features. An important result of experimental studies of early conceptual development that a number of broad ontological categories correspond to specific principles, which (1) orient the child's attention to particular perceptual cues for each ontological domain, (2) constrain the child's inferences derived from those cues, and (3) develop in relatively autonomous developmental trajectories. As Gelman puts it, 'the initial principles of a domain establish the boundary conditions for the stimuli that are candidates for feeding coherent development in that domain' (Gelman 1990: 83). This is observed at the level of categories such as person, animal, plant or artefact. Clearly, categorical discriminations along ontological lines are present from infancy, as concerns person as opposed to the rest (Morton and Johnson 1991; Meltzoff 1994) and artefacts versus non-artefacts (Mandler and Bauer 1989; Mandler, Bauer and McDonough 1991). At 18 months 'children do not differentiate dogs from horses or rabbits in the same way that they differentiate dogs from sea or air animals' (Mandler et al. 1991: 290). The identification of objects as belonging to such categories as person, animal, plant or artefact triggers specific forms of inference which focus on particular aspects of the objects considered and only handle information pertinent to that aspect. This is clearly visible in such domains as the representation of number (Gallistel and Gelman 1992; Antell and Keating 1983; Starkey, Spelke and Gelman 1990), the understanding of the physical properties of solid objects (Baillargeon 1987; Baillargeon and Hanko-Summers 1990; Spelke 1990), biological inferences (Gelman *et al.* 1986; Massey and Gelman 1988; Becker and Ward 1991), and the representation of mental states (Baron-Cohen 1995). In the domain of 'intuitive physics', infants from 6 months and even earlier are sensitive to such properties as the 'solidity' or 'continuity' of objects, as well as to constraints on the way objects can support other objects.

Other ontological domains emerge later. Consider for instance the child's specific expectations about living kinds. From an early age, the identification of types of artefact and types of living thing involves the use of rather different perceptual cues. This early categorical distinction between animates and inanimates is enriched by a variety of specific principles which describe biological aspects of live beings (an 'intuitive biology'). Categories of living things are organized in terms of mutually exclusive, jointly exhaustive taxa (Atran 1990), between which hierarchical proximity is a good predictor of overall similarity (Carey 1985: 79–87; Inagaki and Hatano 1987; Inagaki and Sugiyama 1988), while artefact categories are not structured in that way. Also, children gradually develop a number of quasi-theoretical beliefs that apply exclusively to the biological domain, to do for instance with the fact that

Pascal Boyer

kind-membership overrides perceptual resemblance as a predictor for certain essential properties (Gelman and Markman 1987; Gelman 1988). This kind-essentialism underpins children's doubts about the possibility of kind-transformation (Keil 1986), as well as their notions about the growth of living things (Rosengren *et al.* 1991), inheritance of properties or the transfer of features by contagion (Springer and Keil 1989; 1991), and more generally their construal of the mechanisms whereby kind-essence causes external features (Rosengren *et al.* 1991).

Another set of complex aspect-specific principles underpins the psychological explanation of behaviour. Principles here specify a range of mental entities and their causal connections with observable action (see for instance Wellmann and Estes 1986; Perner 1991; Whiten 1991; Gopnik and Meltzoff 1997). From the earliest stages of cognitive development, children readily interpret the behaviour of animate beings, particularly persons, in terms of the causal role of unobservable entities such as beliefs and intentions. They also assume that definite causal links can be readily inferred postulated from actual situations to perceptions, from perceptions to beliefs, from beliefs to desires, while causal links in the other direction are non-standard (Wellmann 1990). Specialized principles, present from infancy, allow the child to detect gaze-direction and directed attention in others as a prelude to understanding the causal structure of their mental states (Baron-Cohen 1991; Baron-Cohen and Cross 1992). Changes in the handling of meta-representations (e.g. 'I know that Sally thinks that "X"') allow the child gradually to build more complex intentional accounts of own and others' behaviour and in particular accounts of behaviour based on erroneous belief (Wimmer and Perner 1983; Perner, Leekam and Wimmer 1987). As a result of this quasi-theoretical understanding of others, the child also develops a more refined explanation and description of her own mental states and behaviour (Gopnik and Astington 1988; Gopnik 1993).

Intuitive ontology, then, emerges as the combination of two functionally distinct kinds of structure: (1) a set of broad perceptually grounded categories and (2) a set of aspect-specific inference engines. Intuitive ontology directs the child's attention to particular cues and their inferences from those cues. Intuitive ontology is not just a phenomenon of early childhood, although it is particularly clear in developmental studies. The reason for using developmental data here is that it is quite clear that children must go 'beyond the information given' in order to build conceptual structures. It is also interesting that they do not have the benefit of sophisticated meta-cognitive abilities, and must therefore build on intuitive expectations delivered by various specialized capacities, in order to respond to the strange stimuli used in typical developmental experiments.

On the whole, adult representations in the domains described here seem to become more complex by gradual enrichment of principles that can be found in the pre-schooler. Obviously, this enrichment requires massive input from experience and interaction. But it is significant that the core principles themselves are not substantially modified in the course of development. For instance, people develop a gradually more complex understanding of other people and their own motivations and behaviours. This however never challenges basic principles about the nature of mental representations and their causal links with real states of affairs. In the same way, adult intuitive physics or adult biological representations are principally extensions and complexification of early developed intuitive principles, except (and very partially) as a result of scientific training that challenges those principles.

Anthropological illustrations: varieties of religious ontology

At first sight, cultural representations concerning religious agencies or entities and their causal powers may appear extremely diverse, and wholly determined by local historical or social conditions. However, this diversity may be more superficial than real, if we focus not on the details concerning various agencies/entities but on their connections with the limited resources of intuitive ontology. This will become clearer with a few illustrations.

Consider first a type of religious ontology that is widespread the world over. Among the Fang of Cameroon, the 'ghosts' or 'spirits' (*bekong*) are commonly characterized as the immaterial presence of dead people. (See Boyer 1992; 1994b: 91–124 for more details.) Some features are central to the characterization of the *bekong*. First, the ghosts have extraordinary physical properties. They are invisible, probably immaterial, can easily go through physical obstacles, and usually move extremely fast. Also, they have powers that set them off from most other kinds of being. They can throw tiny 'darts' at people to pierce the skin and 'thicken' (i.e. poison) the victim's blood. These powers, and notably the physical properties of the ghosts, are clearly and explicitly construed as out of the ordinary, as what makes the category *bekong* of particular interest. Such intentional agents with non-standard physical properties are given various names in anthropological descriptions (gods, spirits, souls, etc.). Their common characteristic is the combination of standard cognitive powers with counter-intuitive physical properties.

Another familiar feature of religious ontologies is the assumption that some inert physical objects have some of the typical properties of animate beings, among which intentionality is central. Consider for instance James's (1988) account of 'ebony divination' among the Uduk-speaking peoples of Sudan. The main ritual in this recent and successful cult centres on the interrogation of wands made from branches of ebony. The wands are first kindled on a fire, and then held over a gourd of water. Divination messages are 'read' in the way the wand burns and in the smudges on the surface of the water. The crucial assumption here is that the wand gives messages simply by 'telling' what the tree overheard (James 1988: 10). The concept of 'listening ebony' seems to bridge the gap between the categories plant and person: something that is identified as a member of a particular living kind is given standard features of intentional beings: perceptions, thoughts, memories, and communicative intentions.

In many cultural environments, this projection is directed at artefacts. Many religious traditions include some assumptions concerning the intentional features of particular religious artefacts. As an illustration, consider for instance Severi's account of shamanistic ritual among the Cuna of Panama: 'The [shaman's] song is chanted in front of two rows of statuettes facing each other, beside the hammock where the ill person is lying. These auxiliary spirits drink up the smoke, whose intoxicating effect opens their minds to the invisible aspect of reality, and gives them the power to heal. In this way [the statues] are believed to become themselves diviners' (Severi 1993: 231).

To turn to another type of assumption, consider the connections established in some religious systems between biological properties of live things and the structure of non-live natural objects. In his account of the religious representations of an Andean community, Bastien for example (Bastien 1978) describes how a particular mountain is construed as a live body, with a trunk, a head, legs, and arms. The mountain is represented as having physiological properties; it 'bleeds' for instance, and also 'feeds' on the meat of sacrificed animals that are left in particular places (Bastien 1978: 37). A whole domain of ritual action is based on assumptions that transfer properties of live organisms to a non-living natural object.

Finally, a less common, but more spectacular form of religious speculation is the notion of zombie as found in Haiti. Zombies are the bodies of dead people that a sorcerer has taken out of their tombs and 'animated'. They can eat, drink, move and work for their 'master', and are totally unaware of their condition (Métraux 1958: 280–1). This notion in a sense constitutes the converse of the notion of spirits described above.

Spirits are ontologically peculiar in that they seem to be persons without being physical objects. Zombies have material bodies but they seem to have lost some crucial properties of persons, notably intentions and self-awareness.

These examples, however cursory, convey some of the conceptual diversity to be expected in the domain of religious concepts. They also make clear that ontological assumptions are crucial here. What makes the Cuna statuettes special, for the Cuna, can be described as a particular combination of features of two distinct ontological categories, that of artefact (the statuettes are artefacts) and that of person (the statuettes are described as intentional agents); the same remark applies to the ebony sticks used in Uduk divination. The Aymara mountain, too, combines features of two different ontological domains, that of live beings and that of inanimate objects. Zombies are remarkable in virtue of a violation of central features of the category person, i.e. self-awareness and volition. The same applies very generally to concepts of gods and spirits, but in this case it is another typical property of person, the possession of a body that is a solid physical object, that seems to be violated.

In each of these cases, it is quite clear that the overt, socially transmitted part of the religious concept is only a fragment of the conceptual representation that drives people's inferences. For instance, the artefacts described by W. James as 'listening ebony' are counter-intuitive in that they are described as having certain properties of intentional beings. But one must notice that these properties themselves need not be directly specified by the cultural input. No one needs to specify that the trees only hear what is said, that they form a memory of what was said after perceiving it (not before), and so on. The ebony trees have perceptions which are caused by external states of the world, as do human beings. Also, the way the ebony twigs 'communicate' with human beings complies with ordinary, intuitive principles of intentional communication. As in the case of spirits, all the assumptions concerning the alleged perceptual cognitive activities of the religious agencies are a straightforward projection of ordinary, self-evident understandings of such processes in persons. They need not be specified because they are spontaneously hypothesized by people equipped with a normal 'intuitive psychology'. For all its bizarre aspects, even the notion of a zombie includes a host of non-counter-intuitive assumptions. Zombies are characterized as persons and this carries the intuitive assumption that they are solid physical objects, with one definite location in space and with the possibility of interacting with other objects in accordance with intuitive physical expectations. In all these cases, then, we can see that intuitive ontology (1) makes certain representations salient because of their contrast with (or violation of) intuitive expectations and (2) governs people's inferences by activating principles that need not be culturally transmitted.

In the absence of precise and reliable statistical data, it would be difficult to go further as regards the relative spread or distribution of religious ontologies. However, it seems not too unsafe to claim that:

1. some of these combinations (spirits and artefacts with cognitive powers in particular) are so widespread that it would be difficult to find human groups that do not have them;
2. these and other types of religious ontology always require some background input from intuitive ontology;
3. one does not find culturally widespread ontologies that do not combine such categories as person, animal, artefact, and plant with violation or transfer of intuitive psychology, intuitive biology or intuitive physics;
4. when scholarly elites put forth a version of religious ontology that deviate from these combinations, these are generally 'normalized' by popular representations towards one of the cases described here.[2]

The distribution of cultural representations seems to confirm the prediction that religious concepts include violations of core expectations found in intuitive ontology, rather than violations of information at the basic level. Also, these illustrations suggest that in most cases only the overt violations of intuitive expectations are socially transmitted. The intuitive, default background that allows inferences is spontaneously added by people. We must now turn to the mechanisms that produce such recurrence.

Experimental evidence: recall for violations

Let me now turn to experimental studies of differential recall for violations and other types of conceptual representation. That some representations are better recalled than others is a familiar phenomenon, abundantly evidenced in psychology. If we can show that concepts with the particular structure described above have an advantage in terms of recall, this should go some way towards explaining why they can be found in so many cultural systems. Whatever the particular circumstances in which they first appear – these circumstances may differ from one place or time to another – they are simply more likely than others to become stable in a group.

The present model would predict that, all else being equal, counter-intuitive elements are better recalled or recognized than representations that conform to intuitive expectations. However, one of the few direct studies of recall for such material, Bartlett's famous study of transmission chains for mythical stories, seemed to suggest the opposite (Bartlett 1932). For Bartlett, subjects tend to normalize stories to familiar 'schemata' and discard their strange or exotic elements. So one could think that whatever conflicts with 'schemata' or intuitive ontology would be discarded too. However, Bartlett's studies were very limited and could confound two causes for poor recall and distortion. The subjects might have discarded particular items from exotic stories either because they were culturally alien or because they were counter-intuitive, and Bartlett's conclusions about 'schemata' do not distinguish between these two aspects. Although Bartlett's conclusions are often cited and commented on, very few people have bothered to pursue this line of inquiry, or indeed to replicate the original studies. So what I present here is a report on preliminary explorations by J. Barrett and myself, focused on the following questions: Is recall better for counter-intuitives than for intuitive descriptions? Is this a question of 'strangeness'? Is this affected by cultural familiarity? Does the effect obtain in different cultures? For want of space I will give results without detailed descriptions of methods, protocols, and statistics.

Barrett (1996) tried to address Bartlett's original questions in a more controlled and systematic way. These studies used quasi-stories in which a variety of items (PERSONS, ARTEFACTS, ANIMALS) were described as exhibits in an intergalactic museum. Barrett studied transmission of items on three 'generations' of subjects. Recalled items from each generation subjects were used as stimulus material for the next generation. Such studies show that violations of intuitive expectations are the most 'culturally fit' category of items in such conditions. That is, they are not just recalled better but also transmitted in a way that preserves the violations, while control items are sometimes distorted and become 'stranger' with the transmission process.

With slightly different stimuli, Boyer and Ramble (in preparation) chose to measure immediate recall without further transmission to other generations of subjects. A first study included standard items (Sn items) as well as *breaches* of intuitive expectations (Br items, e.g. artefacts that have no shadow or suddenly disappear, people with extraordinary cognitive powers). In both types of item the properties were applied to the appropriate category of objects: the artefacts had physical properties, the persons had psychological properties. The study shows a significant advantage of counter-intuitive items over standard ones. A second study tested standard items against *transfers* of intuitive expectations (Tr items). Here the properties themselves were in conformity with intuitive expectations. Some were applied to the appropriate category (Sn items, e.g. a person with a psychological property) or to the inappropriate one (Tr items, e.g. an artefact with a psychological property). Results showed a significant advantage of Tr items over Sn items. In both studies, then, counter-intuitive items seemed to carry a significant advantage in terms of recall over control items.[3]

Such results may not seem too surprising, as a vast literature documents the recall advantage of 'distinctive' material, that is, representations that do not match the predictions of currently activated conceptual schemata (see Schmidt 1991 for a survey). However, studies of recall generally use material that violates basic-level conceptual information (e.g. a table that is made of chocolate) rather than violations of ontological expectations (e.g. a table that feels pain). Are these two different in terms of recall? If basic-level incongruities and category-level violations were similar in terms of recall, it would be surprising to find that religious concepts generally focus on the latter rather than the former. Indeed, there seem to be differences in terms of recall. Barrett's first studies of transmission made use of three levels of items: violations, basic-level oddities, and standard items. Barrett found a significant transmission advantage for violations and odd items over standard items in the artefact category. In the person category there was an advantage of counter-intuitive material over both odd and standard items. This was only found in the first generation. In further transmission, basic-level violations were often distorted into category-level violations.

If violations of intuitive ontology are recalled better than 'mere oddities', this might suggest that the more bizarre the material, the better. We should expect culturally successful concepts to pile violation upon violation. But this is not the case. Actual religious concepts generally conform to the template described at the beginning and include only a few major violations for a particular category. In the terms of the present model this is because religious concepts are culturally successful if it is possible to derive inferences from them, on the basis of default assumptions. To test whether this had any direct effect on recall, Boyer designed another study with four item-types: standard (Sn), breaches of expectations (Br), transfers of expectations (Tr) and combinations of breaches and transfers (BrTr). For instance, the stories mentioned artefacts with a single location in space (Sn), artefacts that disappear every now and then (Br), artefacts that have offspring (Tr), and artefacts that have offspring of a different 'species' (BrTr). This last item-type combines the activation of an inappropriate domain of expectations for the category (biology in this case) and a breach of expectations within that domain (things that have a biology are assumed to have offspring of the same species). These items are certainly counter-intuitive but they would seem to block ordinary inferences. For instance, from the information that a washing-machine has telephones as offspring it is difficult to infer any other standard artefact properties (since the artefact is obviously strange) or even standard biological properties (since the only one it has violates expectations for objects with a biology). The point of this design was that, if mere strangeness or distance from experience was the factor driving recall, then the subjects' performances would be best for (BrTr) items which were twice removed, as it were, from intuitive ontology. If on the other hand inferential potential was an important factor in recall, then (Br) and (Tr) items should be recalled better than (BrTr). This is precisely what happened and we observed a significant interaction between the presence of breaches and that of transfers. Recall for a combination of breach and transfer is lower than that for either breaches or transfers.

A major prediction of the anthropological model is that, since intuitive ontology does not display major cultural differences, sensitivity to violations of intuitive expectations should be similar in otherwise very different cultures. This would help explain why religious concepts are invariably chosen among the limited list described above. To test this, further experiments with roughly similar material were conducted in Nepal and Gabon (Boyer forthcoming). In the same way as in the French and American studies, a narrative frame embedded a list of items with various counter-intuitive and intuitive descriptions, as well as oddities (basic-level violations). The Nepal experiment involved Bon-Po monks from Tibetan monasteries of Kathmandu. These were all literate scholars, specialized in one particular religious tradition. They were tested on their recall of a text they had read. The Gabon experiments mainly involved illiterate non-specialists and were conducted orally. As an additional difference, it must be noted that religion in a Tibetan context is mainly transmitted through the teachings of literate specialists whereas in Gabon it is only acquired through participation in ritual.

In both Nepal and Gabon, the recall results were fairly similar to those of Western studies.[4] The items that produced the best recall rates were category-level violations for both artefact and person items, with lower recall for oddities and lowest for intuitive descriptions. There were cultural differences too. First, recall for basic-level incongruities would seem to be affected by cultural familiarity; that is, whether one has heard folk-stories that depict similar situations enhances recall. For counter-intuitive items on the other hand, cultural differences seemed to work in the other direction. Tibetan participants are trained in a tradition that emphasizes mental powers and a reflection on consciousness. But they recalled counter-intuitive artefact items much more than person items. This effect was not found among Gabon participants, who are familiar with notions of magical objects. In other words, it would seem that familiarity enhances the recall of oddities, whereas 'exoticism' makes counter-intuitive representations more salient. In both contexts people could readily see a similarity between our 'stories' and the stuff of folk-tales or superstitions, but they did not perceive the similarity with religious concepts.

To sum up: Much remains to be done, and many factors to be controlled before we reach a more precise view of the effect of recall on religious concepts. However, beyond the simple but important point, that it is possible to test anthropological claims in a fairly controlled manner, our experimental studies suggest the following:

1. violations of intuitive expectations do result in high recall, compared to representations that are compatible with intuitive expectations;
2. they also produce higher recall than violations of basic-level inform- ation ('mere oddities');
3. counter-intuitive representations with no inferential potential are not well recalled;
4. these effects are not affected by cultural familiarity (i.e. whether one has heard of similar concepts before), against one possible inter- pretation of Bartlett's results;
5. this is not dependent on the context being marked off as 'religious';
6. the effect is cross-cultural: people from very different locations and cultural settings show similar sensitivity to violations of intuitive expectations, relative both to intuitive understandings and to 'mere oddities'.

These points connect in a fairly direct way with anthropological claims about cultural transmission. Points 1 and 3 would explain why there is a limited catalogue of counter-intuitive concepts in religious ontologies. Point 2 would explain why, although we find departures from basic level information in many religious concepts (e.g. 'spirits like to drink Cologne instead of water'), these are invariably based on departures from intuitive ontology ('spirits are invisible agents'); the latter assumptions are also more central and more stable than the former. Points 4–6 suggest that there is a cross-cultural sensitivity to violations that is used mainly but not exclusively by religious concepts. Whether one finds a concept of 'ghost' in one particular location obviously depends on the history of the group concerned. But the mental equipment that makes people receptive to this local concept is non-cultural, and could accommodate a broader range of possible religious concepts, within the limits described here.

Further queries: religious concepts

So far, I have summarized evidence on three fronts (anthropological record, developmental data, memory experiments) that helps us to describe religious concepts in a fairly rigorous way, as well as to understand their recurrence. To better describe the model, as well as its relevance to cultural transmission, we must answer a few additional questions.

First, is the violation+default principle specific to religious concepts? Using default premises to produce inferences about an otherwise counter-intuitive representation is certainly not an exclusive feature of religious concepts. From an early age, children's pretence play is often based on such combinations.[5] The point also applies to some domains of scientific theories, as mentioned above, as well as to whole domains of fiction and fantasy that are not religious in content. Cartoon-physics and ghost-physics are based on similar principles.

Second, is this exhaustive of religious concepts? No, for the reason given earlier. The present model only applies to ontological concepts. 'Religion' is a combination of a set of ontological commitments with a specific morality, with notions of group-identity, with representations of particular forms of action and of particular experiences. There is no reason to think that all these are represented in similar ways. That diverse 'registers' of religious concepts are represented in different ways could imply that they are transmitted in different ways, a point to which I return below.

Third, is recurrence only a matter of recall? Recall is a crucial aspect of cultural survival, but only one aspect. I do not want to suggest that cultural representations are just recalled representations and that cultural transmission is a monotonic function of memorability. The point here is more modest; differences in recall can cause differences of cultural survival in a way that accounts for some recurrent cultural representations. There are many other aspects of transmission beyond recall, and we have anecdotal evidence that some aspects can even override memory factors. Jokes for instance are notoriously difficult to recall, yet seem extremely stable as a set of cultural representations. They can be construed as the analogue of germs that have few physiological effects yet are extremely contagious. In this case it is fast transmission (and motivation) rather than recall that results in a transmission advantage.

Beyond these simple effects, one must remember that particular modes of transmission can impose strong constraints on the concepts transmitted. Consider for instance the contrast between religious concepts acquired though salient, sensorily rich experiences such as initiation rituals, and those acquired through rote-learning and systematic teaching. These are not simply different routes towards the same conceptual structures. They seem to have a direct influence on the representations acquired and their organization, because different kinds of experience activate different memory processes (Whitehouse 1992; 1995). So the salience and inference constraints described here are only one dimension in the complex dynamics of acquisition. Still, there is definite evidence that, all else being equal, religious concepts tend to display particular combinations of salient assumptions and background inferences in a way that constrains religious ontologies.

Fourth, what assumptions get violated? There seem to be limits to the range of counter-intuitive representations included in religious concepts. 'Counter-intuitive' here only means that religious concepts include explicit assumptions which go against expectations about ontological domains as evidenced in normal five-year-olds (and enriched at later stages). It is quite interesting in this respect that most religious ontologies violate or transfer not sophisticated aspects of intuitive ontology that are acquired late and may be sensitive to particular cultural input, but those core principles that are acquired very early with little cultural variation. For example, spirit-concepts generally involve violations of core physical intuitions about physical objects, such as solidity or continuity, rather than later-acquired notions about the relations between force and momentum for instance. We do not know why this is so, nor do we have good experimental evidence that recall for violations of very early assumptions is better than for violations of later-acquired ones.

Moreover, the present account is very much a 'domain-general' view of salience and recall. It states that violations of intuitive ontology are in general better than other types of representation, and the experiments support this general claim. But we know that some specific counter-intuitive concepts are far more frequent than others. In particular, the notions of (1) physically counter-intuitive but cognitively standard agents and (2) artefacts or natural objects with cognitive processes are quasi-universal, whereas the notion of a zombie (standard physics+counter-intuitive intentional properties) is rare.[6] Guthrie argued that religious concepts generally extend human characteristics to non-human things (Guthrie 1993). It would seem that the extension is in fact more limited. It is only intentional agents' characteristics that are extended in this way.

This may be an effect of the inferential constraint; a religious concept has better survival potential if it allows rich inferences. Now intuitive 'theory of mind' is the richest inference domain humans have, so it should not be surprising that extension of intentionality to non-intentional things has good cultural fitness (Boyer 1996). Still, this remains an ad hoc explanation so long as we have no direct experimental evidence of privileged recall for some particular violations.

Fifth, do violations replace intuitive principles? As I said above, people can get trained in cultural knowledge domains, e.g. scientific physics, whose principles are incompatible with intuitive expectations. It is still debated whether training can override prior intuitions even in such cases of intensive training. In the domain at hand, one might wonder whether intensive cultural training in religious concepts would change people's intuitions. The present model predicts the opposite, because violations are represented explicitly and therefore do not penetrate the cognitive functioning that delivers intuitions. As a consequence, it should be possible to find domains for which people have both (1) cultural representations that conform to intuitive expectations and (2) cultural representations that contradict them. In a sense, this is a familiar situation in cultural anthropology. In discussions of magic and rationality, one often finds the observation that people who hold certain counter-intuitive claims very seriously, as descriptions of real states of affairs, also seem to maintain a generally rational and practical outlook on most everyday affairs. However, the point here is more specific; the model predicts that we should find these contradictory representations in the same domain. For instance, the same person would have divergent representations of the same situation, depending on whether contextual cues make one anticipate violations or not. There are very few systematic investigations of this phenomenon. An exception is Walker's study of Yoruba adults' explanations for natural-kind transformations in ritual versus non-ritual contexts (Walker 1992). Yoruba adults from south-western Nigeria refused to accept, for example, that in an everyday context a cat could turn into a dog. Their explanations centred on the immutability of natural kinds. In contrast, when a cat was disguised as a dog and used as such in a ritual context (the efficacy of a particular Yoruba ritual depending on sacrifice of a dog), the same subjects who had just denied that one animal could turn into another now declared unequivocally that the cat had become a dog. Yoruba adults clearly demonstrated their solid knowledge of causal principles with respect to natural kinds, yet in contexts allowing for violations of those principles, their explanatory accounts were consistent with an understanding of the special nature of those violations.

Sixth, are violations really 'explicit'? So far I have presented a somewhat simplified account of the acquisition of religious concepts, in which people are given an 'explicit' violation of intuitive expectations and they spontaneously activate some 'tacit' information that allows further inferences. This is over-simplified in that violations are themselves inferred from cultural input. Obviously, people are not given information like 'spirits are persons that violate intuitive physics'; that would be meaningless, since people do not explicitly represent their intuitive physics. Rather, people are given information like 'this spirit was here and then went through the wall and reappeared on the other side'. If this is the case, there might be variations in individual interpretations of a single item of cultural input. Anthropologists have quite a lot of anecdotal evidence for this, though the question has generally not been thoroughly investigated. For instance, the Fang people with whom I worked readily assert that 'ghosts cannot normally (i.e. outside visions, dreams, possession) be seen'. However, my – admittedly unsystematic – probing of their representations of that representation produced the most diverse results. Some people thought that ghosts were just transparent, others that ghosts moved too fast to be detected, others still that ghosts were two-dimensional, etc. These divergent interpretations do not interfere with the literal transmission of the 'official' statement that 'ghosts cannot normally be seen'.

A spectacular demonstration of this effect is a study by J. Barett and F. Keil of concepts of 'God' and other counter-intuitive agents in both believers and non-believers (Barrett and Keil 1996). Participants were first asked to produce explicit descriptions of God. These generally centre on counter-intuitive claims for extraordinary cognitive powers. Most subjects describe God as an agent who can perceive everything at once, focus his attention on multiple events simultaneously, and so on. The subjects were then tested on their recall of simple stories involving God in various scenarios where these capacities are relevant. On the whole, subjects tended to distort the stories in ways that were directly influenced by their tacit, intuitive principles of psychology. For instance, they recalled (wrongly) that in the story God attended to some problem and then turned his attention to another, although this contradicts what was said in the original stories. This is particularly impressive in that intuitive principles that specify limitations on cognitive powers (e.g. attention is a serial process) are diametrical to the subjects' explicit beliefs about God.[7] Barrett and Keil use the term 'theological correctness' to denote this tendency for subjects explicitly to entertain a description of supernatural agents that is not actually used in representing or predicting their behaviour.

This study shows, first, that default assumptions do support people's inferential processes about the religious agent, as predicted in the model. Although no one told people that God has a mind that works according to the principles of intuitive 'theory of mind', they routinely activate these principles when wondering what God will do. Second, Barrett and Keil's results also show that the transmission of counter-intuitive representations is more complex than described above. People's explicit and official concept of God includes such propositions as 'God perceives everything at the same time'. However, their 'on-line' concept of God seems to distort this into something like 'God can perceive things beyond obstacles' that is counter-intuitive too but more inference-friendly. Note that this is very likely to happen in cultural settings where a literate elite produces descriptions of religious agents that everyone keeps citing although they routinely use a rather different concept. Whether 'theological correctness' is also found in other settings is a matter for further research, and requires the kind of controlled experiments used by Barrett and Keil.

Further queries: cultural inheritance

This concept-based account of religious ontologies can illustrate more general questions of cultural transmission. A suggestive model of trans-mission is based on an analogy between genes and what Dawkins called 'memes' (Dawkins 1976). These are mentally represented units of information passed along from mind to mind, thereby forming relatively stable 'cultural pools' in analogy with gene-pools. Parallels and inter-actions between genetic and cultural inheritance tracks are described in sophisticated terms in the cluster of models known as 'co-evolution theories' (Cavalli-Sforza and Feldman 1981; Dawkins 1976; Lumsden and Wilson 1981; Boyd and Richerson 1985; see Durham 1991 for a synthetic account of co-evolution and Boyer 1994a for a discussion). Co-evolution theories are based on a selectionist account of cultural transmission. As Durham puts it, 'culture evolves through the differential transmission of ideas, values and beliefs in a population' (1991: 156). All else being equal, certain representations are more likely than others to survive cycles of transmission, and therefore become what anthro-pologists call 'cultural'. The recurrent features of representations within a group, and the recurrence of certain features among groups, are just the outcome of many iterations of this probabilistic selection mechanism.

This selectionist viewpoint is very much the stance taken here in the description of religious ontologies. However, explanations of cultural representations in terms of 'meme-dynamics' include rather implausible assumptions about acquisition and communication. Among them is the notion of replication borrowed from population genetics. The idea is that cultural representations are units of information found in one mind that lodge copies of themselves in other minds. If for instance I hear a song, I form a mental copy of its melody which causes me to sing it sometimes, thereby causing whoever hears me to form a copy of that representation, and so on.

This view of cultural transmission suggests:

1. that cultural concepts themselves are transferred from mind to mind;
2. that all the information that structures those concepts is derived from communication;
3. that concepts formed by different members of a cultural group are identical; and
4. that the acquisition process depends on some general capacity for 'learning culture'.

Each of these points can be revised in the light of the present account of religious ontologies.

1.   Whatever information is passed along is generally not the religious concept itself, but cues that lead people to build that concept. As we saw above, the overt, accessible part of religious concepts is inferred rather than directly 'downloaded' from one mind to another. Concepts of spirits as intentional agents with non-standard physics, or of God as an agent with non-standard cognitive capacities, are acquired through social interaction with cultural peers and elders who hold beliefs about the existence and properties of such entities. But they are obviously not transmitted in that general, descriptive, contextless fashion, but recon-stituted from particular statements about particular circumstances. This is an inferential process that may differ from one mind to another, with corresponding changes in the explicit part of the religious concept.

2.   The overt, salient component that is culturally communicated is only part of the conceptual structure of religious categories. Assumption-violations (e.g. 'an agent that goes through solid obstacles') or assumption transfers (e.g. an artefact with biological properties) are completed with a set of intuitive assumptions (from intuitive psychology, intuitive biology, etc.) which support inferences about the agents or artefacts in question. Now these assumptions need not be acquired through communication. No one needs to 'learn' the principles of intuitive-psychology in the sense of having them passed through communication, or to 'learn' that if they apply to human agents they should apply by default to other types of

agent. These additional assumptions are activated spontaneously. So one crucial part of religious concepts is a set of assumptions that do not form a 'meme'.

3.   The concepts are not necessarily identical. First, people's recall for explicit statements is generally not perfect. In our experiments, recall data show that people very often modify the stimuli and generally add to the original formulation. Second, inferential processes (see point 1 above) introduces further differences. Third, additional background assumptions (point 2 above) may be activated in different ways by different people. So my claim here is not (and in fact cannot be) that a part of a religious concept (a 'meme') replicates itself from mind to mind. Rather, the idea is that, in the long run, people's representations tend to gather around a certain number of particularly robust combinations of assumptions (what Sperber calls 'attractors', Sperber 1994).

4.   Cultural transmission does not require a general capacity for culture. In this account, religious representations are acquired and built in relatively stable ways because of the specific interaction between certain overt, publicly available representations on the one hand and intuitive ontology on the other. Notice that this interaction is specific, that is, it only describes representations that tap the special attention-grabbing quality or salience of counter-intuitive descriptions in a way that activates particular background inferential capacities. The particulars of this model apply to religious ontologies, but other domains of cultural representations may evoke cognitive predispositions of a different nature and interact with them in a different way.

This last point is particularly important. The present model accounts for a domain of representations that does not correspond to traditional anthropological labels. The domain includes recurrent features of religious ontologies, what it aimed to explain in the first place, but also counter-intuitive 'cartoon-physics' and science-fiction stories. Belief in psycho-analysis, too, may well be based on the kind of combination described here, with overt assumption violations (there is an intentional agent inside you – the unconscious – but it's not you) and intuitive inferential processes (that agent can be understood in terms of intuitive psychology: it perceives, knows, believes, intends, etc.).[8] But the model does not apply to the whole of 'religion' as commonly understood. As I said at the beginning of this chapter, religion comprises ontology, but also a morality, particular aspects of ethnic identity, and sometimes varieties of private experience. There is no reason to think that these domains are acquired in the same way as religious ontological concepts. Each of them certainly activates cognitive predispositions. Morality and group-identity for instance may activate predispositions for certain kinds of social exchange, reciprocal altruism, and the representation of kinship ties. But these have little to do with assumption-violations and assumption-transfers as described here. 'Religion' may seem an integrated package, where ontology underwrites a morality that is the basis for a certain group-solidarity between followers, so that there seem to be strong connections between the various aspects of the package. This, however, does not mean that their different parts depend on similar transmission processes.

More generally, there seem to be many different types of cognitive predisposition, all of them of a strictly domain-specific nature. It follows that there is no such thing as 'learning culture' in general, and probably no such thing as a 'culture-learning' capacity. In various domains, cultural representations made manifest by other people activate this or that specialized predisposition. People's patterns of social exchange are acquired through activation of predispositions for exchange, altruism and cheater-detection (Barkow, Cosmides and Tooby 1992). People's statements about group identity may activate predispositions for certain types of representation of social categories and kinship ties (Hirschfeld 1989; 1994). There is no evidence that all these have the same acquisition and transmission patterns. Note, too, that talking about 'predispositions' in no way implies that there is nothing to acquire from cultural input, quite the opposite. It is precisely because predispositions are rich, specific, and complex that they allow people to acquire vast ranges of cultural representations, within the boundaries of each domain.

To sum up: *pace* co-evolution theories, there may be no single 'inheritance track' for cultural representations but a variety of specific cognitive tracks, each with its particular dynamics. Rather than try to describe the acquisition and transmission and evolution of culture, it may be more rational to talk about the acquisition of various competencies. The taxonomy of such competencies does not follow traditional distinctions (e.g. politics, religion, kinship) because it depends on distinctions between evolved predispositions, and these are geared to specific domains of adaptive value (exchange, sexual preferences, kinship-based behaviour, etc.).

Epilogue: genes, development and culture

We can now return to the general question of transmission, cultural epidemics, and the general framework for cultural evolution that includes evolution as its causal background. Before getting into the detail of that question, it may be of help at this point to distinguish those questions that are tractable for those that are not. Debating what is the best explanation for a phenomenon is worthwhile only inasmuch as there is agreement on what the phenomenon is and what a satisfactory explanation would be. This rules out pseudo-controversies between projects that cannot be compared simply because they do not have the same goals. For instance, many anthropologists are interested in describing what is distinctive about particular cultural environments. In this kind of project, considerations about the general abilities of the species might be of value as a general background but they cannot be a central point of interest. There is no principled discussion that could establish whether it is intrinsically 'better' or 'more scientific' to be interested in the Fang of Cameroon as opposed to other human groups, rather than in humankind as opposed to other species. In the same way, there is no principled way of deciding whether it is a more worthwhile project to try to build a 'phenomenologically valid' account of cognition, as C. Toren proposes in Chapter Five, or a scientific one.

By contrast, there is a (potentially) tractable debate between projects that agree that human culture has general features and that these are connected to the evolution of the species through natural selection. In this respect, it may be of interest briefly to compare the claims made here with the kind of 'interactionist' view put forward by T. Ingold in Chapter Four. Ingold argues against naturalized views of culture that include Darwinian accounts of cognitive predispositions. For Ingold, there is a *reductio* here, in that naturalizing anthropologists and evolutionary psychologists are led to think that properties of organisms are 'written in' the genome and 'read off' during development. But, as Ingold rightly points out, there is no way one could 'read off' genotypes in that way and there is no way cultural concepts could be 'read off' universal cognitive capacities. DNA strings under-determine the development of cognition and cognitive capacities under-determine cultural concepts, because development consists of an 'interaction' between prior information and external circumstances.

This argument may be based on a slight misunderstanding of the specific claims of naturalizing anthropology and evolutionary psychology. The point about genetic properties is not that they are 'contained' in strings of genetic code, although popular representations of modern genetics may give this false impression. The point is that, given a particular genotype, certain developmental consequences are practically inevitable in normal circumstances. This is a *ceteris paribus* clause. Unless very strange conditions prevail, children will develop a first set of teeth, then lose it and grow the permanent set during middle childhood. Vitamin-deprived children may have a different developmental trajectory, to be sure, and we know nothing of children raised in zero-gravity or fed by an intravenous drip instead of chewable food. We can exclude these circumstances as exceptional, not just because they are rare (they could become common) but because they were not part of the conditions prevailing when the genes in question were selected. In much the same way, children have a step-wise linguistic development that will invariably include a vocabulary explosion between two and five (with a 'noun spurt' as its main component), a one-word stage followed by two-word utterances followed by syntactic development with recursive structures and rich morphology. This is not 'written' in the code, but will occur in normal circumstances. Children raised in isolation will not develop like that, because normal circumstances include the presence of adult speakers.

To say that a full phenotype should be 'written' in DNA strings, for evolutionary biology to be taken seriously, seems a mistake either about causation in genetics or about the notion of information used in evolutionary theory. Let me first consider the question of causes. The problems here may result from a confusion between the 'cause' for an event and what Mill called the 'total cause', the sum of all necessary conditions. If you strike a match in a wood and start a forest-fire, it is safe to say that your imprudence was the cause of the fire. Now one could say that it is not the whole story, for the fire would not have developed without a set of background necessary conditions: the wood was dry, wood is flammable, there was oxygen around, gravity pulled the burning match to the ground, etc. A 'cause' is simply what will produce the effect given standard conditions, and in this sense striking a match really caused the fire. And having genes of a certain type will cause particular patterns of tooth-growth and lexical acquisition during early childhood, given standard developmental conditions. It is the cause of those phenotypic properties, in the sense that in similar conditions other genes would have triggered the development of different teeth or a different pattern of lexical growth.

If causes are not too difficult to sort out, then information may be the problem, and is indeed a trickier concept. The only sense in which DNA strings carry 'information' is in the strict, information-theoretic sense, that properties of the string reliably trigger systematic changes in protein manufacture, which reliably cause changes in cell structure and so on. It is difficult to underestimate the distance between this technical concept of information, as a causal connection between states of a source and states of a target system, and the commonsense notion. We usually think that information is 'contained' in some source and readily say that a book 'contains' a narrative or that airline timetables 'include' information about flight departures. But this is just a loose way of speaking. Books and time-tables only contain ink-patterns. A complex combination of visual recognition, phonological identification, lexical access, parsing, and pragmatic inference is required to produce cognitive effects on the basis of those ink-patterns. Trivial incidents illustrate how wrong this notion of information as 'contained' in the source may be. If you try to read with the wrong software a computer file that 'contains' your article, you will soon find out that the file only 'contains' garbled code, except for the application programme that created it. The same goes for DNA strings, which 'contain' recipes for organism-building only for the complex bio-chemical factory they happen to be in. Tooth-growth and lexical acquisition are no more 'contained' in the genome than a tragic love story is 'contained' in my copy of *Anna Karenina*. But the ink-patterns in that volume are structured in such a way that they cause me, a normal reader, to follow a tragic love story if I read them sequentially. Arrangements of genes cause the cell factory to develop in such a way that tooth-growth and lexical acquisition follow the usual patterns, typical of the species.

This leads us, finally, to the question of 'innate' modules, propensities, sensitivities and suchlike. To many people, it is quite clear that having an evolutionary approach to cognitive capacities means that those capacities are 'innate'. It is much more difficult to understand what those opponents of evolutionary psychology mean by 'innate', a term that is not really used these days in either evolutionary biology or evolutionary psychology. Conceptual capacities are probably not 'innate' in the sense of being present in the newborn human, any more than teeth or a fully-formed larynx are there. There is a lot of information processing that infants do very badly or cannot do at all. I do not think that anyone seriously interested in evolutionary biology would deny that. In fact, there seems to be a confusion here between a capacity being evolved, a result of adaptation by natural selection, and that capacity being 'innate', whatever that means. The distinctions presented above should make things a bit clearer and show why the term is profoundly misleading. To say that some capacity is evolved means that, given the human genotype and standard epigenetic environments, they are bound to appear in the normal adult. That is, had evolutionary environments been different, that capacity would not have been selected for in the course of evolution.

It is not altogether clear in what sense 'interactionism' goes against this Darwinian view of human capacities. 'Interactionism' is certainly true, if the claim is that no DNA string could ever contain a description of full organisms and full developmental patterns. These depend on the complex embryological factory DNA strings interact with. On the other hand, if the interactionist claim is that all background conditions are causes in the development of organisms, then it seems clearly false. We are trying to explain why humans have the capacities they have, for instance the capacity to make inferences about living kinds (even unknown or imaginary ones) that they do not make about artefacts. There are two absurd explanations of this capacity. One is what Tooby and Cosmides call 'incoherent environmentalism', the view that there must be something in developing environments that lead subjects to have that capacity (Tooby and Cosmides 1992). The problem is that we don't know what that 'something' is, and in fact we could not find out. Environments differ wildly and the capacity does not. Another magical explanation is that the capacity is already contained in the newborn infant's mind. This would leave us with the difficult question of why the capacity develops instead of being there from the start. A third possibility has none of the absurdity of these alternatives, but it is far more difficult to investigate. It assumes that the genotype results in the type of neural structure which, faced with stimuli from a normal environment, would tend to favour slightly different types of categorization processes for things that move by themselves and things that do not. This may be based on computational differences which by themselves carry no presumption about the domain to which they will be applied. In other words we need not suppose that there are concepts of living thing and artefact to start with. Computational differences may be very subtle and result in very deep conceptual differences, and finally in full-blown conceptual distinctions. (On such developmental dynamics, see Thelen and Smith 1995 and Whitehouse's account of Edelman's selectionist model, in the concluding chapter of this volume.) It is true that we know practically nothing about how this computational development unfolds. But we know this is where we must look. The same goes for higher capacities and more complex acquisition processes, including those relevant to cultural transmission.

Notes

1. Otherwise the claim that 'religious concepts violate intuitive expectations' might degenerate into a series of ad hoc assumptions. For each religious concept we would postulate an ontological expectation that is violated.

2. This is a familiar phenomenon. A scholarly elite can devise representations that go far beyond the violation-transfer system described here and, for instance, postulate an ontology that contradicts intuitions of identity (in the case of the Holy Trinity) or assumptions about agency (in the case of the non-anthropomorphic universe of literate Buddhism). Such constructions are transmitted in their own right through scholarly transmission, and routinely ignored (in Christianity) or supplemented (in the case of Buddhism) by popular culture.

3. The first study, comparing Sn to Br items, used different versions of a story with 24 test sentences and 10 fillers, describing both artefacts and persons. The participants (N=18) recalled an average of 10.22 items out of 24, over all categories. The following table breaks down results in terms of category (artefact vs person) and item-type (Sn vs Br), with standard deviation (S.D.) between brackets, out of six items in each cell.

	Sn items	*Br items*
Artefact items	2.61 [1.15]	3.61 [1.04]
Person items	1.11 [1.2]	2.89 [1.67]

The second study, comparing Sn to Tr items, had similar stories with 24 test sentences and six items in each cell. The participants (N= 22) recalled an average of 11.86 items out of 24. The results, broken down by category and item-type are given in the table below.

	Sn items	*Tr items*
Artefact items	2.91 [1.72]	3.5 [1.4]
Person items	2.22 [1.45]	3.23 [1.2]

In both studies the main effect of item-type (Sn vs either Br or Tr) was significant, $p<.05$. In these studies, participants also had to fill out questionnaires about all the items, rating first their 'divergence' from ordinary experience and second their familiarity, i.e. whether these items had been encountered before in fiction, dreams, fantasies, etc. There was a strong correlation between recall performance and intuitive distance from everyday experience, as we expected, but no correlation with cultural familiarity. The fact that an item was rated as 'encountered before' did not correlate with that item being recalled more than novel ones. See details in Boyer and Ramble (in preparation).

4. The Gabon experiment was run with non-literate Fang speakers in Libreville (N=81). The stories were adapted from the materials used in the French studies. They combined three types of item: Sn (control), Bs (basic level violations) and Ov (Ontological violation) with six items per cell. The category variable was a between-subject variable. Here are the results broken down by category and item-type, giving average recall out of six items, with S.D. between brackets:

	Sn items	Bs items	Ov items
Artefact items	1.56 [1.12]	1.82 [1.1]	2.31 [1.59]
Person	1.81 [1.17]	2.02 [1.26]	2.6 [1.5]

The Katmandu experiments were run with male monks at the Triten Norbutse monastery (N=30). The stories were similar to the ones used in Gabon, with category as a between-subject variable. The table below breaks down results by category and item-type out of six items, with S.D. between brackets:

	Sn items	Bs items	Ov items
Artefact items	2.15 [1.14]	2.62 [1.26]	3.31 [1.7]
Person	1.59 [1.42]	2.06 [1.43]	2.41 [1.06]

In both experiments there was a significant effect of item-type, $p<.05$. See Boyer and Ramble (in preparation) for details and discussion.

5. For instance, children who pour pretend-water from pretend-containers nevertheless assume that liquids flow downwards; children who talk to an imaginary (invisible) companion still assume that the companion's body has only one location in space, etc.

6. In all cultural environments where one finds concepts of 'zombies', these non-intentional agents are invariably construed as 'remote-controlled' by other agents, and the latter always have all the standard features of intentional agents.

7. Incidentally, it is striking that neither the explicit concept nor the inferences produced by subjects show any difference correlated with the subjects' particular faith or denomination, or even their general attitude towards religion. Atheists, Hindus and Christians of various denominations have similar performance. The study was replicated by Barrett in India with Hindu participants, using a combination of Hindu deities and novel counter-intuitive agents, with similar results.

8. For Gellner, the success of psychoanalysis as a cultural phenomenon resulted from the combination of (1) the cognitive 'shock' caused by its strange claims and (2) the profound banality of its assumptions about cognitive functioning (Gellner 1979).

References

Antell, E. and Keating, D.P. (1983), 'Perception of numerical invariance in neonates', *Child Development*, 54: 695–701.

Atran, S. (1990), *Cognitive Foundations of Natural History: Towards an Anthropology of Science*, Cambridge: Cambridge University Press.

Baillargeon, R. (1987), 'Young infants' reasoning about the physical and spatial characteristics of a hidden object', *Cognitive Development*, 2: 179–200.

—— and Hanko-Summers, S. (1990), 'Is the top object adequately supported by the bottom object? Young infants' understanding of support relations', *Cognitive Development*, 5: 29–53.

Barkow, J., Cosmides, L. and Tooby, J. (eds) (1992), *The Adapted Mind: Evolutionary Psychology and the Generation of Culture*, New York: Oxford University Press.

Baron-Cohen, S. (1991), 'Precursors to a theory of mind: understanding attention in others', in A. Whiten (ed.), *Natural Theories of Mind*, Oxford: Blackwell.

—— (1995), *Mindblindness: An Essay on Autism and Theory of Mind*, Cambridge, Mass: MIT Press.

—— and Cross, P. (1992), 'Reading the eyes: evidence for the role of perception in the development of a theory of mind', *Mind and Language*, 6: 173–86.

Barrett, J.L. (1996), *Anthropomorphism, Intentional Agents, and Conceptualizing God*, PhD dissertation, Ithaca, NY: Cornell University.

—— and Keil, F.C. (1996), 'Conceptualizing a non-natural entity: Anthropomorphism in God concepts', *Cognitive Psychology*, 31: 219–47

Bartlett, F.C. (1932), *Remembering: A Study in Experimental and Social Psychology*, Cambridge: Cambridge University Press.

Bastien, J.W. (1978), *Mountain of the Condor: Metaphor and Ritual in an Andean Ayllu*, St. Paul: West Publishing Company.

Becker, A.H. and Ward, T.B. (1991), 'Children's use of shape in extending novel labels to animate objects: identity versus postural change', *Developmental Psychology*, 6: 3–16.

Boyd, R. and Richerson, P. (1985), *Culture and the Evolutionary Process*, Chicago: University of Chicago Press.

Boyer, P. (1992), 'Explaining religious ideas: outline of a cognitive approach', *Numen*, 39: 27–57.

—— (1994a), 'Cognitive constraints on cultural representations: natural ontologies and religious ideas', in L.A. Hirschfeld and S.A. Gelman (eds), *Mapping The Mind: Domain-Specificity in Cognition and Culture*, New York: Cambridge University Press.

—— (1994b), *The Naturalness of Religious Ideas: A Cognitive Theory of Religion*, Berkeley/Los Angeles: University of California Press.

—— (1996), 'What makes anthropomorphism natural: intuitive ontology and cultural representations', *Journal of the Royal Anthropological Institute* (N.S.), 2: 1–15.

—— and Ramble, C., 'Cognitive templates for religious concepts: cross-cultural evidence for recall of counter-intuitive representations' (forthcoming *Cognitive Science*).

Carey, S. (1985), *Conceptual Change in Childhood*, Cambridge, Mass.: MIT Press.

Cavalli-Sforza, L.L. and Feldman, M.W. (1981), *Cultural Transmission and Evolution: A Quantitative Approach*, Princeton, NJ: Princeton University Press.

Dawkins, R. (1976), *The Selfish Gene*, New York: Oxford University Press.

Durham, W.H. (1991), *Coevolution, Genes, Cultures and Human Diversity*, Stanford: Stanford University Press.

Gallistel, C.R. and Gelman, R. (1992), 'Preverbal and verbal counting and computation', *Cognition*, 44: 43–74.

Gellner, E. (1979), 'Notes towards a theory of ideology', in I.C. Jarvie and J. Agassi (eds), *Spectacles and Predicaments: Essays in Social Theory*, Cambridge: Cambridge University Press.

Gelman, R. (1990), 'First principles organize attention and learning about relevant data: number and the animate-inanimate distinction as examples', *Cognitive Science*, 14: 79–106.

Gelman, S.A. (1988), 'The development of induction within natural kind and artefact categories', *Cognitive Psychology*, 20: 65–95.

——, Collman, P. and Maccooby, P. (1986), 'Inferring properties from categories versus inferring categories from properties: the case of gender', *Child Development*, 57: 396–404.

—— and Markman, E. (1987), 'Young children's inductions from natural kinds: The role of categories and appearances', *Child Development*, 58: 1532–41.

Gopnik, A. (1993), 'How we know our minds: the illusion of first-person knowledge of intentionality', *The Behavioural and Brain Sciences*, 16: 1–14.

—— and Astington, J.W. (1988), 'Children's understanding of representational change and its relation to understanding false belief and the appearance-reality distinction', *Child Development*, 58: 26–37.

—— and Meltzoff, A.N. (1987), 'The development of categorization in the second year and its relation to other cognitive and linguistic developments', *Child Development*, 58: 1523–31.

—— (1997), *Words, Thoughts, and Theories*, Cambridge, Mass.: MIT Press.

Guthrie, S.E. (1993), *Faces in the Clouds: A New Theory of Religion*, New York: Oxford University Press.

Hirschfeld, L.A. (1989), 'Rethinking the acquisition of kinship terms', *International Journal of Behavioral Development*, 12: 541–68.

—— (1994), The acquisition of social categories', in L.A. Hirschfeld and S.A. Gelman (eds), *Mapping The Mind: Domain-Specificity in Cognition and Culture*, New York: Cambridge University Press.

Inagaki, K. and Hatano, G. (1987), 'Young children's spontaneous personification as analogy', *Child Development*, 58: 1013–20.

Inagaki, K. and Sugiyama, K. (1988), 'Attributing human characteristics: developmental changes in over- and under-attribution', *Cognitive Development*, 3: 55–70.

James, W. (1988), *The Listening Ebony: Moral Knowledge, Religion, and Power among the Uduk of Sudan*, Oxford: Oxford University Press.

Keil, F.C. (1986), 'The acquisition of natural kind and artefact terms', in A.W.D. Marrar (ed.), *Conceptual Change*, Norwood, NJ: Ablex.

Lumsden, C.J. and Wilson, E.O. (1981), *Genes, Minds and Culture*, Cambridge, Mass.: Harvard University Press.

Mandler, J. and Bauer, P. (1989), 'The cradle of categorization: is the basic level basic?', *Cognitive Development*, 4: 247–64.

—— and McDonough, L. (1991), 'Separating the sheep from the goats: differentiating global categories', *Cognitive Psychology*, 23: 263–98.

Massey, C. and Gelman, R. (1988), 'Preschoolers' ability to decide whether pictured unfamiliar objects can move themselves', *Developmental Psychology*, 24: 307–17.

Meltzoff, A. (1994), 'Imitation, memory, and the representation of persons', *Infant Behavior and Development* 17: 83–99.

Métraux, A. (1958), *Le Vaudou Haitien*, Paris: Gallimard.

Morton, J. and Johnson, M. (1991), 'CONSPEC and CONLERN: A two-process theory of infant face-recognition', *Psychological Review*, 98: 164–81.

Perner, J. (1991), *Understanding the Representational Mind*, Cambridge, Mass.: MIT Press.

Perner, J., Leekam, S.R. and Wimmer, H. (1987), 'Three year olds' difficulty with false belief', *British Journal of Developmental Psychology*, 5: 125–37.

Rosengren, K.S., Gelman, S., Kalish, C.W. and McCormick, M. (1991), 'As time goes by: children's early understanding of growth in animals', *Child Development*, 62: 1302–20.

Schmidt, S.R. (1991), 'Can we have a distinctive theory of memory?', *Memory and Cognition*, 19: 523–42.

Severi, C. (1993), 'Talking about souls', in P. Boyer (ed.), *Cognitive Aspects of Religious Symbolism*, Cambridge: Cambridge University Press.

Spelke, E.S. (1990), 'Principles of object perception', *Cognitive Science*, 14: 29–56.

Sperber, D. (1994), 'The modularity of thought and the epidemiology of representations', in L.A. Hirschfeld and S.A. Gelman (eds), *Mapping the Mind: Domain-Specificity in Cognition and Culture*, New York: Cambridge University Press.

Springer, K. and Keil, F.C. (1989), 'On the development of specifically biological beliefs: the case of inheritance', *Child Development*, 60: 637–48.

Springer, K. and Keil, F.C. (1991), 'Early differentiation of causal mechanisms appropriate to biological and non-biological kinds', *Child Development*, 62: 767–81.

Starkey, P., Spelke, E.S. and Gelman, R. (1990), 'Numerical abstraction by human infants', *Cognition*, 36: 97–127.

Thelen, E. and Smith, L.B. (1995), *A Dynamic Systems Approach to the Development of Cognition and Action*, Cambridge, Mass.: MIT Press.

Tooby, J. and Cosmides, L. (1992), 'The Psychological foundations of culture', in J. Barkow, L. Cosmides and J. Tooby (eds), *The Adapted Mind: Evolutionary Psychology and the Generation of Culture*, New York: Oxford University Press.

Walker, S. (1992), 'Developmental changes in the representation of word-meaning: cross-cultural findings', *British Journal of Developmental Psychology*, 10: 285–99.

Wellmann, H. (1990), *The Child's Theory of Mind*, Cambridge, Mass.: MIT Press.

—— and Estes, D. (1986), 'Early understandings of mental entities: a re-examination of childhood realism', *Child Development*, 57: 910–23.

Whitehouse, H. (1992), 'Memorable religions: transmission, codification and change in divergent Melanesian contexts', *Man* (N.S.), 27: 777–97.

—— (1995), *Inside the Cult: Religious Innovation and Transmission in Papua New Guinea*, Oxford: Oxford University Press.

Whiten, A. (ed.), (1991), *Natural Theories of Mind: The Evolution, Development and Simulation of Everyday Mindreading*, Oxford: Blackwell.

Wimmer, H. and Perner, J. (1983), 'Beliefs about beliefs: Representation and constraining function of wrong beliefs in young children's understanding of deception', *Cognition* 13: 103–28.

3

Some Elements of a Science of Culture
Henry Plotkin

Culture is the product of interacting human minds, and hence a science of culture will be a science of the most complex phenomenon on Earth. It will also be a science that must be built on interdisciplinary foundations including genetics, neuroscience, individual development, ecology and evolutionary biology, psychology and anthropology. In other words, a complete explanation of culture, if such a thing is ever possible, is going to comprise a synthesis of all human science. Such a synthesis poses significant conceptual and methodological problems, but also difficulties of another kind for those contributing to this science. Scholars from different disciplines are going to have to be tolerant of one another, open to ideas from other areas of knowledge; and they will have to relinquish old territorial claims or renounce grandiose and imperialist intellectual aims. A science of culture belongs to all of us. It continues to surprise those of us who watch events from the sidelines how entrenched positions are maintained, and also at the persistence of old and wholly unfounded fears. It is, of course, true that down the years some biologists have made occasional preposterous statements about the human sciences; a more recent phenomenon is the sometimes absurd and incorrect assertions made about contemporary biology by social scientists. None of this is con-structive and neither is it necessary because the old fears of a rampant reductionist biology taking over the social sciences have not, and never will be, realized.

The unnecessary defensiveness of the social sciences

Most animals are not intelligent and have other adaptive capacities for adjusting their behaviour in order to satisfy their energy and other requirements. Intelligence, defined broadly as the capacity adaptively to alter behaviour based upon some form, no matter how elementary, of internalized representations of the world (i.e. neural network states that correlate with features of the world), caused by individual experience and individual history, probably evolved hundreds of millions of years ago, perhaps soon after the appearance of multicellular animals. There presently is no understanding exactly why a comparatively small number of animals evolved intelligence. Since intelligence is a costly adaptation there must have been strong selection forces for its evolution, these most likely relating in part to amounts and rates of environmental change. If the rates of change in the world do not exceed the rates at which evolutionary processes work, then, put crudely, these processes result in the gene pools of populations having arrays of genes present in high frequencies which furnish individuals with the starting conditions (not the only conditions) such that they develop, given the necessary other conditions, into viable but unintelligent phenotypes. But if certain features of the world are relatively unstable, then evolution cannot establish the starting conditions by which adaptation to these features of the world might occur. If these features of the world are significant, then one solution to these selection pressures is to evolve semi-autonomous tracking devices which form the basis for intelligence-guided, adaptive behavioural responses to these rapidly changing events.

This is a massively truncated account of the evolutionary origins of intelligence; the fuller argument can be found in Plotkin (1995). I present it here to make a point, which is another way of telling the same story. Intelligence evolved because evolutionary processes on their own were unable under certain circumstances to provide appropriate and viable behavioural repertoires. What this means is that in intelligent creatures, some of the causes of their behaviour are generated within their own brains, and this is so precisely because of the limitations of the evolutionary processes. Were these limitations not present, intelligence probably would not have evolved. But once evolved, any causal analysis of the behaviour of intelligent creatures must accord with this shift in causation. Brains are a source of behavioural causation no less than are genes. Moreover, as Waddington recognized in his notion of the exploitive system (Waddington 1958), which he defined as 'the capacity of animals to select, out of the range open to them, the particular environments in which they will pass their life, and thus to have an influence on the type of natural selective pressure to which they will be subjected', intelligence can have a causal force on the course of evolution itself, most directly in terms of mate choice, and less directly in matters such as habitat choice (see Plotkin, 1988 for a review).

If this argument is correct, then a genetic reductive account of the behaviour of any intelligent animal is literally impossible. Since I take culture to be a special manifestation of human intelligence, precisely the same arguments apply to ourselves, but with even greater force. The social sciences operate within a domain that simply cannot be reduced. As with intelligence, the line of argument can be extended by noting how culture has entered as a causal force into human evolution. There are a number of empirically certain examples, the best known being lactose tolerance, details of which can be found in Durham (1991). What follows is a brief and hence somewhat inaccurate account.

Approximately two-thirds of all people in the world have varying degrees of difficulty in digesting lactose, a sugar found in mammalian milk. Prior to weaning, the enzymes that allow lactose absorption are present in the alimentary tracts of all people. Around the time of weaning these enzyme levels decline in most people, and the illness that results from drinking milk in those who are lactose intolerant can be severe – indeed in those suffering from illness or malnourishment, it can be fatal. Most people from Africa, South Asia and South-east Asia are lactose intolerant. However, 95 per cent of Scandinavians are lactose tolerant. Across Europe there is a marked gradient in the ability of adults to absorb lactose, being high in the north and declining towards the south and east. Correlating with this gradient are customs of animal husbandry, milk production, and milk-product preparation such that in Northern Europe there is largely consumption of unprocessed milk and its products like cream which are lactose rich, whereas as one moves towards the Levant processed milk products like yogurt and kefir, which have greatly reduced lactose levels, become common. There are also culturally propagated myths about milk consumption which accompany the dietary and food-preparation practices. It is widely accepted that lactose tolerance is caused by a mutant gene which has become fixated at high frequencies in populations that in the past combined high nutritional stress with vitamin D deficiency, the latter being prevalent among people who live in regions of low sunlight levels. The benefit to the peoples of northern Europe of being able to consume milk without it making them ill is clear. The result was strong selection for the mutant gene which bestowed this benefit. However, the engine driving this evolutionary event was not the mutant gene. The engine was the invention and propagation of animal husbandry and dairying practices, all part of the agricultural revolution, which, of course, was one of the most significant achievements of human culture in human history.

A similar story can be told using migration, genocide, and warfare, among many other cultural examples. The moral of these stories is that biology and culture relate to one another as a two-way street of causation.

As will be argued below, evolutionary forces must have played a part in the formation of the human capacity to enter into and participate in culture, and culture has been a force in human evolution. The latter is an instance of what Campbell (1974) called downward causation, which is an additional counter to the claims of what genetic reductionist arguments can achieve.

Why must evolution enter into an understanding of culture?

Why, in other words, is it a two-way street? Why not just accept that culture is a trait that humans have and that it has affected the evolution of our species? In order to answer that question, especially in a book such as this one which presents such diverse views, all of us should be explicit about what Bohm (1969) referred to as one's metaphysics, i.e. those most basic assumptions that scientists have about the phenomena that we study and what we consider to be an adequate explanation of them. Virtually all scientists, and I assume that includes social scientists – it certainly includes me – are materialists or physicalists (to use a word from a somewhat different philosophy of science tradition) and ontological reductionists. That is, most scientists believe that all things are physical things and nothing else. There is no untouchable or unmeasurable force or property of life beyond an immensely complex organization of chemicals and the physical forces that act on them. The mind is the workings of the brain, including the connectivity of billions of individual brain cells, not some non-physical essence that hovers about our heads and follows us around. Because culture, as already pointed out, is some kind of complex interlocking organization of many minds, it is the most complicated thing in the known universe. Nonetheless, culture too is not some kind of untouchable non-physical essence that fills the spaces between people making up a society. Culture is what happens in people's minds when they interact in certain ways with other minds and with the artefacts that are often central to those interactions.

If we are all ontological reductionists adopting a materialist stance and accepting that there must be psychological processes and mechanisms which give rise to culture, then there seem to be only two possible ways of thinking about how these arose. The one is that whatever these processes and mechanisms are (more of which later), they all arose by chance without selection. The other is that at least some of these are based upon processes and mechanisms which were selected for other purposes or were selected de novo because culture is a powerful force in human survival, or some mixture of both. For me the notion that all the constituent processes that make culture possible have not been fashioned by selection is simply inconceivable. My sense of it not being conceivable is based both on the notion of complexity and on the view that culture is the outcome of a number of processes and mechanisms. There are, doubtless, processes and mechanisms of mind that are not the result of evolution, but these are not likely to be complex processes and mechanisms. That is the point. At least two of the aspects of mind that I will consider below are complex, and complexity has long been held to point to the workings of evolution. For several complex features of the human mind to have arisen entirely by chance, all of which are essential for people to be creatures of culture, invokes likelihoods so remote as not to be worth considering.

Furthermore, if we are indeed all ontological reductionists, and if we do all accept that culture is a complex, many-tiered phenomenon that can only be fully understood through its study at all these tiers, and if as ontological reductionists we all accept that a causal explanation of culture must be in terms of processes and mechanisms operating within and between these tiers, then I am at a loss to account for the continuing hostility of some social scientists to biological approaches to the human sciences, including culture, as evidenced by some of the chapters in this book. Yes, some of us will concentrate our thoughts and studies on one tier, others on another tier. Some will confine attention just to a single tier, while others might busy themselves with the relationships between tiers. Why, though, should anyone evince hostility to such a pluralist approach to culture? Why the intolerance?

It could, I suppose, be misunderstanding, but I rather think not. There are too many good, accessible, and easily available accounts of evolutionary theory in libraries and bookshops, and the hostility is coming from widely-read people of high intelligence. For example, Ingold asserts that for biologists, or at any rate conventional evolutionary biologists, 'evolutionary change is fundamentally genetic' (Chapter Four, p. 163). This is simply incorrect. Ingold is either ignorant of modern evolutionary biology, a possibility which I doubt, or the assertion is driven by some other, and rather mysterious, motive. I have before me Ridley (1996), which is an excellent broad-based and conventional text on evolutionary biology. It comprises five parts, one of which is on evolutionary genetics. The rest, historical accounts of changing evolutionary theories aside, is devoted to adaptations, units of selection, diversity, bio-geography, speciation, the fossil record, co-evolution, and extinction. Genes will enter in a small way into all of these topics, and in a big way on the question of the units of selection. The rest is about whole organisms.

Evolution refers to the transformation of biological forms and systems in time. It is about dynamical, changing entities and events. Its recognition in the last century marked the switch to modern thinking about the living world and a departure from an older more static view of life. Darwin built his theory without any knowledge of genetics. He did not need genetics to create a viable theory, even though it was incomplete (as he knew it was). Now we understand that genes, both as a part-source of variation and as a transmission system (and also as a metric of change, but the metric of transformation does not enter into a causal explanation of basic processes), are indeed important in evolutionary biology. But it is simply a travesty to say that evolution is considered to be about genetics alone. I would hazard the guess that in any account of evolution, genetics is a prominent but minority component of any exposition. As conventionally understood, e.g. Mayr (1978), evolution is a two-stage process. One concerns the development of phenotypes and their selective filtering through a complex set of interactions with their environment. This is natural selection. The second is the correlation between the characteristics of successive generations brought about *in part* by the transmission of genes between individuals.

'In part' is emphasized because transmission need not involve just genes. Phenotypes are often active constructors of their own world and that of their offspring (e.g. Odling-Smee 1988; Laland, *et al.* 1996). There is a real sense in which constructed niches are passed on across generations. And then there is the specific case of the evolution of language in humans, which is recognized by evolutionary biologists (e.g. Szathmary and Maynard Smith 1995) as a major evolutionary event, on a par in importance with any of the previous major evolutionary events in the history of life on Earth. Both of these elements, the effects that phenotypes have on their world and that of succeeding generations and the evolution of non-genetic channels of transmission between the phenotypes of some species, have transformed and are transforming the way contemporary evolutionists think, especially about human evolution.

Culture is the pre-eminent example of both niche-construction and extra-genetic transmission of information. This is why human evolution and cultural evolution are two-way streets of causal interactions.

Even if one wants to argue the (in my view, absurd) case that there is just one cognitive process that allows humans to share knowledge, beliefs, and skills, some single associative or selectionist learning mechanism that is a *tabula rasa* device responsible for any and all learning which we share with other species of learner, the architecture of the neural networks that underpin such learning must itself have evolved, probably hundreds of millions of years ago. The fact is, then, that if we are all materialists, hostility to evolutionists with an interest in human science is plainly unsupportable on scientific grounds. The source of that hostility must lie elsewhere, best understood and explained by a sociologist of science rather than myself.

The Great Game

It is around the notion of a *tabula rasa* that a deep conceptual schism has divided psychology. The arguments between those who support and those who oppose it have marked some of the most important debates within psychology in the twentieth century, and the inevitable attempts to bridge the divide have been played out as the great game of our discipline. The schism has been present in the study of emotions, personality, psycho-pathology, and learning (including learning in non-human animals), among other areas of the subject. It has been especially prominent in writings on human intelligence and language. On the one side have been psychologists who believed that the human mind at birth is relatively unstructured, and that perception, feeling, thought, the acquisition of skills and knowledge, and all the rest are consequences of the operation of general processes and mechanisms of learning, shared perhaps with other species. There has been conflation and confusion as to what 'general' means (Plotkin, 1997), but the central image has indeed been that of a blank slate upon which experience writes. On the other side of the divide are those who believe that at birth the mind is highly structured, such structures operating according to specific processes and mechanisms, some of which are unique to our species – such processes and mechanisms being different from one another.

The extent to which the latter camp insists on separation of structures in terms of mechanisms and functions varies with what aspect of mind is being spoken of. For example, personality theorists may or may not encompass differences in traits such as learning within their theories. But the fundamental difference between personality theorists who operate on either side of this great divide is this: one set of theorists argues that personality types are as numerous as there are differences in individual life experiences (this is the *tabula rasa* position); the other set of theorists argues that personality is the product of a small number of component features which are shared by all humans, the so-called 'big five' (or seven, or however many basic features are subscribed to) theories of personality.

It is in the study of language that the schism has been most clearly present and most famously fought over. Since language is central to any science of culture, it is on language that I will briefly dwell. While many (lesser) figures have been involved, over the last four decades the most influential proponent of the anti-*tabula rasa* view has been Chomsky. The general process position has been championed by Skinner and Piaget in the period 1950–1980, and more recently by connectionist neural network modellers. In part the matter was, and is, an empirical one which remains unresolved. But there are also key theoretical issues that decide which position scientists have taken, and these will have an important bearing on how the argument is eventually settled.

One in particular is important, often referred to as the argument from the poverty of the stimulus. This is a general argument deployed by Chomsky (1980, for example) and presented at length also by Fodor (1983) to claim that in this significant respect, the brain and mind are no different from any other part of our bodies. In a nutshell, the poverty-of-the-stimulus argument asserts that because of the action of 'internal' causes which are impossible to observe directly, the outputs of biological systems are richer than the proximal inputs. This is such a commonplace of biological observation and thought, noted Chomsky, that it is always taken for granted, and in modern biology, with the exception of psychology, it is never stated out aloud. For example, the proximal inputs to the human foetus and infant constitute a set of chemical nutrients, among many other externally originating events, that do not constitute an adequate explanation for the differentiated form of the human body. The argument, of course, applies to any animal or plant. It is impossible to explain, say, the form of the human hand or the vascular system in terms just of meals eaten, liquids drunk, objects manipulated, and the loving attention of parents and other care-givers. Such explanation has to include 'innate factors (that) permit the organism to transcend experience, reaching a high level of complexity that does not reflect the limited and degenerate environment' (Chomsky 1980: 2). That is to say, no account of the form of an organism, including humans, can leave genetics out of such explanation. There must be another source of order and information apart from partial and unreliable experience that is the cause of exquisitely differentiated forms. That source must lie in the genes. There are no other possibilities.

Very few biologists would question this position, which, it should be noted, neither denies the role of experience nor excludes principles such as self-organization. It merely asserts the necessary causal force of genes. In order to make his case more clear, Chomsky drew a distinction between the triggering and shaping effects of the environment during development, a distinction not dissimilar to that drawn by others (e.g. Gottlieb 1976).

Triggering occurs when some event, or set or sequence of events – temperature, perhaps, and the presence of water or nutrients – initiates an intrinsically determined process that results in an end-state that bears little or no resemblance to the triggering conditions. Hence the lack of resemblance across any dimension of form between the food that we eat and the form of our hands or ears. Shaping, by contrast, describes a relationship between environmental events and organismic states whereby the former initiates and guides the latter, and the end result is a demonstrable resemblance between the two. Instrumental learning and antibody formation are examples of shaping. Most characteristics of animals (and plants) are the result of triggering where an internal or endogenous set of causes, genes, and cascades of developmental pathways is supported by necessary environmental events. Some characteristics are due to a combination of triggering and shaping. Shaping by itself, I would argue, cannot account on its own for any characteristic.

Now why, asked Chomsky, should not a similar distinction be adopted when we are trying to understand the human mind? What special plea can be made that places the human mind outside of the realm of accepted biological thinking? The answer from all ontological reductionists, of course, is that there is none. So, for Chomsky, language is viewed as an organ of mind whose development is triggered and which is an innately determined feature of every member of our species, the grossly pathological aside. For Chomskians, the argument from the poverty of the stimulus is powerfully supported by evidence from studies of language development in children (Pinker 1994).

Two general points must be made here. First, it has become a form of 'intellectual' correctness for social scientists, supported by some biologists, to frown at the use of the word 'innate'. This fastidiousness derives from the controversies of the 1960s and has little importance thirty years on. Innate quite simply means part-caused (not wholly caused) at any time in a life cycle by the sequence of base pairs in an individual's DNA. Put in other words, something is innate when the characteristic would be absent or altered if the DNA sequences that code for the central nervous system were randomized. Claims that the notion of innate is crude biologizing, or that biologists think that the genome contains information, are red herrings. While it is difficult to document with certainty the relative influence and significance of one person's work over that of another, I have no doubt that the evidence overwhelmingly favours the Chomskian position. In my view, the Skinnerians (most now extinct) and the Piagetians had nothing like the conceptual firepower or empirical support that the Chomskians have (Plotkin 1997). No one denies, of course, that language acquisition has a learning element. It is trivially true that French children come to speak French and Russian children acquire Russian. The real point at issue here is whether learning a language involves writing onto a blank slate – how blank is the *tabula rasa*? Can humans learn any language, or are we restricted by constraints on what we can learn to learning one or a few of only the tiniest subset of all possible languages? As already said, in my opinion, the evidence favours the view that the slate is not blank. Language-learning is not a *tabula rasa* affair. We are indeed constrained to learn only one – or, at best, a few – of the world's languages, the approximately 5,500 documented languages being a tiny subset of all possible languages.

The second, and much more general, point of the Chomskian approach, which is now widely held among evolutionary psychologists, doubtless to Chomsky's amusement or chagrin since he himself is no follower of mainstream evolutionary biology, is that human cognition, of which language is but one part, is not the outcome of a single general learning process. There cannot be more than one truly general learning process, so the existence of more than one learning process, general or otherwise, negates the notion of a *tabula rasa*. Thus the case of language alone blows a hole in the notion of a *tabula rasa* big enough for a large coach and horses to be driven through. But the argument goes beyond language. No one these days believes that the cognitive processes that allow for learning a skill like riding a bicycle are the same as those by which we know the faces of our friends. The task demands are different. The anatomical location of the neural networks are different. And the psychological mechanisms are different. Each cognitive device ('module' is now a word with little agreed meaning, though Fodor was originally quite specific) is thought to be separate, innate, hence evolved, genetically part-caused, and triggered during normal development. While triggered, each device has a specific shaping function, but the nature of the shaping is specific to each device. The shaping function is nested within the innate, evolved device. Humans, and other animals that can learn, come into the world knowing what it is they must learn and think about (Plotkin 1995). Thus evolution and learning coalesce into a unity within the conception of evolved cognitive devices, which is a commonplace conception now in evolutionary psychology. Anyone who asserts, as does Ingold, that evolutionists continue to propagate a dichotomy between the innate and the acquired – whereas one of Ingold's claims for a superior distinctiveness is that he and a very small number of enlightened developmentalists do not do this – either misunderstands the literature or does not know it.

Another point to make about general process theory is that my view that no psychologists worth their salt now believe that previous theorists like Skinner and Piaget contributed much to our understanding of language and language acquisition, a very recent and exceedingly interesting general process account by Deacon (1997) may succeed where others have failed. But Deacon's theory is cast in terms of general mechanisms such as attention and memory which themselves are not unconstrained, and is a determinedly co-evolutionary account of language. And even connectionist neural network modellers, the nearest contemporary exponents of a kind of general process theory, concede the likelihood of innate constraints on these networks, even if these constitute a form of 'minimal nativism' (Clark 1993; Elman, *et al.* 1996).

One final general point needs to be made about the cognitive process and mechanisms that psychologists invoke when trying to account for culture. There is no doubting the existence of associative learning processes and mechanisms that are sensitive to a wide range of environmental events. This is because spatial and temporal contiguity are prominent features of the causal texture of the world. As already stated, associative learning is probably almost as old as the nervous system and phylogenetically quite widespread. Humans share this form of learning with other species (Dickenson and Shanks 1995). This does not alter the dominant view within present-day psychology that there are forms of learning and memory other than those that are associative.

So, those in this book who espouse the modularity approach to human cognition which has descended from Chomsky and Fodor are doing no more than reflecting this consensus view. Rather than somewhat mysteriously and arbitrarily disapproving of the widely agreed views of a neighbouring discipline, our colleagues in the human sciences outside of psychology need to be telling psychologists precisely where and why their data contradict psychological theory. While many of the ideas and much of the data given in Part Two of this book are deeply interesting, they simply do not undermine the position advanced in Part One. For instance, I can see nothing in Toren's exposition of Fijian child development that contradicts the views of any evolutionary psychologist that I know. The particular sensitivities and developmental trajectories of Fijian children are the product of a range of experiences particular to that culture played out upon a universal structure of mind. I fail to understand her question as to the 'sort of knowledge in the body (that) is pre-supposed by psychological models of child cognitive development' (Chapter Five, p.230), the language use being unconventional to say the least. But what is clear is that she does indeed on her own admission caricature cognitive models of mind and child development, especially those cognitivists of an evolutionary bent who are acutely aware of the importance of social relations and of cognitive development within a social environment.

Development and evolutionary psychology

Part of the intellectual correctness of many social scientists not only – and quite rightly – emphasizes the importance of development but also seems to assume that anyone with an interest in evolution probably doesn't understand development, is ignorant of the literature on development, and certainly doesn't care about it. I doubt that the assumed lack of interest in or knowledge of development is now an accurate description of most evolutionary biologists. The doyen of living British evolutionists wrote a book more than ten years ago (Maynard Smith 1986) in which development figured large as one of the key issues in modern biology. A major lecture at the London School of Economics in May 1997 by Maynard Smith was concerned with development. For many evolutionarily-minded psychologists, including Piaget, C.H. Waddington was a seminal influence and it would be hard to say whether Waddington was an evolutionist or a developmentalist. He surely was both and anyone who has read anything of his work will know that Waddington accorded as much importance to the role of genes in development as he did to their role in evolution.

Waddington was a kind of Renaissance man of twentieth century biology precisely because he understood the inseparable relationship between evolution and development and the linking role of genes in this. Waddington certainly would not have asserted, as does Ingold, that 'there is ... no genotype', which is simply an instance of biological illiteracy. Waddington understood that Darwin had taught us that history matters, to use Gould's (1986) phrase, a lesson that one would think should resonate powerfully with the thinking of social scientists. It certainly should with Toren, who makes several appeals to the importance of history yet rejects 'a natural science model of mind'.

However contradictory social scientists can sometimes be in their criticisms of biology in particular and natural science in general, adherence to the importance of development certainly is correct. Ingold's endorsement of Oyama's (1985) asserion that the link between 'the genome and the formal characteristics of the organism is none other than the developmental process' cannot but be right; but it is also the case that one of the links between successions of individual developmental processes – that is, of individuals – is genes which carry the causal force of history into our present. My reading of Oyama is that while she is correct in asserting

Developmental new — innate individual differences

that it simply isn't enough to say that traits are inherited, she is incorrect if she also claims, as she seems at times to do, that it is enough to deal only with the construction of traits during epigenesis without their causal attachment to genes.

The child-development literature in psychology contains more and more reports and reviews from developmentalists who are coming to the view that a whole host of psychological traits, including cognitive capacities, display a high degree of developmental invariance and are subject to the argument of the poverty of the stimulus. That is, like language, they appear to be innate. Such developmental studies are, I suggest, the best of evolutionary psychology which is faced with the considerable difficulty, as is all of evolutionary biology, of studying the past in the present. What developmental studies do not have to do is creatively to construct scenarios of ancient selection processes operating within fictions called the environment of evolutionary adaptedness which are then held to be the causes of traits known with empirical certainty to exist in the present. Developmental studies point to present causes of present traits, which include suites of genes whose presence was part-caused by past selection pressures, whatever these were and however difficult it might be to characterize them.

It is ironic that the developmental studies which Ingold and others believe is the way and the light are proving to be the source of the best evidence of how the past reaches into the present. That is, of how evolution has caused the human mind to be what it is. I come back to the analogy with the human hand. The hand is universal in form, it is constructed and triggered during development, and there is a set of genes which is transmitted from individual to individual which partly causes both that construction and that triggering. There is now impressively deep knowledge about what causes limbs of many different creatures including ourselves to be as they are (Shubin, *et al.* 1997), a depth of knowledge that has come from unashamedly pluralist pursuit of that knowledge. Comparative anatomists have not chided molecular biologists, nor have embryologists derided the work of geneticists. It does seem to me that that is the model of how to do science that should be followed as we slowly construct a science of culture.

Reconciliation through possible psychological processes and mechanisms

Appeals for tolerance and pluralism are no stronger in changing views in science than they are in any other area of human activity. Scientists, that is those who do work within the framework of natural science models of any aspect of the world including the human mind, are more likely to be moved by causal explanations cast in terms of mechanism and process. Thus it is that I take as a starting point to reconciling different approaches to a science of culture the assertion by Kitcher, that scourge of the undiscriminating and insouciant biologizing of the human sciences, that one of the essential starting points for introducing evolutionary biology into human social behaviour and culture is 'serious psychological theory onto which the considerations about cultural transmission can be grafted' (Kitcher 1987: 95). I take this to mean that a broad theory of culture grounded in the natural sciences has to be based on plausible psychological processes and mechanisms.

There have been several suggestions down the years as to what these might be, ranging from Freud's psychoanalytic approach (e.g. Freud 1913) to the emphasis of more recent theorists on imitation (e.g. Cavalli-Sforza and Feldman 1981; Boyd and Richerson 1985). Most have concentrated on information transmission and, to a lesser extent, social factors like prestige and rank. Most have been either implausible, like Freud's culture-as-organism notion, or incomplete. In the latter case there has been a strong tendency to concentrate on transmission mechanisms that do not include language. What follows is a summary of my suggested processes and mechanisms that are essential to culture. Because they have been discussed elsewhere (Plotkin 1996, 1997), I will be concerned more with why my choice is what it is, rather than any details as to what is known about these psychological mechanisms.

I cannot imagine that any human scientist would argue against the essential nature of language to human culture, even though, inexplicably, most biological models have ignored it. The rate of information flow, the relative precision of reference, the astonishing richness of scope, and of course, the fact that language is an extra-genetic route of information transmission, all make language a unique form of communication. There is nothing like it in any other species; and precisely because of its extra-genetic characteristics and its centrality to human culture, its appearance in our species was a major evolutionary event (Szathmary and Maynard Smith 1995). There is an important sense in which it really doesn't matter how the language debate of dedicated cognitive capacity versus general process learning is eventually settled. Whatever its history and underlying mechanisms, there seems little reason to question the role of language as the major transmission device of culture.

There is enormous variation in the claims made about when language first appeared, ranging from two million and more years ago to just a few tens of thousands of years before the present. It is not clear that this is an argument that is ever going to be settled. My own cautious, middle-of-the-road view is that language evolved slowly, and over a relatively long period of time. There is simply too much to language in terms of its anatomical demands for the chance occurrence of a single gene, or a small suite of genes, to have made the rapid and chance transition from an animal without language to one with it. There are strong arguments for the likelihood that language evolved alongside, and closely interwoven with, the evolution of manual skills, imitation, and tool use (e.g. Greenfield 1991). So I would not want boldly to assert that language and language alone has been the only transmission device in human culture. I would argue though that, once evolved beyond some level of referential precision and richness, language became the primary vehicle for social transmission.

Now it seems to me that social constructions are among the most extraordinary features of human culture. I take my definition of social constructions from Searle (1995), who considers them instances of collective intentionality; they are complex belief systems, often embodied in some partial physical form, like money, and associated structures and institutions, like banks and markets of many forms, and whose existence depends upon the agreement of all, or most, members of a group. Money only has value because we agree that it does. Social constructions are powerful causal forces in cultures, and explaining them is not some optional extra to a science of culture. Understanding and explaining social constructions is absolutely essential. I do not believe that language, its power and precision of reference notwithstanding, can approach a complete explanation of social constructions. I have suggested that at least two other psychological mechanisms are necessary. Both centre on the matter of agreement.

The first I will refer to generically as social force, which takes in many phenomena described variously by social psychologists as conformity, cohesiveness, and obedience. The classic studies of Sherif (1936) form the beginnings of a long line of empirical research on social force. Its existence is not in doubt, though the translation of such phenomena into psychological mechanisms consonant with present-day cognitive theorizing is lacking. The clue as to how to do this, perhaps, lies in considering the conditions of human evolution, going back seven million years and more to the ancestor common to humans and the other social great apes. I am highly sceptical of the notion of the environment of evolutionary adaptedness (see Tooby and Cosmides 1990, for example) because there never has been just a single environment in the history of any species and because it is almost always a product of imaginitive

Important → because adaptations have appeared to continue → take over domain, see earlier text.

Henry Plotkin

reconstruction of circumstances that cannot be empirically supported. Comparative evidence, however, indicates that there has indeed been one constant feature of the environment within which all species of Australopithecus and Homo evolved, and hence was likely to have been a powerful source of selection in human evolution. This is that life was lived in relatively small social groups. (See Dunbar 1993 for varying estimates of group size by commentators.) The reasons for this sociality are less important here than the consequences, which must have been a sensitizing of psychological mechanisms to the maintenance and continuation of the group. I am speculating, of course, but my guess is that mechanisms that reduced differences in perception and judgement, and hence which reduced the likelihood of conflict within the group, would have been selected for. Some innate constraints which nudge individual judgement in the direction of group consensus would have been the result.

It is conceivable that a social force mechanism (or, more likely, set of mechanisms) coupled to language is sufficient to account for the agreement that allows social constructions to be formed and maintained. But a second mechanism may also be operating to achieve this, which has come to be known as theory of mind, mindreading, social intelligence, or intentional mental state attribution. (See Baron-Cohen 1995; Gopnik 1993; Leslie 1994 for differing views as to the mechanisms underlying theory of mind.) The reason for including a theory-of-mind mechanism is that knowing that others know and believe is an essential prerequisite of being able to match ones own intentional mental states to those of others. If agreement is at the heart of social constructions, then theory of mind must form one of the bases by which that agreement is understood and achieved. The central point about agreement is that whether by implicit modelling, explicit education, coercion, or some combination of these, people are enculturated into acceptance of the set of social constructions that characterize their culture.

Finally, there is a cautionary note on which to end. Psychologists in general, and evolutionary psychologists in particular, must listen to what social scientists tell them about real people in real and diverse cultures, and be prepared to be challenged by what we are told. In the case of Toren's vivid account of the development of ideas of personhood in Fijian children, her observations can, in my view, be explained by the operation of language, responsiveness to social force, and the attribution of intentional mental states to others. In making this claim, however, I am uneasy with the realization that in the absence of certain knowledge and more precise theory as to how such mechanisms articulate with one

Cannot be disproved – evo psych

another, and with other psychological mechanisms such as memory and attention, that very little data of the kind Toren offers would disconfirm current psychological theory. That is a poor position to be in, and presents us with another challenge in establishing a science of culture.

References

Baron-Cohen, S. (1995), *Mindblindness: An essay on Autism and Theory of Mind*, Cambridge Mass.: MIT Press.

Bohm, D. (1969), 'Further remarks on order', in C.H. Waddington (ed.), *Towards a Theoretical Biology, Volume 2*, Edinburgh: Edinburgh University Press.

Boyd, R. and Richerson, P. (1985), *Culture and the Evolutionary Process*, Chicago: Chicago University Press.

Campbell, D.T. (1974), 'Downward causation in hierarchically organized biological systems', in F. Ayala and T. Dobzansky (eds), *Studies in the Philosophy of Biology*, London: Macmillan.

Cavalli-Sforza, L.L. and Feldman, M.W. (1981), *Cultural Transmission and Evolution: A Quantitative Approach*, Princeton: Princeton University Press.

Chomsky, N. (1980), 'Rules and representations', *The Behavioural and Brain Sciences*, 3: 1–61.

Clark, A. (1993), *Associative Engines: Connectionism, Concepts and Representational Change*, Cambridge Mass.: MIT Press.

Deacon, T. (1997), *The Symbolic Species: The Co-evolution of Language and the Brain*, London: Allen Lane.

Dickenson, A. and Shanks, D. (1995), 'Instrumental action and causal representation', in D. Sperber, D. Premack and A.J. Premack (eds), *Causal Cognition*, Oxford: The Clarendon Press.

Dunbar, R.I.M. (1993), 'Coevolution of neocortical size, group size and language in humans', *The Behavioural and Brain Sciences*, 16: 681–735.

Durham, W.H. (1991), *Coevolution: Genes, Culture and Human Diversity*, Stanford: Stanford University Press.

Elman, J.L., Bates, E.A., Johnson, M.H., Karmiloff-Smith, A., Parisi, D. and Plunkett, K. (1996), *Rethinking Innateness: A Connectionist Perspective on Development*, Cambridge Mass.: MIT Press.

Fodor, J.A. (1983), *The Modularity of Mind*, Cambridge, Mass,: MIT Press.

Freud, S. (1913), *Totem and Taboo*, New York: Norton.

Gopnik, A. (1993), 'How we know our minds: the illusion of first-person knowledge of intentionality', *The Behavioural and Brain Sciences*, 16: 1–14.

Gottlieb, G. (1976), 'Conceptions of prenatal development: behavioural embryology', *Psychological Review*, 83: 215–34.

Gould, S.J. (1986), 'Evolution and the triumph of homology, or why history matters', *American Scientist*, 74: 60–9.

Greenfield, P.M. (1991), 'Language, tools and brain: the ontogeny and phylogeny of hierarchically organized sequential behaviour', *The Behavioural and Brain Sciences*, 14: 531–95.

Kitcher, P. (1987), 'Confessions of a curmudgeon', *The Behavioural and Brain Sciences*, 10: 89–97.

Laland, K.N., Odling-Smee, F.J. and Feldman, M.W. (1996), 'The evolutionary consequences of niche construction: a theoretical investigation using two-locus theory', *Journal of Evolutionary Biology*, 9: 293–316.

Leslie, A.M. (1994), 'ToMM, ToBy, and agency: core architecture and domain specificity', in L.A. Hirschfeld and S.A. Gelman (eds), *Mapping the Mind: Domain Specificity in Cognition and Culture*, Cambridge: Cambridge University Press.

Maynard Smith, J. (1986), *The Problems of Biology*, Oxford: Oxford University Press.

Mayr, E. (1978), 'Evolution', *Scientific American*, 239: 46–55.

Odling-Smee, F.J. (1988), 'Niche-constructing phenotypes', in H.C. Plotkin (ed.), *The Role of Behaviour in Evolution*, Cambridge Mass.: MIT Press.

Oyama, S. (1985), *The Ontogeny of Information: Developmental Systems and Evolution*, Cambridge: Cambridge University Press.

Pinker, S. (1994), *The Language Instinct*, London: Allen Lane.

Plotkin, H. (1988), 'Learning and evolution', in H. Plotkin (ed.), *The Role of Behaviour in Evolution*, Cambridge, Mass.: MIT Press.

—— (1995), *Darwin Machines and the Nature of Knowledge*, London, Penguin.

—— (1996), 'Some psychological mechanisms of culture', *Philosophica*, 57: 91–106.

—— (1997), *Evolution in Mind*, London: Allen Lane.

Ridley, M. (1996), *Evolution*, Oxford: Blackwell.

Searle, J.R. (1995), *The Construction of Social Reality*, London: Allen Lane.

Sherif, M. (1936), *The Psychology of Social Norms*, New York: Harper and Row.

Shubin, N., Tabin, C. and Carroll, S. (1997), 'Fossils, genes, and the evolution of animal limbs', *Nature*, 388: 639–48.

Szathmary, E. and Maynard Smith, J. (1995), 'The major evolutionary transitions', *Nature*, 374: 227–32.

Tooby, J. and Cosmides, L. (1990), 'The past explains the present: emotional adaptations and the structure of ancestral environments', *Ethology and Sociobiology*, 11: 375–424.

Waddington, C.H. (1958), 'Evolutionary adaptation', in S. Tax (ed.), *The Evolution of Life*, Chicago: University of Chicago Press.

PART TWO

–4–

From the Transmission of Representations to the Education of Attention
Tim Ingold

We human beings know a great deal. But we are able to be so knowledge-
able only because we stand on the shoulders of our predecessors. As
Durkheim noted long ago (1976 [1915]: 435), 'to that which we can learn
by our own personal experience [is added] all that wisdom and science
which the group has accumulated in the course of centuries'. The problem,
which has remained at the heart of anthropological attempts to understand
the dynamics of culture, is to fathom how this accumulation occurs. How
is the experience that we gain during our lifetimes enriched by the wisdom
of our ancestors? And how, in turn, does that experience make itself felt
in the lives of descendants? More generally, in the creation and maintenance of human knowledge, what contribution does each generation
make to the next?

One approach to answering this question, though it has venerable
antecedents, has undergone something of a revival in recent decades
thanks, in large measure, to parallel developments in cognitive science.
It holds that knowledge exists in the form of 'mental content' which,
with some loss and replenishment, along with diffusion at the margins,
is passed on from generation to generation as the heritage of a culture-
bearing population. Among the leading anthropological exponents of this
approach is Dan Sperber. My aim here is to review some of the central
strands of Sperber's arguments, and then to show why I think they are
incoherent. I focus on Sperber's work not because it should be considered
especially representative, but rather because it has the virtue of rendering
unusually explicit the assumptions built into much contemporary theorizing about culture and cognition, and of driving them through to their
logical conclusions. If the conclusions are absurd, as I believe they are,
then there must be something wrong with the founding assumptions.[1]

These assumptions are, specifically, that knowledge is information, and that human beings are devices for processing it. I shall argue, to the contrary, that our knowledge consists, in the first place, of skill, and that every human being is a centre of awareness and agency in a field of practice. Building on these latter premises, I shall go on to suggest an alternative approach – one that owes more to phenomenological, eco-logical and 'practice-theoretical' perspectives on perception and cognition than to classical cognitive science – which, in my view, offers a more promising way forward. I realize there is currently a vigorous counter-movement within cognitive science itself, which is following a path very similar to the one proposed here. My critique, therefore, is directed against cognitivism in its 'classical' guise, rather than against its 'emergentist' alternative. (For an excellent account of the latter, see A. Clark 1997.) It is fair to say, however, that the classical perspective remains the dominant one in cognitive psychology; moreover its continued dominance is reinforced by a powerful alliance with evolutionary biology in its modern, neo-Darwinian formulation. Thus to take issue with classical cognitive science is inevitably to call into question some of the founding precepts of neo-Darwinism.

In both biology and psychology, as I shall show, the crux of the problem lies in understanding processes of ontogenetic development. Following an outline of Sperber's approach to the explanation of culture, I shall consider the problem of development as it figures first in neo-Darwinian biology and secondly in cognitive science. The solution, I argue, is to move beyond the dichotomy between innate capacities and acquired competencies, through a focus on the emergent properties of dynamic systems. Skills, I suggest, are best understood as properties of this kind. It is through a process of enskilment, not enculturation, that every generation grows into and beyond the wisdom of its predecessors. This leads me to conclude that in the growth of human knowledge, the contribution that each generation makes to the next is not an accumulated stock of representations but an education of attention.

The transmission of representations

More than fifty years ago, Alfred Kroeber was reflecting on the apparent analogies between cultural and biological phenomena. It would be wrong, he observed, to compare the individuals of a culture to members of a species. For the elements that combine to establish the particular pattern of thought and behaviour for a people cannot be traced to a common ancestral source but are of the most diverse origin. Following the convention of the time, Kroeber called these elements 'culture traits'. And if anything is comparable to a species, he thought, it is the trait (or trait cluster) itself. Where the species exists as a population of individual organisms of a certain kind, so likewise, the trait exists as a population of exemplars. Every act of making a stone axe of a particular form, or every utterance of a phrase with a particular grammatical construction, would be a member of such a population. And these individuals of diverse trait-species associate together to form the manifold patterns of human life, just as individuals of different organic species associate to establish the distinctive patterns of fauna and flora characteristic of particular locales. Thus, 'it is ecological aggregates to which cultures can be compared: local associations of species of diverse origin' (Kroeber 1952 [1943]: 93).

Kroeber's original idea has recently resurfaced, in a strikingly similar form, in Sperber's call for an 'epidemiology of representations' (Chapter One). One has only to substitute for the currently unfashionable notion of 'trait', with its somewhat behavioural overtones, the rather more mentalistic notion of 'representation', and the two formulations become virtually identical. Just as the trait, according to Kroeber, is realized in its countless exemplars, so for Sperber, every representation exists on the level of concrete reality as the population of its 'tokens', whether these be found inside human brains or in the bodily behaviour which they set in train. There are, for example, millions of tokens of the story of Little Red Riding Hood, in the heads of everyone who can tell it, and in every event of telling. And where Kroeber compared traits to the plant and animal inhabitants of a locale, Sperber compares representations to the disease-causing micro-organisms that inhabit the body. Studying the proliferation and distribution of representations in brains is thus akin to the epidemiological study of the proliferation and distribution of micro-organisms in bodies: 'cultural phenomena are ecological patterns of psychological phenomena' (Sperber 1996: 60).

If knowledge consists in the representations that populate human brains, then the question which I posed at the outset concerning the contribution, in the accumulation of knowledge, that each generation makes to the next, may be rephrased as follows: *How are representations transmitted*? In other words, how does a representation in your brain find its way into mine, and from my brain into the brains of yet other people? To this question, Sperber offers a kind of answer quite different from that originally suggested by Kroeber. 'Man', Kroeber had pronounced (as long ago as 1917), 'is . . . a tablet that is written upon' (1952 [1943]: 32). The structure and nature and texture of humanity is such that it can be inscribed with any kind of cultural message you please; the critical distinction between the human and the animal is simply that the former is inscribable and the latter is not. This view of the human organism (or more specifically, of the brain) as a *tabula rasa*, however implausible, has served ever since to underwrite the more relativistic claims of cultural anthropology. It implies that students of culture need be no more concerned with the psychology of human nature than, say, journalists with the technology of paper-making.

Sperber's contention is that this traditional model of enculturation, as a simple process of inscription, rests upon an impossible psychology. Even if, in my behaviour, I 'write out' representations in my brain, this is not equivalent to 'writing them down' in yours. The chain of causation that leads from the concrete presence of a representation in one brain to its establishment in others is less direct. Sperber explains it by means of a distinction between 'mental representations' and 'public represent-ations'. I have a tune in my head: that is a mental representation. I whistle the tune as I walk down the street: that is a public representation. It is public because it exists as a sound pattern that can be heard by other people in the vicinity. For some hearers it may form no lasting impression; for others, however, it may be not only heard but also remembered. For these latter, the tune is now established as a mental representation inside *their* heads. And they, too, may find themselves whistling it as they walk down the street, just as I did. A transmission of information has thus been effected, but only because every step of behavioural externalization (which transforms the mental representation into a public one) is complemented by a further step of perceptual internalization (which transforms the public representation 'back' into a mental one). And this latter step calls for the operation of a computational device capable of processing the input of sensory data, such as that generated by the impact of my whistling on the receptor organs of hearers, into an enduring representational form.

In short, some sort of cognitive processing device must already be installed, in human brains, before any transmission of representations can take place at all. A *tabula rasa* could not learn, since it would have no means to convert the sensory input into mental content. Once this point is recognized, however, we have also to admit that the processing device (or devices) may be better able to handle some kinds of input than others. We all know that some things, even when they are long and complicated like a story, are easy to remember, while other things like lists of eleven-digit telephone numbers tax our abilities to the limit. This, Sperber tells us (1996: 74–5), is simply because the brain's inbuilt cognitive mechanisms are specially equipped to handle objects with a narrative structure. If knowledge in non-literate cultures largely takes the form of myths and stories, this is because these forms are readily memorable. What cannot be easily remembered will naturally fall out of circulation and will not, therefore, be retained in the culture. Insofar as the mechanisms of cognition determine what is memorable and what is not, they have a quite immediate impact on the organization of cultural knowledge.

Given that these cognitive mechanisms, or processing devices, must be in place prior to any transmission of cultural information, where do they come from? Of course the devices could themselves have been learned. The child, in other words, may first acquire representations that specify the mechanisms for processing subsequent input. Yet how could those initial representations have been established in the child's mind unless some devices were already installed for selecting and processing the relevant, mechanism-specifying input? The problem is analogous to the one about how to send a message, in code, to a recipient who lacks the key. First you have to send another message, which specifies the key. But then the recipient must already be in possession of another key, in order to decode *that* message . . . and so on and on, in an infinite regress. Unless, at some basic level, both sender and recipient possess a common set of interpretative devices, or 'framings', the communication of information could never get off the ground at all.

The bottom line, then, is that every human being must come into the world pre-equipped with cognitive mechanisms that are specified quite independently, and in advance, of any process of learning or development.[2] For John Tooby and Leda Cosmides, whose investigations into the psychological foundations of culture have followed a path very close to Sperber's, these mechanisms amount to what they call 'human meta-culture', a bedrock of universals bequeathed to each and every one of us by virtue of our shared evolutionary ancestry. It is thanks to these metacultural framings that human beings are able to learn the variable features of their particular cultural traditions. Were it not for them, it would be impossible for the already enculturated adult to communicate with the new-born infant who 'arrives in the culture free of any knowledge about its particularities' (Tooby and Cosmides 1992: 92). Like the ethnographer in a world of strangers (Sperber 1985: 62–3), the infant can fall back on the ready-made information-processing devices which it shares with those around it, in order to gain admission to an otherwise closed world of cultural understanding.

I shall return below to the efforts of Tooby and Cosmides to establish an 'evolutionary psychology'; for the present it suffices to stress their conclusion, fully endorsed by Sperber, that the cross-generational transmission of variable cultural information depends upon the presence, in all human minds, of innate, species-typical mechanisms of cognition. These mechanisms, it is supposed, are the outcomes of a Darwinian process of variation under natural selection, and as such, they are built to specifications that are not cultural but genetic, included within the common biological endowment of humankind.

The evolution of cognition

According to a now well-established scenario, it was during the Pleisto-cene era, while living as hunters and gatherers, that human beings evolved to be the kinds of creatures they are today. Since natural selection, as a rule, adapts organisms to their prevailing conditions of life, we can expect that the properties or 'design features' of the human mind, just as much as those of the body, would have evolved as solutions to the particular problems and challenges that would have been faced by ancestral populations of hunter-gatherers in Pleistocene environments. Moreover there is good reason to believe that a cognitive architecture consisting of a collection of relatively discrete modules, each specialized in a particular domain of problem-solving, would have a selective advantage over a more general-purpose design. A specialized module that already knows, in a sense, what the problem is and how to deal with it, can deliver a more rapid and effective response, causing minimal interference to other cognitive tasks that may be going on at the same time. Thus there might be one module for navigation and orientation in the environment, another for handling social co-operation with conspecifics, another for the recognition and classification of animals and plants, another for language acquisition, another for tool-use, and so on (Hirschfeld and Gelman 1994).

The environments of ancestral hunter-gatherers, however, were very different from those encountered by the majority of the world's inhabitants today. Many of the challenges they faced have all but disappeared, while others have arisen that they could not have anticipated. Thus cognitive modules designed by natural selection for one purpose have, throughout history, been turned to account in other ways. Anyone can learn to drive a car, Sperber speculates (1996: 93), because the skills of driving call for computations of space and movement that the brain is innately pre-equipped to carry out. The requisite processing devices would have evolved in what Sperber calls their *proper* domain, that is, in the solution of cognitive tasks faced by hunter-gatherers in moving around in the terrain. But in driving a car they are mobilized in the *actual* domain of the motorist who has to make his way on the road. Though the circumstances could not be more different, the underlying cognitive operations are much the same. Indeed the implication of Sperber's argument is that any mode of locomotion that could not draw upon evolved cognitive capacities of one kind or another would probably be unlearnable, and could never become a part of culture.

More generally, while the natural environment of human beings has been largely replaced or overlain by a cultural one – that is, by an environment consisting of 'all the public productions . . . that are causes and effects of mental representations' (Sperber 1996: 115) – the various domains of culture in which human cognition actually operates have been shaped by a selective bias in favour of representations that mimic the inputs of evolved cognitive modules in their original, proper domains. To rephrase the point in terms of another distinction suggested by Sperber, the human mind-brain is peculiarly *susceptible* to representations that are compatible with its innate *dispositions*. Such representations will proliferate and spread, and so establish themselves within the culture, whereas others, failing to satisfy the input conditions of the cognitive modules, will decline and disappear. Culture, in short, is parasitic upon the universal structures of human cognition.

Now behind the linked oppositions between dispositions and susceptibilities, and between proper and actual cognitive domains, there clearly lies a more fundamental distinction, namely between *innate* devices and *acquired* representations. A disposition is a function of a genetically specified cognitive device that has evolved within its proper domain as part of the human adaptation to the original environmental conditions of hunter-gatherer life in the Pleistocene. A susceptibility lies in the receptivity of a particular device to mental representational content of a certain kind, that happens to be current within the actual domain of the cultural life of a human population, a form of life which may not remotely resemble that of their earliest ancestors. It must follow, however, that those competencies that have an innate dispositional basis – that we are 'born with' – have to be clearly distinguished from those that are founded in acquired mental content. The first are products of an evolutionary process, the second belong to a process of history. Whereas evolutionary change is fundamentally genetic, the history of a population consists, according to Sperber (1996: 115), in changes in its pool of cultural representations. And throughout the entire course of history, despite the turnover in the composition of this pool, the evolved architecture of the human mind has remained essentially constant.

Tim Ingold

Plotkin (in Chapter Three, p. 132) has seized upon my use of the phrase 'evolutionary change is fundamentally genetic' as a gross misrepresentation of what biologists in general, and evolutionary biologists in particular, actually believe. In response, I can only reiterate that my aim up to this point has been to summarize as accurately as possible the position of one author who is not, and does not pretend to be, a biologist, namely Sperber. And this is what Sperber says: 'Human, genetically determined cognitive abilities are the outcomes of a process of natural selection' (1996: 66). On the question of the significance of genetic change as an index of evolution, biologists themselves are divided. Some adhere to the textbook definition of evolution as change over time in gene frequencies in populations of organisms, and distinguish evolution from history on the grounds that the latter is independent of (though it may have consequences for) genetic change. Others, including Plotkin, distinguish on precisely the same grounds between 'biological' and 'cultural' evolution, and conclude that there is nothing fundamentally genetic about evolutionary change per se. My concern is not with the choice of terms, but with the epistemological basis of the distinction itself – that is, with the idea that one kind of change (cultural, historical, call it what you will) is set within the parameters of another (biological, evolutionary). As for Plotkin's objection that conventional accounts of evolution devote comparatively little space to genetics, and much more to other things, this is simply irrelevant. A good book on evolution might have a lot to say about the fossil record. The fact that it does so is neither here nor there as far as our understanding of the causes of change is concerned.

Taking account of development (1): biology

I should like to begin my critique of Sperber's epidemiological theory of culture by focusing on its evolutionary implications. My purpose is to do away with the opposition between innate cognitive mechanisms and acquired cultural content by showing how the forms and capacities of human beings, like those of all other organisms, arise within processes of *development*. This leads me to a conception of evolution which, though radically at variance with the orthodox neo-Darwinian account, no longer forces us to reserve a separate ontological space for human history. And this, in turn, will eventually open the way to a quite different answer to our original question: how does each generation contribute to the knowledgeability of the next?

Sperber's obsession, widely shared in cognitive science, with the discovery of innate, genetically determined information-processing devices is at first glance rather puzzling, given his explicit appeal to neo-Darwinian evolutionary biology.[3] For most biologists claim that they have long since discarded the distinction between innate and acquired structures. According to what is often called the 'first law of biology', the actual characteristics of organisms are neither innate nor acquired, but are products of the interaction, throughout the life-cycle, between endogenous, genetic causes and exogenous, environmental ones. Thus interactionism has long since replaced innatism as the dominant creed within biological science. In fact, however, a doctrine of genetic pre-formation still lurks beneath the surface of orthodox interactionism, since it is built into biology's own master theory: the theory of evolution under natural selection. The synergy between neo-Darwinian biology and classical cognitive science is thus, after all, closer than meets the eye, and both fail for the same reason: they are unable to offer an adequate account of ontogenetic development. Let me show why.

Interactionism describes development as an unfolding relation between genes and environment. In this relation, however, it is the genes that are supposed to hold the essence of form, whereas the environment is conceived merely to furnish the material conditions for its realization.[4] Each gene is taken to represent a unit of pure, digital information, encoded in the molecular structure of DNA. Put together, these units make up what is called the *genotype*, a formal specification of the organism-to-be which, by definition, is given independently and in advance of any real-world context of development. At the commencement of every new life-cycle, this genotypic specification is introduced, by way of the DNA of the germ cells, into a particular environmental context. In development, the information carried in the genes is then said to be outwardly 'expressed' in the *phenotypic* form of the resultant organism. Only the elements of the genotype, however, and not the characteristics of the phenotype, are transmitted across generations. Over many generations within a population, through accidents of mutation and recombination coupled with the effects of differential reproduction, the informational content of the genotype changes. These changes, it is claimed, add up to a process of evolution.

This is all very neat, save for one problem. To be sure, every organism starts life with its complement of DNA. But if genes are to be understood, as the theory requires, as the carriers of a formal design specification, shaped up through natural selection, from one locus of development to another, then there must be some systematic correspondence between the elements of this specification and the actual DNA of the genome *that is independent of any developmental process*. The existence of such a correspondence has been generally assumed, but it has never been demonstrated (see Cohen and Stewart 1994: 293–4). In practice, what happens is that biologists seek to redescribe the observed phenotypic characteristics of organisms as the outputs of a formal system of epigenetic rules (much as linguists seek to redescribe spoken utterances as outputs of a generative syntax). These rules are then read 'in' to the genome, so that development can be seen as the 'reading off' of a programme or specification that is already there, and that is imported with the genome into the site of inauguration of a new life cycle. In short, as an account of the evolution of form, neo-Darwinian theory rests on a simple circularity. That is one reason why it has proved so hard to refute.

At root, the issue comes down to one about copying. The orthodox account has it that the formal characters of the incipient organism are copied along with the DNA, in advance of its interaction with the environment, so that they can then 'interact' with the environment to produce the organism. I would argue, to the contrary (and as illustrated schematically in Figure 4.1), that copying is itself a process that goes on within the context of organism-environment interaction. In other words, the 'missing link' between the genome and the formal attributes of the organism is none other than the developmental process itself. There is, then, no design for the organism, no genotype except, of course, as this might be constructed by the observing biologist. Organic form, in short, is *generated*, not expressed, in development, and arises as an emergent property of the total system of relations set up by virtue of the presence and activity of the organism in its environment. And if that is so – if form is a property not of genes but of developmental systems – then to account for the evolution of form we have to understand how these systems are constituted and reconstituted over time.

These arguments are not new. One of their most influential proponents in recent years has been Susan Oyama (1985). The nature of an organism, as she points out, 'is not genotypic . . . but phenotypic', and therefore 'depends on developmental context as profoundly and intimately as it does on the genome . . . Evolution is thus the derivational history of developmental systems' (Oyama 1989: 5). Yet however much she has been at pains to distinguish her views from orthodox interactionism, her critics continue to confuse the two, claiming that there is nothing in a developmental-systems approach that is not perfectly consistent with the premises of neo-Darwinian evolutionary biology. (For an example, see Dunbar 1996.) In Chapter Two, Pascal Boyer has reacted in precisely the same way to the arguments I adduce here. Indeed he portrays me as an advocate of the view that 'development consists of an "interaction"

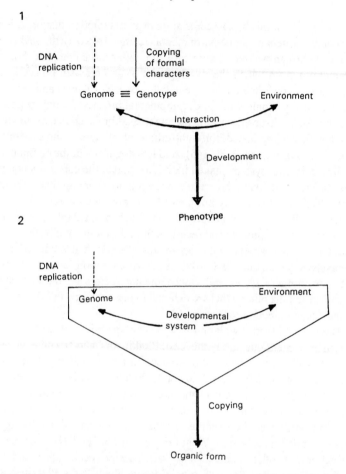

Figure 4.1 Two theories of copying: (1) in the orthodox, Darwinian account, a design for the organism is copied with the DNA of the genome, which is then 'brought out' in the course of development within an environmental context; (2) in the 'developmental systems approach' proposed here, the process of copying is equivalent to that of the organism's development in its environment.

between prior information and external circumstances'. And he wonders why this should be incompatible with a neo-Darwinian view of the evolution of human capacities. Of course there is no incompatibility here! Some kind of mental block, however, appears to prevent Boyer, and many others who think like him, from realizing that to regard form as emergent within the developmental process is anything other than a version of gene-environment interactionism.

Tim Ingold

The source of this block seems to lie in an assumption that organisms are *effects* of genetic and environmental *causes*. However the reality, as Daniel Lehrman warned many years ago, is far more complex. For the interactions from which the development of an organism proceeds are not between genes and environment, but between *organism* and environment. At every moment of the developmental process, formal structures or behavioural dispositions already established in the course of previous interaction are implicated, through further interaction, in the generation of new ones (Lehrman 1953: 345). And it is not in any of the components of the interacting systems, taken individually, that the constraints on the process are to be found, but rather in the relations among them (Oyama 1993: 8). Thus it is simply not possible to apportion causality between genetic and environmental factors. 'The web of causality', as Esther Thelen writes, 'is intricate and seamless from the moment of birth' (1995: 94). Or to put it another way, organisms are both cause and effect of themselves (Goodwin 1988: 108). In short, causation is not a relation between things – genes and environmental factors on the one hand, organisms on the other – that are external to one another, but is immanent in the developmental process itself.[5]

Having said that, my claim that the genotype does not exist is likely to remain contentious, to say the least. Plotkin, in Chapter Three, goes so far as to call it 'an instance of biological illiteracy'! Let me, then, make my position absolutely clear. I do not doubt the existence of the genome, or that it sets in train processes that are crucial to the development of the organism at every stage of its life-cycle. Nor, moreover, do I deny that the composition of the genome changes across generations through a process of natural selection. What I *do* deny is that the DNA sequence in the genome encodes a context-independent design specification, and with it, the idea of natural selection as a design agent. Now Plotkin might possibly accept the first of these denials, since he dismisses as a 'red herring' the claim that biologists 'think the genome contains information'. It is difficult to know what to make of this dismissal, however, since it follows hard on the heels of an equally forthright insistence that the source of the order and information that cannot be found in environmental experience 'must lie in the genes'. I certainly have no problem with Plotkin's definition of evolution as 'the transformation of biological forms and systems in time', and he appears to agree with me (and Oyama) that development is the link between the genome and organic form. But what Plotkin fails to recognize is that if the idea of the genome as a carrier of information is indeed a red herring, then the theory of variation under natural selection, though it can account for changes in gene frequencies over successive generations within a population, is powerless to explain the evolution of biological form.

Genes, after all, are but segments of molecules that may or may not have unspecified consequences for the organisms they are in. It is perfectly possible, as Cohen and Stewart have demonstrated, for two quite different creatures to have precisely the same DNA in the genome. Not only can creatures evolve without any genetic change at all, they can also retain a more or less constant form despite considerable modification at the genetic level (Cohen and Stewart 1994: 309). Thus natural selection, leading to changes in the composition of the genome, occurs *within* evolution, but does not explain it. Nor does it even furnish a partial explanation, since to determine what part is due to natural selection, and what part is not, would require an apportionment of causal responsibility for the development of form between genes and environmental experience. And this, as I have shown, cannot sensibly be done. Only by going beyond the theory of evolution through variation under natural selection, and by considering the properties of dynamic self-organization of developmental systems, can we hope to discover the possible consequences of those changes that *can* be explained by natural selection for the evolutionary process itself.

Taking account of development (2): psychology

I should now like to return from biology to psychology, and to the problem that cognitive science has with its persistent appeal to innate structures. Just as neo-Darwinian biology has to posit a design for the organism, the genotype, that is specified in advance of its development, so cognitive science posits a design for the mind that pre-exists and underwrites all subsequent learning or knowledge acquisition. In so far as this design is assumed to have a genetic basis, and to have been fashioned by natural selection, it must form one component of the genotype. Yet here cognitive science runs into the very same dilemma that, as we have seen, derails neo-Darwinian theory – but in an even more pronounced form. It is more pronounced since the genetically specified cognitive devices that are supposed to make possible the transmission of representations must already exist, not merely in the virtual guise of a design, but in the concrete hard-wiring of human brains. In other words, it has to be assumed that DNA replication not only copies a design for the mind into the embryonic human being, but also copies out the mechanisms specified in that design into its head. Somehow, in order to kick-start the process of ontogenetic development, strands of DNA have miraculously to transform themselves into computational modules. This is rather like supposing that merely by

Tim Ingold

replicating the design of an aircraft, whether on the drawing board or on the computer screen, one is all prepared for take-off.

By and large, in the literature of cognitive science, the postulation of innate structures is taken to require no more justification than vague references to genetics and natural selection (e.g., Johnson-Laird 1988: 35). Where the issue of development is addressed at all, the arguments are confused and contradictory. A case in point lies in the work of Tooby and Cosmides, to which I have already referred. Recalling the biological distinction between genotype and phenotype, Tooby and Cosmides argue that an equivalent distinction needs to be recognized in the study of mind between *evolved* psychology and *manifest* psychology. Every situation, then, may be analysed into 'environmental conditions, evolved archit-ecture, and how their interaction produces the manifest outcome' (1992: 45–6). This sounds like a restatement of orthodox interactionism. Yet if what they call the 'architecture' of the mind were truly analogous to the genotype, it would exist only in the programmatic form of a 'building design' regulating the construction, in the course of ontogenetic develop-ment, of a suite of cognitive mechanisms. Not all the features specified in this design, as Tooby and Cosmides go on to recognize, will be realized at once for any single individual. Thus different mechanisms will come on line at different moments in the life cycle; moreover they may be revealed in some individuals but not others, depending (among other things) on the environmental circumstances they have encountered.

From this it would appear that the mechanisms themselves should be understood as aspects of manifest rather than evolved psychology. Confusingly, however, Tooby and Cosmides more often use the phrase 'evolved architecture' to refer to these manifest structures than to the underlying design. Indeed they openly admit that their usage is ambig-uous, that they do not bother to distinguish terminologically between 'expressed adaptive architecture' and the more fundamental programmes that underwrite its construction (1992: 82). Presented as a matter of expository convenience, this conflation of the manifest and the evolved is more in the nature of a cover-up that enables them to get away with talking about cognitive mechanisms *as if* they were already in place and fully operational, constructed by the great master-builder of evolution, natural selection, before any development can get under way at all. And it enables them to claim, almost in the same breath, that the 'evolved architecture' *selects* what is developmentally relevant in the environment, and that the environment is implicated in the very development of the architecture (1992: 84–7).

Sperber runs into precisely the same dilemma, though it is not elaborated to the same degree. In this case, the problem revolves around the status of the innate dispositions which, as we have seen, are defined as functions of evolved, genetically determined, and domain-specific cognitive modules. Let us suppose, in accordance with orthodox evolutionary biology, that the genotype includes a set of instructions for constructing the modules, and the dispositions that are given in their operation. It would follow that the dispositions themselves emerge in the course of ontogenetic development. Sperber confirms this inference, noting that dispositions will only develop if 'appropriate environmental conditions' are fulfilled (1996: 67). Yet elsewhere, he assures us that the dispositions are there to begin with, and that they cause the developing child to attend selectively to information from the surrounding environment that is relevant to his or her becoming 'a competent speaker, a competent climber, thrower, catcher, eater, drinker, a competent manipulator of objects, a competent recogniser of animals, a competent predictor of other people's behaviour, and so on' (1996: 117). In this account of development, the process starts not with a plan for constructing cognitive modules that is *as yet unrealized*, but with preconstituted modules whose 'needs' for information are *as yet unsatisfied*. The structures are already in place, but they are initially empty of informational content. Development is about filling up the modules, not about their construction.

The core of the problem, however, lies in the seemingly innocuous phrase 'appropriate environmental conditions'. For the development of dispositions, according to Sperber, the appropriate conditions are those of the module's proper domain, the domain for which it originally evolved as an evolutionary adaptation. If the conditions are significantly altered, so that they are no longer appropriate in this sense, then we would expect that the dispositions would either not develop at all or develop along different lines. Yet Sperber appeals to the 'innateness' of dispositions to assert the contrary: that the dispositions are there anyway, whatever environmental conditions happen to obtain, and that environmental differences are registered in development solely through the susceptibility of modules to diverse representational content. Tooby and Cosmides advance much the same claims, arguing on the one hand that the concrete mechanisms making up the evolved architecture are 'reliably constructed' under all normal environmental circumstances, but on the other that these universal mechanisms proceed to work on 'variable environmental inputs' to produce the diversity of manifest competencies and behaviours that we actually observe (1992: 45).[6]

Let me unpack these claims (illustrated schematically in Figure 4.2) with reference to a specific and much-vaunted example, that of language acquisition. Here, the alleged universal mechanism is what has come to be called the 'language acquisition device' (LAD). During a well-defined

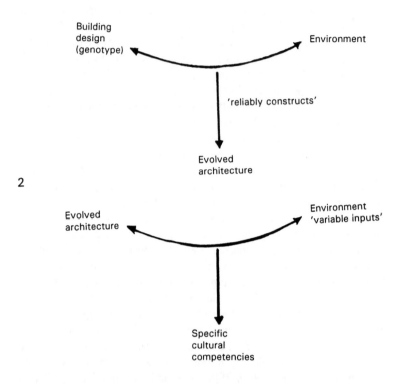

Figure 4.2 Two claims for the construction of mind, following the model presented by Tooby and Cosmides (1992). (1) A universal building design (one component of the genotype) interacts with the environment to 'reliably construct' the 'evolved architecture' consisting of a number of cognitive mechanisms including, for example, the 'language acquisition device'. (2) The architecture (presumed universal) interacts selectively with the environment, accepting information specifying diverse cultural competencies such as, for example, the ability to speak English, Dutch or Japanese.

stage of infancy, this device is said to be activated, operating upon the input of speech sounds from the environment so as to establish, in the infant's mind, the grammar and lexicon of the particular language (or languages) spoken in his or her community. An infant reared in social isolation, and thus deprived of the relevant environmental input, would not learn a language, but would still possess a fully formed LAD (Tooby and Cosmides 1992: 45). It would thus appear that language acquisition is a two-stage process: in the first, the LAD is constructed; in the second

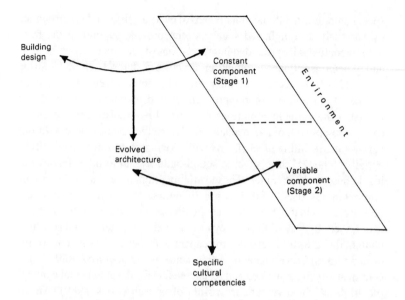

Figure 4.3 Putting the two claims of Figure 4.2 together yields a two-stage model of cognitive development. Note, however, that this model depends on factoring out those features of the environment that are constant, or 'reliably present' in every conceivable developmental context, from those that represent a source of 'variable input' from one context to another. Only the former are relevant in the first stage (the construction of 'innate' mechanisms); only the latter are relevant in the second (the acquisition of culturally specific competencies).

it is furnished with specific syntactic and semantic content. That, at least, is the theory, but is it borne out in practice? Is there any basis in reality for separating out the construction of 'innate' psychological mechanisms from the transmission of 'acquired' cultural representations, as shown in Figure 4.3, or is the division into these two stages no more than an artefact of our own analytic procedures? In what follows, I shall argue that the latter is the case.

Beyond the innate/acquired dichotomy

The first point to note is that the mechanisms (if we can call them that) underwriting the child's ability to speak are not constructed in a vacuum, but rather emerge in the context of his or her sensory involvement in a richly structured environment. From birth, if not before,[7] the infant is immersed in a world of sound in which the characteristic patterns of speech mingle with all the other noises of everyday life, and is surrounded by variously accomplished speakers who provide support in the form both of contextually grounded interpretations of the infant's vocalizations and of demonstrations, or 'attention-directing gestures' (Zukow-Goldring 1997: 221–3), to accompany their own. This environment, then, is not a source of variable input for pre-constructed mechanisms, but rather furnishes the variable conditions for the self-assembly, in the course of early development, of the mechanisms themselves. And as the conditions vary, so the resulting mechanisms will take manifold forms, each differentially 'tuned' both to specific sound-patterns and to other features of local contexts of utterance. These variably attuned mechanisms, and the competencies they establish, are of course the neurophysiological correlates of what appear to us as the diverse languages of the world. It is not, then, by way of the conveyance of specific syntactic and semantic content that the child develops the capacity to speak in the manner of his or her community. Language, in this sense, *is not acquired*. Rather, it is continually being generated and regenerated in the developmental contexts of children's involvement in worlds of speech (Lock 1980). And if language is not acquired, then there can be no such thing as an innate language-acquisition device (Dent 1990).

What applies specifically in the case of language and speech also applies, more generally, with regard to other aspects of cultural competence. Learning to throw and catch, to climb, or to eat and drink, to cite a few of Sperber's examples (1996: 117), is a matter not of acquiring *from* an environment representations that satisfy the input conditions of preconstituted modules, but of the formation, *within* an environment, of the necessary neurological connections, along with attendant features of musculature and anatomy, that establish these various competencies. To underline the contrast between Sperber's position and mine, let me return to the question of copying. For Sperber, a design for the mind is copied, along with the DNA of the genome, at the inception of every new lifecycle. And this design, prior to being opened up to the differentiating influences of the environment, magically turns itself into concrete mechanisms in the brain, ready and prepared to process relevant environmental input. I have argued, to the contrary, that copying is itself a developmental process, that this process takes place in an environmental context, and that it alone provides a link between the genome and the formal properties of the organism – including those of its brain (see Figure 4.1).

In a sense, then, the architecture of the mind *is* a result of copying; that copying, however, is not an automatic transcription of cognitive devices (or instructions for building them) from one head to another, but a matter of *following*, in one's actions, what other people do. In this sense, of imitation rather than transcription, copying is an aspect of a person's life in the world, involving repeated tasks and exercises or what White-house (1996: 113) aptly calls 'the labours of maturation'. It is through the work of copying, then, that the neurological foundations of human competencies are established. This is not to deny that the resulting neural organization may take a modular form; it is to insist, however, that *modularity develops* (Ingold 1994: 295),[8] and that the precise way in which this packaging occurs will depend upon the particularities of environmental experience.

To dispel any possible misunderstanding, I should stress that my purpose is not to argue for the priority of nurture over nature, or to substitute for the innatist bias of Sperber's account a doctrine of the environmental determination of human capacities. My argument is not caught, as is Plotkin's in Chapter Three, between the two poles of what he calls the 'great game', with one side positing the mind as a blank slate and the other insisting that it comes with a ready-made architecture.[9] These are not the only theoretical alternatives, and indeed both are fallacious for the same reason, most succinctly expressed by Oyama, namely that the information specifying the capacities in question, whether its source be supposed to lie inside the organism or outside in the environment, must be presumed to 'pre-exist the processes that give rise to it' (Oyama 1985: 13). My point is that these capacities are neither internally pre-specified nor externally imposed, but arise within processes of development, as properties of dynamic self-organization of the total field of relationships in which a person's life unfolds.

An example is the ability to throw things with some precision, and to catch them by hand. Like walking on two feet, this appears to be one of the hallmarks of our species. Yet there are, in practice, any number of different modes of throwing, and of catching, appropriate to different activities and settings. Hurling a javelin, putting shot, and bowling in cricket all call for different patterns and sequences of muscular tension, and for different judgements of pace, angle, and spin. There is no 'essence' of throwing and catching, however, underwriting these variations in actual performance (Thelen 1995: 83). In every case, the particular capacities of perception and action constituting the motor skill are developmentally embodied into the modus operandi of the human organism through practice and training, under the guidance of already accomplished practitioners, in an environment characterized by its own textures and topography, and littered with the products of previous human activity. To adopt a felicitous expression from Kugler and Turvey (1987), the components that actually produce the limb trajectories involved in throwing and catching are not hard-wired but 'softly assembled'.[10]

Though it is customary to speak of a capacity such as throwing/catching as a human universal, as distinct from its particular manifestations, we can do so only by artificially 'bracketing out' all variations of context, and by focusing exclusively on what every conceivable situation of development has in common. For comparative analytic purposes, such attempts to sift the general from the particular, or to establish a lowest common denominator of development, may have their uses. But if universal capacities are nothing more than abstract precipitates of this analytic procedure, to claim that they are concretely instantiated in the heads of individuals, in the form of evolved mental modules, is patently absurd (Shore 1996: 17). This is the crux of my disagreement with Boyer (Chapter Two). Given the human genotype, he says, 'certain developmental consequences are practically inevitable *in normal circumstances*'. But how are we to decide what circumstances are normal? For Boyer, circumstances are exceptional rather than normal if 'they were not part of the conditions prevailing when the genes in question were selected'. In that sense, most children in the world today are growing up in rather exceptional circumstances. Yet barring accident or handicap, they are nevertheless supposed to be equipped with the full suite of evolved capacities specified by naturally selected genes.

It must, then, be possible to adduce a core of concrete circumstances – what Boyer calls a 'standard epigenetic environment' – that is common to all situations in which humans learn, for example, to throw things, from the hunting ground to the cricket pitch. I cannot fathom what these circumstances might be. Or to take another example, we might admit that infants, in learning to walk, normally find themselves in situations where there is ground to walk on. Yet how could the infant encounter 'ground', as a concrete condition of development, not only as distinct from, but also prior to, such diverse 'walk-on-able' surfaces as sand, asphalt, meadow, and heath, all of which call for different modalities of gait, balance, and footwork? And how, again, could such a ground be free from all contours? Bizarre as it may seem, this is precisely how the ground beneath our feet would have initially to be experienced, if we are to hold on to the notion that culturally and environmentally particular modalities of walking are added on to a universally innate capacity for bipedal locomotion. And just the same kind of partitioning of the child's experience of the environment is entailed by the notion that competence in his or her mother tongue is acquired on the basis of a preformed 'language instinct' (Pinker 1994).

If, however, there are no innate psychological structures – no built-in architecture nor even any context-independent design specifications – then what, if anything, evolves? Earlier, with regard to the general problem of form in biology, I argued that since form arises within developmental systems, to account for its evolution we need to focus on the temporal unfolding of these systems and on their properties of dynamic self-organization. Reconceptualized in this way, the evolutionary process becomes one in which organisms, through their presence and their activities, set up the developmental conditions under which their successors are destined to live out their lives. Likewise the manifold capacities of human beings, from throwing stones to bowling cricket balls, from climbing trees to scaling ladders, from whistling to playing the piano, emerge through the labours of maturation within fields of practice constituted by the activities of predecessors. It makes no sense to ask whether the capacity to climb lies with the climber or the ladder, or whether the capacity to play the piano resides in the pianist or the instrument. These capacities exist neither 'inside' the body and brain of the practitioner nor 'outside' in the environment. They are rather properties of environmentally extended systems that crosscut the boundaries of body and brain (A. Clark 1997: 214). It follows that the work people do, in establishing environments for their own and future generations, contributes quite directly to the evolution of human capacities.

In his study of the computational tasks involved in maritime navigation, Edwin Hutchins observes that 'humans create their cognitive powers by creating the environments in which they exercise these powers' (1995: 169). This, for him, is the process of culture, though one could just as well call it history. But is there anything specifically human about this process? Hutchins compares the human navigator to the ant, which owes its apparently innate ability to locate food sources with uncanny accuracy to the trails left in the environment by countless predecessors. Wipe out the trails, and the ant is lost. So, indeed, would humans be, without culture or history. Hutchins's conclusion is that the capacities of the ant, too, are constituted within a historical process of culture. Alternatively (and amounting to much the same thing) we could conclude that the supposedly 'cultural' capacities of human beings are constituted within a process of evolution. My point is that history, understood as the movement wherein people create their environments, and hence themselves, is no more than a continuation of the evolutionary process, as defined above, into the domain of human relations (Ingold 1995a: 207–12). Having dissolved the distinction between the innate and the acquired, we find that the parallel distinction between evolution and history falls with it.

Capacity, competence, and skill

Up to now, I have used the words 'capacity' and 'competence', loosely and interchangeably, to describe aspects of human knowledgeability. Neither word, however, seems entirely appropriate for this purpose. The trouble with the concept of capacity is that it is rooted in the metaphors of container and content, of human psychology as a set of preconstituted, modular compartments or 'acquisition devices', waiting to be filled up with cultural information in the form of mental representations. The image of mind as container is shared both by Sperber and by many of those with whom he claims to take issue: orthodox cultural relativists who, as he puts it, are naive enough to believe that 'human mental abilities make culture possible and yet do not in any way determine its content and organisation' (1996: 57). What I find naive, to the contrary, is Sperber's belief that culture stands as 'content' to human psychology (Lave 1988: 85). Without doubt, people raised in different environments learn to perceive their surroundings, and to act within them, in different ways. We may even agree to call these differences cultural. As such, however, they are not so much received into the 'capacities' of a universal psychology as immanent in that field of relations wherein human beings undergo the organic processes of growth and maturation, and in which their powers of action and perception are developed and sustained.[11]

But the notion of competence is equally problematic, largely because of the way its meaning has come to be constituted, particularly in the literatures of psychology and linguistics, through an opposition to performance. The notion suggests a knowledgeability that is detached from action and from the contexts of actors' bodily engagement with the world, and that takes the form of interior rules or programmes capable of specifying, in advance, the appropriate behavioural response to any given situation. Competence, as Dreyfus and Dreyfus have pointed out (1986: 26–7), underwrites the kind of process that, according to cognitive science, lies at the heart of *all* intelligent action, namely 'problem-solving'. The approach of the intelligent problem solver, in this view, is always to act on the basis of a plan, which is formulated by bringing a given set of decision rules to bear upon a representation of the existing situation. Thus the notions of capacity and competence are closely bound up with one another: where the former implies a built-in readiness to accept certain types of rules and representations, the latter inheres in this received mental content. The individual equipped with a capacity for language can acquire competence in English; the individual equipped with a capacity for throwing/catching can become a competent cricketer, and so on.

To think in these terms, however, is to treat performance, such as that of the English-speaker or the bowler in cricket, as nothing more than the mechanical execution, by the body, of a set of commands generated and placed 'on line' by the intellect. It is to suppose that the performance begins with a plan which, since it contains a precise and complete specification of the behaviour to follow, is necessarily a structure of a very complex kind. The process of implementation, on the other hand, is assumed to be of clockwork simplicity. This is the approach taken by Sperber, and indeed generally in the classic tradition of cognitive science. But as David Rubin has pointed out (1988: 375), we could equally well take the opposite tack: that is, to presuppose a simple structure, or even no structure at all, and to account for the performance as the unfolding of a complex process. Consider, for example, the movements of the woodsman, in felling a tree with his axe. A complex-structure, simple-process model would regard every swing of the axe as the mechanical output of a mental computational device installed inside the woodsman's head, designed to calculate the optimal angle of the swing and the precise force of the blow. A complex-process model, by contrast, would regard the movement of the axe as part of the dynamic functioning of the entire system of relations constituted by the presence of the man, with his axe, in an environment that includes the tree as the current focus of his attention (Bateson 1973: 433). More generally, a model of the latter kind would treat performance not as the discharge of representations in the mind but as an achievement of the whole organism-person in an environment (Thelen 1995).

This calls for a fundamentally ecological approach, and that is the approach I adopt here.[12] Its basic premise is that human knowledgeability is founded not in some combination of innate capacities and acquired competence, but in *skill* (Rubin 1988; J.E. Clark 1997). How, then, might an ecological account of skilled practice take us beyond what classical cognitive science describes as competent performance? We have seen that the competent performer of cognitive science is bound to the mechanical execution of a predetermined plan. Once set upon a course of action, he cannot therefore alter it without interrupting the execution in order to reconfigure the plan in the light of new data. The movement of the skilled practitioner, by contrast, is continually and fluently responsive to perturbations of the perceived environment (Ingold 1993a: 462). This is possible because the practitioner's bodily movement is, at one and the same time, a *movement of attention*; because he watches, listens, and feels even as he works. It is this responsiveness that underpins the qualities of care, judgement, and dexterity that are the hallmarks of skilled workmanship (Pye 1968: 22). As Nicholai Bernstein wrote, 'the essence of dexterity lies not in bodily movements themselves but in the *tuning of the movements to an emergent task'*, whose surrounding conditions are never precisely the same from one moment to the next (Bernstein 1996: 23, original emphasis).

Moreover the more skilled the practitioner, the less 'working out' is needed: thus what distinguishes the expert from the relative novice is not the complexity or elaborateness of his plans or representations but the extent to which he can dispense with them. 'When things are proceeding normally', as Dreyfus and Dreyfus put it, 'experts don't solve problems and don't make decisions; they do what normally works' (1986: 30–1). This is not to deny that experts lay plans or formulate objectives. The woodsman has to select which tree to fell, and to decide upon the orientation of the notch so that it will ultimately fall in a direction that will not risk damage to surrounding vegetation. To observe him doing this, however, is to watch as he paces the woods, casting his eyes over different trees, sizing them up. In other words, it is to observe him feeling his way, in an environment, towards a goal that is conceived in anticipation of a future project. This kind of preparatory work, as Leudar and Costall have pointed out, 'is itself a mundane social activity, not a purely "intellectual" enterprise' (1996: 164). As such it calls, just as any other skilled practice, for powers of perceptual discrimination finely tuned through previous experience. Furthermore the 'plans' that the woodsman arrives at through this activity in no sense specify or determine the movements that follow, or the circumstances attending them, in all their concrete detail. What they do, rather, is to place him in a position of readiness, from which to launch into the subsequent project with a reasonable chance of success. Once the project is under way, he must fall back on bodily skills that he has already perfected (Suchman 1987: 52).

Now it is one thing to characterize the knowledge of the expert in terms of skill, but quite another to claim, as I have done, that skill is the foundation of *all* knowledge. It would of course be foolish to imagine that we are experts in everything we do. In the course of anthropological fieldwork among reindeer herdsmen in Finnish Lapland, I had to learn to cast a lasso. Despite my best efforts, I remain incapable of capturing a moving animal of my choice amid the swirling mass of deer in the roundup enclosure. The trouble is that lacking the intimate coordination of perception and action of the expert herdsman, I have to stop to think before casting the rope, in order to figure out how to proceed, by which time the reindeer, which is a good deal more skilled at evading the lasso than I am in casting it, has already moved out of reach. Indeed an account of how I set about casting the lasso, according to a series of precalculated moves, would at first glance appear to conform rather closely to the picture that classical cognitive science presents of the competent practitioner at work. For me it is indeed a puzzle, a problem to be solved. In what sense, then, can it be claimed that my rudimentary competence is nevertheless founded in skill? To answer this question I need to introduce a distinction, which is critical to my argument, between knowledge and information.

Consider a cookbook. The book is packed with information about how to prepare a selection of mouth-watering dishes. But is it in this inform-ation that the knowledge of the cook consists? Sperber would have it so. Thus the recipe for Mornay sauce, to cite one of his favourite examples, includes everything you need to know to prepare the sauce in your own kitchen. Nothing more is presupposed than the ability to read. Once the instructions have been transcribed into your head, all you have to do is to 'convert [them] into bodily behaviour' (Sperber 1996: 61). The conversion, however, is easier said than done. No known cookbook comes with such precise instructions that its recipes could be converted into behaviour just like that. When the recipe instructs me to 'melt the butter in a small pan and stir in the flour', I am able to follow it only because it speaks to my own prior experience of melting and stirring, of handling such substances as flour and butter, and of finding the relevant ingredients and utensils from the various corners of my kitchen (Leudar and Costall 1996: 163). The verbal commands of the recipe, in other words, draw their meaning not from their attachment to mental representations in my head, but from their positioning within the familiar context of my activity in the home. Like signposts in a landscape, they provide specific directions to practitioners as they make their way through a field of related practices or what I have elsewhere called a 'taskscape' (Ingold 1993b: 158). Each command is strategically located at a point which the original author of the recipe, looking back on previous experience of preparing the dish in question, considered to be a critical juncture in the total process. Between these points, however, the cook is expected to be able to find his or her way around, attentively and responsively, but without further recourse to explicit rules of procedure – or in a word, skilfully.

Thus the information in the recipe book is not, in itself, knowledge. Rather, it opens up a path to knowledge, thanks to its location within a taskscape that is already partially familiar by virtue of previous experience. Only when placed in the context of skills gained through this prior experience does information specify a route that is comprehensible and that can practicably be followed, and only a route so specified can lead to knowledge. It is in this sense that all knowledge is founded in skill. Just as my knowledge of the landscape is gained by walking through it, following various signposted routes, so my knowledge of the taskscape comes from following the several recipes in the book. This is not knowledge that has been communicated to me; it is knowledge I have built up for myself by following the same paths as my predecessors and under their direction. In short, the growth of knowledge in the life history of a person is a result not of information transmission but of guided rediscovery. I shall return to this distinction below, since it has a critical bearing on how we understand the process of copying.

It is here, finally, that we can identify what distinguishes the real-life novice from the competent practitioner as classically depicted by cognitive science. Both may proceed in the same 'stop–go' fashion, periodically interrupting the flow of action in order to take stock of the situation and to plot a new course. But the deliberations of the novice are carried on not in an inner mental sanctum, closeted from the multiple domains of practical life, but in a real world of people, objects and relationships. The environment, then, is not merely a source of problems, of adaptive challenges to be resolved; it becomes part of the means for dealing with them. As Andy Clark nicely puts it, the mind is a 'leaky organ' that refuses to be confined within the skull but shamelessly mingles with the body and the world in the conduct of its operations (A. Clark 1997: 53). Every step of problem-solving is itself an exploratory movement within that world.

When, for example, lasso in hand, I adjust my body posture so as to be suitably poised for the next cast, I do not place my limbs into precalculated positions; rather, the preparatory adjustments of my posture are integral to the process of calculation itself. The 'calculator', in other words, is not a device inside the head but the whole person in the world (Lave 1988: 154). Along with parts of the body, aspects of the environmental setting are incorporated as integral parts of the 'device'. But this means, too, that calculation and implementation, far from being separate, successive stages of any operation, are merged as one and the same. As with a journey through the landscape, to have found your way to a place is to have actually arrived there, and not merely to have plotted a course for the trip. In the final analysis, then, there can be no distinction between solving a problem and carrying out the solution in practice, since every step of problem-solving is itself a step along the way to implementation. And each step follows the next as successive movements of the perceptually aware agent, the 'person-acting' (Lave 1988: 180–1), in the settings of practice.

The education of attention

How, then, to return to my original question, does each generation contribute to the knowledgeability of the next? The answer cannot lie in the transmission of representations – or of what D'Andrade (1981: 179) calls '"pass it along" type information' – since, as I have shown, this rests upon the impossible precondition of a ready-made cognitive architecture. In this penultimate section I want to offer an alternative suggestion: namely, that the contribution each generation makes to its successors amounts to an *education of attention.*

Earlier, I argued that there is no 'reading' of the molecules of DNA making up the genome of an organism apart from the process of development itself. We have now arrived at an almost identical conclusion with regard to human learning: there is no reading of a verbal script such as that contained in the cookbook that is not part of the novice's practical engagement with his or her environment. Once again, the issue comes down to one about copying. Recall that in Sperber's epidemiological model of cultural transmission, knowledge comes in the form of representations which pass from head to head by way of successive steps of behavioural externalization and perceptual internalization. But the copying of a public representation, perceived in the world, into a corresponding representation in the mind forms no part of the process by which the representation, once copied, is put into practice.

In its public form, for example, the recipe for Mornay sauce exists in the cookbook as 'an ink pattern on a piece of paper which can be read' (Sperber 1996: 61). To turn the public representation into a mental one, the aspiring cook need only be equipped with cognitive mechanisms for processing the input from this pattern into a corresponding set of images in the mind. In principle, the recipe could be reread, by generation after generation, without any cookery having to take place at all. Cooking, in Sperber's account (and as shown schematically in Figure 4.4), is not copying, it is the expression of copies that are already established in the mind of the cook. This view has its precise analogue in orthodox evolutionary biology which, as we have seen, supposes that development is the expression of a formal specification that has already been copied into the organism, through genetic replication, at the point of conception. Just as evolutionary theory imagines that the specifications of organic form, coded in genes, can be passed down the generations independently of the processes of development, so cognitive science imagines that cultural knowledge, coded in words or other symbolic media, can be passed on independently of its practical application in particular tasks and contexts.

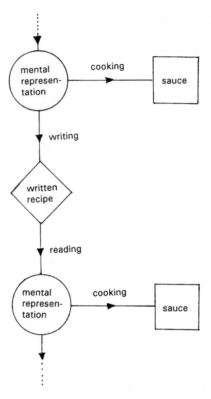

Figure 4.4 According to cognitive science, the copying of mental representations is quite distinct from their behavioural expression. This is illustrated schematically, with reference to Sperber's example of cookery. In terms of the diagram, copying is a 'vertical' process, whereas conversion into behaviour is 'horizontal'.

But Sperber plays a trick with his Mornay sauce example. For if reading the recipe were really a matter of processing the visual input from an ink-pattern, then the resulting mental representation would consist of nothing more than an image of the written script. And the reader would implement the representation not by cooking at all, but by writing out the words of the recipe onto another piece of paper. The trick is to suppose that by forming an image of the ink-patterns, the aspiring cook has also formed in his or her mind an image of what those patterns are supposed to represent, namely a programme for activity in the kitchen. However Sperber's other example, the story of Little Red Riding Hood, gives the game away. He explains that the child whose mind contains a representation of the story may, if she so wishes, turn it 'into bodily, and more specifically vocal, behaviour' (1996: 62), simply by telling the tale. By the same token, the cook would convert the remembered recipe into behaviour by writing it down. To claim, as Sperber does, that the cook turns the mental representation of the written recipe into bodily behaviour by *preparing the sauce* makes about as much sense as supposing that the child converts the story of Little Red Riding Hood into behaviour by setting off to her grandmother's with a pot of butter and a cake!

A device capable of scanning the pages of a cookbook, and of processing the input data into stored images, could also be equipped, at least in principle, with a facility for printing out the received information. Yet such a device – which is what Sperber imagines the human being to be – would be quite unable to cook. How, then, do real-life human beings, as opposed to the animated processing devices of Sperber's imagination, learn the arts of cookery? They do so, of course, by copying the activities of already skilled cooks. To reiterate my earlier point, copying is not the automatic transcription of mental content from one head to another, but is rather a matter of following what other people do. The novice watches, feels, or listens to the movements of the expert, and seeks through repeated trials to bring his own bodily movements into line with those of his attention so as to achieve the kind of rhythmic adjustment of perception and action that lies at the heart of fluent performance (Gatewood 1985). As Merleau-Ponty has observed, we do not so much copy other persons as copy their actions, and 'find others at the point of origin of these actions' (1964: 117).[13] This process of copying, as I have already shown, is one not of information transmission but of guided rediscovery. As such, it involves a mixture of imitation and improvisation: indeed these might better be understood as two sides of the same coin. Copying is imitative, insofar as it takes place under guidance; it is improvisatory, insofar as the knowledge it generates is knowledge that novices discover for themselves. Thus conceived, improvisation in Bourdieu's terms is 'as remote from a creation of unpredictable novelty' as is imitation 'a simple mechanical reproduction of the initial conditionings' (Bourdieu 1977: 95). Both are aspects of the situated and attentive engagement that is fundamental to becoming a skilled practitioner (Ingold 1996b: 179).

The process of learning by guided rediscovery is most aptly conveyed by the notion of *showing*. To show something to someone is to cause it to be made present for that person, so that he or she can apprehend it directly, whether by looking, listening, or feeling. Here, the role of the tutor is to set up situations in which the novice is afforded the possibility of such unmediated experience. Placed within a situation of this kind, the novice is instructed to attend particularly to this or that aspect of what can be seen, touched, or heard, so as to get the 'feel' of it for him- or herself. Learning, in this sense, is tantamount to an 'education of attention'. I take this phrase from James Gibson (1979: 254), whose attempt to develop an ecological psychology that treats perception as the activity of the whole organism in an environment rather than that of a mind inside a body has been a major source of inspiration for the approach I have adopted here. Gibson's point was that we learn to perceive not by taking on board mental representations or schemata for organizing the raw data of bodily sensation, but by a fine-tuning or sensitization of the entire perceptual system, comprising the brain and peripheral receptor organs along with their neural and muscular linkages, to particular features of the environment (Gibson 1979: 246-8).

This education of attention is quite different from what Sperber has in mind when he suggests that the child is innately disposed to attend to information that specifies particular competencies such as speaking, climbing, throwing, and so on (1996: 117). The difference is twofold. First, the structures of attention to which Sperber refers, namely 'dispositions', are given from the start, and do not themselves undergo development within an environmental context. Secondly, their 'education', if we can call it that, lies not in their sensitization to certain features of the world, but in their receipt of specific informational content. To put it rather crudely, Gibson's novices are 'tuned up', Sperber's are 'filled up'. Thus from a Gibsonian perspective, if the knowledge of the expert is superior to that of the novice, it is not because she has acquired mental representations that enable her to construct a more elaborate picture of the world from the same corpus of data, but because her perceptual system is attuned to 'picking up' critical features of the environment that the novice simply fails to notice. The accomplished woodsman – to revert to our earlier example – looks around him for guidance on where and how to cut: he consults the world, not a picture in his head. The world, after all, is its own best model (A. Clark 1997: 29). Adopting one of Gibson's key metaphors, we could say that the perceptual system of the skilled practitioner *resonates* with the properties of the environment. Learning, the education of attention, is thus equivalent to this process of attunement of the perceptual system (Zukow-Goldring 1997).

We are now, at last, able to provide an answer to the question with which I began. In the passage of human generations, each one contributes to the knowledgeability of the next not by handing down a corpus of disembodied, context-free information, but by setting up, through their activities, the environmental contexts within which successors develop their own embodied skills of perception and action. Rather than having its evolved capacities filled up with structures that *represent* aspects of the world, the human being emerges as a centre of awareness and agency whose processes *resonate* with those of its environment. Knowing, then, does not lie in the relations between structures in the world and structures in the mind, mediated by the person of the knower, but is immanent in the life and consciousness of the knower as it unfolds within the field of practice – the taskscape – set up through his or her presence as a being-in-the-world. Cognition, in this sense, is a process in real time. 'Rather than speaking of ideas, concepts, categories and links', Gatewood suggests, 'we should think of flows, contours, intensities and resonances' (1985: 216).[14] These are terms that describe, on the one hand, the features of the taskscape in which practitioners are situated and, on the other hand, the course of their own attention as they make their way through it. But since the taskscape through which any person moves is constituted by the practices of all the others, each plays a part in establishing the conditions of development for everyone else. Thus the process of cognition is tantamount to the historical process of social life itself. And the latter, as I have already shown, is but a continuation, into the human domain, of a more encompassing process of evolution.

Conclusion

By way of an epilogue, I should like finally to dispose of three fallacies that lie at the heart of Sperber's approach to the explanation of culture. The first is that cultural knowledge takes the form of representations; the second is that these representations, in their mental modality, are stored within the containers of a universal psychology, whence they have to be retrieved prior to their practical enactment; the third is that in this enactment, a boundary is crossed between mental and public domains.

Sperber's 'representations' are peculiar things. It is not at all clear what they represent, if not themselves. True, the recipe for Mornay sauce is, in some sense, 'about' the activity that goes on in the kitchen. When it comes to the story of Little Red Riding Hood the situation is not so clear, and Sperber's claim that a myth such as this is 'an orally transmitted story which is taken to represent actual events' (1996: 95) is decidedly unconvincing. As for the tune that I whistle as I walk down the street, the claim that it represents something other than itself (ibid.: 32) is quite absurd. Indeed, if we accept that the representation is a 'concrete physical object' (ibid.: 61), which can turn up just as well inside human brains as outside them, in the public form of artefacts, then nothing seems to have been gained by the substitution of 'representation' for the old-fashioned concept of 'trait'.[15] At least the latter does not send us off in a fruitless search for what the object in question is supposed to stand for. Might we not do better, as a last resort, to return to the language of Kroeber, and to regard every cooking of a sauce, every telling of a story, and every whistling of a tune as a particular exemplar of a trait, rather than a particular token of a representation?

The answer is 'no'. Cookings, story-tellings, and whistlings are not representations, they are not traits, indeed they are not objects of any kind; they are rather enactions in the world.[16] When you whistle an original tune, or tell a story for the first time, you do not merely convert, into manifest behaviour, a structure that exists already full-formed in your mind. Rather, the form of the melody or the story arises and is suspended within the current of the activity itself, situated as it is within an environment that includes me, the listener. And when I listen, I do not convert the pattern of acoustic stimulation *back* into a mental structure, but align the movement of my attention so that it resonates with that of your action. To put this another way, I am not – as Sperber would have it (1996: 32) – the 'user' of a form that you have yourself 'produced', but have rather joined *with* you, albeit silently, in the process of its production. The same goes for watching the activity of the cook in the kitchen: again, the movement of my attention 'follows' that of the cook as he goes about his task. To listen or to watch, in that sense, is to accompany another being, to follow – even if only for a short while – the same path that this being takes through the lifeworld, and to share in the experience the journey affords. Critically, in this journey, both observer and observed travel in the same direction. Listening, in short, is not the reverse of whistling or speaking, nor is watching the reverse of doing, for 'both are oriented in the same direction by the movement of consciousness' (Ingold 1986: 273).

How, then, is it possible that having heard you whistle a tune, which I might never have heard before, I am later discovered whistling the very same tune myself? Surely, it will be argued, there is no way to explain this remarkable ability of recall save by supposing that the tune exists, in some form, 'inside my head' – that is, as a mental representation. This, of course, is Sperber's view. It implies that the mind itself, with its several domain-specific compartments, is a repository for an immense accumulation of such representations, and that the act of recall is a matter of accessing or 'calling up' a particular representation from its place of storage, so that it can then be turned into overt behaviour. To adopt this view, however, is to force a distinction between recall and performance. The former is conceived as a purely intellectual operation, carried on exclusively within the space of the mind, whereas the latter is conceived as a purely physical or behavioural operation, subsequently undertaken by the body. This essentially Cartesian distinction is redolent of one to which I have already referred, and which is central to classical cognitive science's account of intelligent action, between problem-solving and the bodily implementation of the solutions reached.

Criticizing this account, I argued that problem-solving is inseparable from the actual movements of the person-acting in the settings of practice, and therefore that to have solved a problem is *ipso facto* to have implemented the solution. On the same grounds, I would now argue that recall and performance are one and the same: that whistling a tune *is* remembering it. This – harking back to Rubin's (1988) point – is to understand remembering not as the accessing of a complex structure, but as the unfolding of a complex process. To whistle a tune or tell a story that you have heard before is like taking a walk in the country along a route that you previously travelled in the company of someone else. You remember as you *go along*, where to 'go along' means to find your own way through the terrain of your experience. Thus the tune or story is a journey made rather than an object found, and to have remembered the way is already to have reached one's destination. Yet if each whistling, or telling, is a separate journey, how can we say of any two journeys that they are actually the same? For Sperber, every performance is the token of a representation, so that to whistle the same tune on different occasions is simply to run off two replicas from the same template. The similarity is given from the start. Journeys, however, can only be compared retrospectively in terms of the ground covered. Just as to follow someone is to cover the same ground through the world of lived experience, so to remember is to retrace one's steps. But each retracing is an original movement, not a replica.

Finally, if the forms things take, whether in the imagination or on the ground, arise within the current of involved activity in a field of practice (Ingold 1995b: 76), then there is no longer any need to suppose that to be perceived by others, a form has to have crossed a threshold from the interiority of my brain to the world outside or, conversely, that to be known by me, it has to have crossed the threshold in the reverse direction, from the surrounding environmnent to my brain. It would be wrong, as I have argued elsewhere (Ingold 1992: 51), to think of the interface between brain and environment as one of contact between two mutually exclusive domains, respectively mental and public; rather each, to use Bohm's (1980: 177) term, is 'implicate' in the other. Thus in the course of development, the history of a person's relations with his or her environment is enfolded in particular, neurologically grounded structures of awareness and response. Likewise, enfolded within the manifold forms and structures of the environment are histories of the activities of persons. In sum, the neurological structures and artefactual forms that Sperber calls representations are not causes and effects of one another, but emerge together as complementary moments of a single process – that is, the process of people's life in the world. It is within this process that all knowledge is constituted.

Notes

1. This chapter originated from discussions in the series of seminars on 'Memory and Social Transmission', held at Queen's University, Belfast, through 1994 and 1995, and funded by the Economic and Social Research Council. I would like to thank the organizers of the series, Elizabeth Tonkin and Harvey Whitehouse, for making these discussions possible, and all the participants for many hours of fruitful exchange, from which I learned a great deal. In revising the chapter, I have benefited greatly from the comments of two very helpful, but anonymous readers.
2. This is also the conclusion reached by Johnson-Laird, who regards learning as 'the construction of new programs out of elements of experience'. Programmes, however, cannot be constructed out of thin air. To learn anything, you must already have a programme governing the construction process. That, too, may have been constructed in the same way, through the processing of experiential input according to yet another programme: 'you can learn to learn, but then that learning would depend on another program, and so on. Ultimately, learning must depend on *innate* programs that make programs' (Johnson-Laird 1988: 133, my emphasis).
3. I use the term 'neo-Darwinian' to refer to the so-called 'modern synthesis' of natural selection and population genetics, and to the claim that taken together, these are both necessary and sufficient to explain the evolution of living things (Maynard Smith 1969). Whether neo-Darwinism represents a refinement or a travesty of Darwin's original ideas is a controversial issue in the history and philosophy of biology which I shall not go into here.

4. That this is so can be confirmed by means of a simple thought experiment. Imagine an organism O1 at time T1, and its descendant (many generations removed) O2 at time T2. Suppose, first, that in the period from T1 to T2, environmental conditions have remained unchanged, but significant alteration has taken place in the organism's genetic constitution. Comparing O1 and O2, we conclude that there has been an evolution of form. Now suppose, secondly, that there has been no change in the organism's genes but that environmental conditions have significantly altered. Superficially, the differences between O1 and O2 are just the same as in the first case, yet on comparing them this time, we conclude that no evolution has taken place at all, and that O1 and O2 are but outward expressions of the same basic design (see Oyama 1985: 40–1). The environmentally induced outcome, in the second case, is said to be a 'phenocopy' of what has been produced through genetic change in the first. Significantly, however, the latter is never referred to as a 'genocopy' of the former (Cohen and Stewart 1994: 307).
5. For a fuller discussion of the difference between the developmental systems approach and standard interactionism, see Ingold (1996a).
6. It is simply impossible to reconcile the claim of reliable construction with Tooby and Cosmides' subsequent admission that 'the genetically universal may be developmentally expressed as different maturational designs in the infant, the child, the adolescent, and the adult; in females and males; or in individuals who encounter different circumstances' (1992: 82).
7. As Dent (1990: 693) points out, 'birth is a transition, not a magic starting point before which experience cannot play a role'. There is evidence that prenatal experience of vocal sounds leads new-born infants to express specific preferences for certain voices or even spoken passages (DeCasper and Spence 1986).
8. Greenfield (1991), for example, has shown how distinct neurological circuits, underlying the capacities of speech and tool-use respectively, emerge in development from a common substrate identified with Broca's area, through the establishment of separate though parallel connections with anterior regions of the prefrontal cortex.
9. According to Plotkin, 'humans, and other animals that can learn, come into the world knowing what it is they must learn and think about'. This statement is founded on a distinction between what is known from the start and what is subsequently taken on board. If this is not an instance of the innate/acquired dichotomy, it is hard to know what is. Almost in the same breath, Plotkin both sets up the dichotomy and

then lambasts social scientists such as myself for supposing that he and his fellow evolutionary psychologists would ever do such a thing!

10. See Thelen (1995) and A. Clark (1997: 42–5) for further discussion of this idea.

11. One indication of the tenacity of the metaphors of container and content, with regard to mind and culture, is that in a work devoted to demolishing the notion of genes as containing information that is replicable across generations independently of the contexts of development, Cohen and Stewart can nevertheless speak of human culture as 'a vast information store', available 'to be poured into each developing child' (1994: 357). This decontextualization of the context of human development, its reduction to a mass of free-floating particles of information, is disastrous for their overall argument. As Laughlin, McManus and d'Aquili have noted (1992: 66), 'any view that construcs learning as a process of pouring . . . information into a passive, "floppy disk" brain, where it is then absorbed and stored in memory, is totally . . . outmoded and erroneous' (1992: 66). See also Shore (1996: 7).

12. Since Sperber, too, sometimes presents his programme in a quasi-ecological idiom, I should explain how my kind of ecology differs from his. Sperber's proposal is to 'recognise only human organisms in their material environment (whether natural or artificial), and focus on these organisms' individual mental states and processes and on the physical-environmental causes and effects of these mental things' (1996: 99). Even if we agree with Sperber that 'mental things' can be 'naturalised' (ibid: 158, fn. 27), that is, treated as specific configurations on a neurological level, this approach sets up what is inside the organism (mental states) and what is outside it (the physical environment) as mutually exclusive entities, or classes of entity, which are only subsequently brought together and caused to interact. By contrast a properly ecological approach, in my view, is one that treats the organism-in-its-environment not as the compound of internal and external factors but as one indivisible totality. That totality is, in effect, a developmental system, and ecology deals with the dynamics of such systems.

13. Merleau-Ponty cites evidence in support of this idea from the pioneering work of Paul Guillaume, originally published in 1926, on imitation among children (Guillaume 1971). Subsequently, Bourdieu has made exactly the same point, in almost the same words: 'The child imitates not "models" but other people's actions' (Bourdieu 1977: 87). Recent empirical confirmation, with regard to imitation

in infancy, is provided by Meltzoff (1993). He shows how through 'babbling', not just with the voice but with the limbs and face as well, infants are able to match the movements they feel themselves to make with the movements they observe on the part of other people around them. This kind of 'active intermodal mapping' (AIM), Meltzoff argues, provides a bridge to the understanding of others as persons with desires and intentions, wherein the observed actions are supposed to have their source.

14. These points are echoed by Hutchins: 'Instead of conceiving the relation between person and environment in terms of moving coded information across a boundary, let us look for processes of entrainment, coordination and resonance among elements of a system that includes a person and a person's surroundings' (1995: 288).

15. Where Sperber speaks of representations, other writers in cognitive anthropology have had recourse to the notion of 'models'. Thus Shore (1996: 46–52) distinguishes between 'mental models' and 'instituted models' in a way that precisely parallels Sperber's distinction between mental and public representations. But the problems and ambiguities inherent in such usage are just the same.

16. I borrow the term 'enaction' from Varela, Thompson and Rosch (1991: 173), who use it as a shorthand for 'embodied action'. By this they mean action that is perceptually guided and grounded in sensorimotor experience.

References

Bateson, G. (1973), *Steps to an Ecology of Mind*, London: Granada.

Bernstein, N.A. (1996), 'On dexterity and its development', in M.L. Latash and M.T. Turvey (eds), *Dexterity and Its Development*, Mahwah, N.J.: Lawrence Erlbaum Associates.

Bohm, D. (1980), *Wholeness and the Implicate Order*, London: Routledge & Kegan Paul.

Bourdieu, P. (1977), *Outline of a Theory of Practice*, Cambridge: Cambridge University Press.

Clark, A. (1997), *Being There: Putting Brain, Body and the World Together Again*, Cambridge, Mass.: MIT Press.

Clark, J.E. (1997), 'A dynamical systems perspective on the development of complex adaptive skill', in C. Dent-Read and P. Zukow-Goldring (eds), *Evolving Explanations of Development: Ecological Approaches to Organism-Environment Systems*, Washington, DC: American Psychological Association.

Cohen, J. and Stewart, I. (1994), *The Collapse of Chaos: Discovering Simplicity in a Complex World*, Harmondsworth: Viking.

D'Andrade, R.G. (1981), 'The cultural part of cognition', *Cognitive Science*, 5: 179–95.

DeCasper, A. and Spence, M. (1986), 'Prenatal maternal speech influences newborns' perception of speech sounds', *Infant Behavior and Development*, 9: 133–50.

Dent, C.H. (1990), 'An ecological approach to language development: an alternative functionalism', *Developmental Psychobiology*, 23: 679–703.

Dreyfus, H.L. and Dreyfus, S.E. (1986), *Mind Over Machine: the Power of Human Intuition and Expertise in the Era of the Computer*, New York: Free Press.

Dunbar, R.I.M. (1996), 'How not to do biology', *Cultural Dynamics*, 8: 363–8.

Durkheim, E. (1976 [1915]), *The Elementary Forms of the Religious Life*, trans. J.W. Swain (2nd edn), London: Allen & Unwin.

Gatewood, J.B. (1985), 'Actions speak louder than words', in J.W. Dougherty (ed.), *Directions in Cognitive Anthropology*, Urbana, Ill.: University of Illinois Press.

Gibson, J.J. (1979), *The Ecological Approach to Visual Perception*, Boston: Houghton Mifflin.

Goodwin, B.C. (1988), 'Organisms and minds: the dialectics of the animal-human interface in biology', in T. Ingold (ed.), *What Is An Animal?*, London: Unwin Hyman.

Greenfield, P.M. (1991), 'Language, tools and the brain: the ontogeny and phylogeny of hierarchically organized sequential behaviour', *The Behavioural and Brain Sciences*, 14: 531–95.

Guillaume, P. (1971), *Imitation In Children*, trans. E. P Halperin, Chicago: University of Chicago Press.

Hirschfeld, L.A. and Gelman, S.A. (1994), 'Toward a topography of mind: an introduction to domain specificity', in L.A. Hirschfeld and S.A. Gelman (eds), *Mapping the Mind: Domain Specificity in Cognition and Culture*, New York: Cambridge University Press.

Hutchins, E. (1995), *Cognition in the Wild*, Cambridge, Mass.: MIT Press.

Ingold, T. (1986), *Evolution and Social Life*, Cambridge: Cambridge University Press.

—— (1992), 'Culture and the perception of the environment', in E. Croll and D. Parkin (eds), *Bush, Base: Forest Farm. Culture, Environment and Development*, London: Routledge.

—— (1993a), 'Technology, language, intelligence: a reconsideration of basic concepts', in K. R. Gibson and T. Ingold (eds), *Tools, Language and Cognition in Human Evolution*, Cambridge: Cambridge University Press.

—— (1993b), 'The temporality of the landscape', *World Archaeology*, 25: 152–74.

—— (1994), 'Tool-using, toolmaking and the evolution of language', in D. Quiatt and J. Itani (eds), *Hominid Culture in Primate Perspective*, Niwot, Colo.: University of Colorado Press .

—— (1995a), '"People like us": the concept of the anatomically modern human', *Cultural Dynamics*, 7: 187–214.

—— (1995b), 'Building, dwelling, living: how animals and people make themselves at home in the world', in M. Strathern (ed.), *Shifting Contexts: Transformations in Anthropological Knowledge*, London: Routledge.

—— (1996a), 'Why four why's? A response to my critics', *Cultural Dynamics*, 8: 377–86.

—— (1996b), 'Situating action V: the history and evolution of bodily skills', *Ecological Psychology*, 8: 171–82.

Johnson-Laird, P.N. (1988), *The Computer and the Mind*, London: Fontana.

Kroeber, A.L. (1952 [1943]), *The Nature of Culture*, Chicago: University of Chicago Press.

Kugler, P.N. and Turvey, M.T. (1987), *Information, Natural Law, and the Self-Assembly of Rhythmic Movement*, Hillsdale, N.J.: Erlbaum.

Laughlin, C.D. Jr., McManus, J., and d'Aquili, E. (1992), *Brain, Symbol and Experience: Toward a Neurophenomenology of Human Consciousness*, New York: Columbia University Press.

Lave, J. (1988), *Cognition in Practice: Mind, Mathematics and Culture in Everyday Life*, Cambridge: Cambridge University Press.

Lehrman, D.S. (1953), 'A critique of Konrad Lorenz's theory of instinctive behavior', *Quarterly Review of Biology*, 28: 337–63.

Leudar, I. and Costall, A. (1996), 'Situating action IV: planning as situated action', *Ecological Psychology*, 8: 153–70.

Lock, A. (1980), *The Guided Reinvention of Language*, London: Academic Press.

Maynard Smith, J. (1969), 'The status of neo-Darwinism', in C.H. Waddington (ed.), *Towards a Theoretical Biology, 2: Sketches*, Edinburgh: Edinburgh University Press.

Meltzoff, A.N. (1993), 'The centrality of motor coordination and proprioception in social and cognitive development: from shared actions to shared minds', in G.J.P. Savelsbergh (ed.), *The Development of Coordination in Infancy*, North Holland: Elsevier Press.

Merleau-Ponty, M. (1964), *The Primacy of Perception and Other Essays on Phenomenological Psychology, the Philosophy of Art, History and Politics*, ed. J.M. Edie, Evanston, Ill.: Northwestern University Press.

Oyama, S. (1985), *The Ontogeny of Information: Developmental Systems and Evolution*, Cambridge: Cambridge University Press.

—— (1989), 'Ontogeny and the central dogma: do we need the concept of genetic programming in order to have an evolutionary perspective?', in M. Gunnar and Thelen, E. (eds), *Systems in Development: the Minnesota Symposia on Child Psychology, Vol. 22,* Hillsdale, N.J.: Erlbaum.

—— (1993), 'Constraints and development', *Netherlands Journal of Zoology*, 43: 6–16.

Pinker, S. (1994), *The language instinct*, London: Allen Lane.

Pye, D. (1968), *The Nature and Art of Workmanship*, Cambridge: Cambridge University Press.

Rubin, D. (1988), 'Go for the skill', in U. Neisser and E. Winograd (eds), *Remembering Reconsidered: Ecological and Traditional Approaches to the Study of Memory*, Cambridge: Cambridge University Press.

Shore, B. (1996), *Culture in Mind: Cognition, Culture, and the Problem of Meaning*, New York: Oxford University Press.

Sperber, D. (1985), *On Anthropological Knowledge*, Cambridge: Cambridge University Press.

—— (1996), *Explaining Culture: A Naturalistic Approach*, Oxford: Blackwell.

Suchman, L.A. (1987), *Plans and Situated Actions: The Problem of Human–Machine Communication*, Cambridge: Cambridge University Press.

Thelen, E. (1995), 'Motor development: a new synthesis', *American Psychologist*, 50: 79–95.

Tooby, J. and Cosmides, L. (1992), 'The psychological foundations of culture', in J.H. Barkow, L. Cosmides and J. Tooby (eds), *The Adapted Mind: Evolutionary Psychology and the Generation of Culture*, New York: Oxford University Press.

Varela, F.J., Thompson, E. and Rosch, E. (1991), *The Embodied Mind: Cognitive Science and Human Experience*, Cambridge, Mass.: MIT Press.

Whitehouse, H. (1996), 'Jungles and computers: neuronal group selection and the epidemiology of representations', *Journal of the Royal Anthropological Institute* (N.S.), 2: 99–116.

Zukow-Goldring, P. (1997), 'A social ecological realist approach to the emergence of the lexicon: educating attention to amodal invariants in gesture and speech', in C. Dent-Read and P. Zukow-Goldring (eds), *Evolving Explanations of Development: Ecological Approaches to Organism-Environment Systems*, Washington, D.C.: American Psychological Association.

–5–

The Child in Mind
Christina Toren

This chapter is based on the premiss that what is wanted in the human sciences is a model of mind that is phenomenologically sound: that is to say, one that contains within itself the potential for acknowledging and explaining its own historicity even while it analyses the historicity of other ideas.[1] In this view a natural science model of mind cannot be viable for it allows no place for reflection on the conditions of its own genesis. Rather, because such a model takes it for granted that mind is 'an information-processing description of the functioning of an organism's brain', the problem for cognitive psychologists in general is to understand how mind works, while evolutionary psychologists want to explain further how mind works as a function of 'solutions to the adaptive problems that regularly occurred in the Pleistocene'.[2] As an anthropologist, I have been compelled by the evidence of ethnographic studies (my own among others) to develop a different approach, in which mind is characterized as a function of the whole person that is constituted over time in inter-subjective relations with others in the environing world (see Toren 1999). Because this perspective recognizes that all human ideas (my own included) are always the outcome of the microhistorical processes that characterize the constitution of mind over time in each and every one of us, it cannot help but challenge certain assumptions that are taken for granted by cognitivists of all persuasions (including cognitive anthro-pologists). It throws into relief the ethnocentricity of the natural science model of mind and in so doing suggests a way forward that does not rely on a claim to objectivity.

Because the questions we ask structure the answers we receive, it makes little sense for me to argue my case in terms of the natural science model of mind that is proposed by the contributors to Part One of this volume. This model takes it for granted that the world is objectively given to the scientific observer, whose premises are self-evidently true, whose being in the world is uncontaminated by history. My argument here is intended

e that a scientifically valid approach to understanding what
nan – for our ideas about this may be more or less valid,
bjectivity is always elusive – should be able to incorporate
recognition of the inherently historical nature of all our explanations.
But insofar as explanation is our project, we are bound to dispute the
adequacy of the models proposed by those others who maintain that it is
their project too – an obligation that is here taken up in the notes, the
body of the text being devoted to following through my own argument.

For me, the fundamental question from an anthropological perspective
is how do people become who they are?[3] To pose this question is to
suggest the necessity for a model of mind that allows us to recognize
human ontogeny as a genuinely historical process and, in so doing, to
challenge the view that biology, psychology, and anthropology/sociology
are conceptual domains of successively greater orders of complexity,
located at different 'levels of analysis'.[4] For when we come to consider
the ontogeny of any given human being, at any time of life and in any
time or place, it becomes clear that the biological, the psychological, and
the sociocultural are not discrete functional domains, but fused aspects
of a unitary phenomenon – the phenomenon of human autopoiesis.

Humans as self-producing systems

Autopoiesis, meaning 'self-creating' or 'self-making', is characteristic
of all organisms. The development of the human foetus out of the zygote
(the single-cell product of the union of egg and sperm) is an excellent
example of autopoiesis for it allows us to realize easily how the growth
and development of the foetus are a function of continuing cell division
and differentiation *within* the human organism itself. In other words, foetal
development is an autonomous process – one that itself specifies what is
proper to it. But foetal development is not independent of conditions in
the womb in which the foetus is carried, so it cannot be independent of
the specific existential conditions lived by the woman whose womb
nurtures it; even so it is the ontogeny of the developing human that
determines what changes occur in the foetus as a function of conditions
external to it at a given time.[5]

When we think about this process of human development in the womb
we realize too that, even before birth, the soon-to-be infant is positioned
in relation to particular others. Once out of the womb, the infant continues
the autonomous process of its own making – what we call 'life' – but its
making of itself, its self-production, depends on (without being determined by) those others who attend to it and live themselves alongside it.

In other words, human sociality is the bedrock condition of human autopoiesis. Or, to put it another way, we can only become ourselves in relations with others: from my very beginning the process of my self-making necessarily co-opts, as it were, all those others alongside whom I live and so my eventual idea of myself as the subject of my own actions is founded in inter-subjective relations. It follows of course that the particular human beings in whom are manifested particular forms of human sociality are at once the producers of their history and its products.

An understanding of historical continuity and transformation is central to the anthropological endeavour; it requires an investigation of how the history of our social relations enters into the constitution of meaning over time by each and every one of us. Which brings us to the problem of how we conceptualize 'history' and its significance for the study of embodied mind.

The prevailing tendency in the human sciences makes history inhere in 'social structures', in 'institutions', in 'ideologies', in 'collective representations', in 'cultural models', in 'social constructs' – which are represented as independent of the living persons whose actions make these abstractions material. Here history is conceived of as what is past but persistent, as inhering in the products of human action as divorced from their producers: in the environment as modified by human practice, in technologies, in ritual, in oral traditions, in what has been written down, in the very categories of language. And because these alienated products of the past are understood to pre-exist any given human being they are taken for granted as 'readymade' – the implicit assumption being that insofar as they carry meaning, that meaning declares itself.[6] But this cannot be so, for people have actively to constitute the categories in whose terms they understand and act in the world, and each one of us does this rather differently as a function of a unique set of relations with others.[7] It follows that even while the past inheres materially in the present, it can manifest in the present only as the constituted, but never finished, always emergent product of particular human minds.

Thus one can argue that mind is the fundamental historical pheno-menon because each one of us, over time, in inter-subjective relations with particular others in the environing world, constitutes mind anew *and* manifests it. In this view, mind cannot be an information-processing function of the nervous system or, more narrowly, of the brain; neither can it be located in 'culture' or 'collective representations' or 'cultural models'; nor can it be the outcome of an 'interaction' in which mind as a pan-human information processor is modified by its encounter with something called 'society' and/or 'culture' to produce 'social' and/or 'cultural constructs'. Rather, mind is a function of the whole person, considered as a particular person with a particular history in inter-subjective relations with other persons who are similarly constituting themselves over time – from birth to death – as unique manifestations of mind.

In this perspective, what are usually considered to be mental or psychological phenomena have also to be recognized as aspects of the microhistorical process that is human autopoiesis. Piaget's work remains useful because he was able to conceive of cognitive schemes as 'self-regulating transformational systems' – i.e. as autopoietic; this explicitly biological concept allows one to understand structure and process, continuity and transformation as aspects of one another.[8] Piaget held that 'symbolism as a general structure of thought is inherent in thought before it is socialized'.[9] I should rather say that historically particular forms of human sociality are inherent in the way humans conceptualize or bring forth their world by virtue of living it alongside others; indeed, inter-subjectivity entails that children socialize themselves: they engage those who care for them in the process of constituting their own understandings of the world.

It can be argued that babies are born with a body scheme, a scheme for human voices, for human faces – all of which seems reasonable enough, given that sociality or inter-subjectivity must, in some minimal sense, be given if its particular forms are to be achieved.[10] Indeed one might say the same for infants' abilities to demonstrate cross-modal matching – for example, of a particular sound with the sight of a particular object, and to conceive of objects in the world as solid and stable across time. But this latter ability does not appear before three to four months old and, given the extraordinary complexity of the human nervous system, the infant's immersion in a world of highly differentiated sensation, and the rapid growth of interneuronal connections, this is surely ample time for its autopoietic development out of much more primitive beginnings. Moreover, as a 'self-regulating transformational system', a Piagetian scheme, *especially* in its early stages, is going to 'look like' what cognitive psychologists call a module – an observation that has apparently escaped evolutionary psychologists for whom modularity has become an article of faith.[11] Assuming that mind is a function of the whole person mediated by his or her relations with others, the 'poverty of the stimulus' argument becomes nothing short of absurd, for it is the infant itself who specifies what, at any point in time, constitutes 'the stimulus'.[12] The newborn infant brings the world into being for itself as a function of the potential for cognitive structuring that is given to it, and there is no reason why the differentiation through functioning of a primitive cognitive scheme for assimilating information (such as that evinced in grasping, or sucking, or looking, or listening) should not be as dramatically rapid as cell differentiation in the developing foetus.

The position I am putting forward here is *not* a theory of so-called social or cultural construction – that is to say, it does not rest on an implicit distinction between individual and society, or biology and culture, in which people are born biological individuals and become socio-cultural by virtue of interaction with others. Neither does it imply that what is social (and/or cultural) in humans can be allocated to one dimension of their being or one domain of knowledge. Nor am I concerned to favour one side or the other of the constructivist versus nativist debate or to argue about what might be universal as opposed to what is relative. Indeed I reject all these forms of explanation as inadequate and, as the reader will note, I make no use of the terms they employ. I am arguing that in humans the biological and the social are *aspects of one another* or, to put it another way, that as humans it is given in us to require the others if we are to achieve our respective poieses. In this case the human being as the subject of his or her behaviour is a function of inter-subjectivity – i.e. inter-subjectivity is the primary condition of human being in the world. While Piaget himself would have objected to this view, it is nevertheless the case that his idea of genetic epistemology and the cognitive scheme that is its always emergent product can be embedded in a foundational inter-subjectivity – an understanding that allows us to show how rooted in our sociality is the process of bringing ideas into being over time and, in so doing, transforming them or, to put the matter more pithily, how we come to embody history.

Thus the way human infants engage with their caregivers suggests that the recursive qualities of language are immanent in human pre-speech cognitive processes: human infants see that others see them seeing them.[13] It is this mode of cognitive functioning that allows specific forms of sociality (or what others may call 'culture') to inhere in pre-speech concepts. In being rendered explicit in language this recursiveness is further elaborated: I attribute to the other the awareness that I am aware that the other is aware of my awareness. It is necessary to assume that this recursiveness is inherent in the processes of human mind because if it is *not*, language becomes an impossible phenomenon. Further, that recursiveness is given in the processes of human mind is suggested by the way that knowledge one has embodied, but which one does not know one has, is brought forth as a function of certain relationships. So, for instance, when one becomes a parent one's 'mothering' or 'fathering' practice is a function not only of what one has consciously observed or, more radically, of what one has decided to be good practice, but of how one was oneself 'mothered' or 'fathered' in infancy. The infant other calls forth knowledge constituted and embodied by the parent in his or her own infancy, knowledge which – to a greater or lesser degree – may have been transformed in later life in the course of other relationships. Thus humans are at once in historical time and themselves incorporate history, such that continuities in human ideas and practices are embedded in the selfsame processes that give rise to transformation.[14]

These general remarks bear on the necessity for analysing *how* our collective history is implicated in the constitution of cognitive processes and thus in our understanding of what constitutes mind. An anthropology that has at its heart a model that is capable of comprehending human historicity can properly claim to be a human science, precisely *because* it provides a way of explaining its own project as valid without implying that it is immune from history. Elsewhere I have described in detail a model of ontogeny as an historical process.[15] The present chapter is devoted to drawing out the contrast that emerges from a consideration of psychological models and Fijian ideas; it is intended to demonstrate how ideologically laden are *all* our ideas and how they suggest the impossibility of 'a natural science of mind'.

Ideas of personhood

All psychological models of mind – whether they be proposed by cognitivists, by social constructionists, or by evolutionary psychologists – take for granted distinctions between society and the individual, culture and biology, mind and body; it is by virtue of this step that 'psychology' comes into being as a discrete domain, as an abstract 'level of analysis' that is allowed to be the locus of the dialectical relation between the equally abstract 'sociocultural level' and 'biological level'.[16] It follows that psychologists have no difficulty in formulating natural science models of mind that are understood to be universal. In this view, what is 'sociocultural' may certainly affect cognitive processes, but it cannot contaminate the models themselves because the model-makers (i.e. the psychologists) are understood to be operating according to standards of rationality that guarantee their findings as objective – in their terms scientific.

Whence comes this confidence in an uncontaminated rationality? Well, unsurprisingly, it is to be found in psychological models of the relation between rationality and emotion. In contemporary cognitive psychology

it is has long been understood that affect is a dimension of problem-solv.
and that emotion inevitably implicates cognition; nevertheless rationalit̲
and emotion are still treated in effect as distinct domains.[17] The person
as agent, as the purposive subject who wills her or his own actions, is
located in the domain of rationality. In the domain of emotion, the person
becomes an object overcome by external forces that arouse anger,
overcome with sadness, make happy, are a source of irritation, render
helpless with laughter and so on. And if the person is to make sensible
judgements, come to logical decisions, and solve problems rationally then
she or he must be in control of emotions which will otherwise be a source
of 'irrational bias'.

Cognitive psychological models of mind suggest that rationality is
given to the subject as the means whereby the subject is given purely to
her- or himself. By contrast, the experience of emotion seems always to
be grounded in our relations with others (i.e. the extent to which we are
angry, loving, fearful, courageous, etc. is understood to be a function of
the nature of our relations with others over time), but it is also the
dimension in whose terms we are understood to differ from one another.
Cognitivist models suggest that if humans were perfectly rational creatures, as logically programmed as the computers on which mind has been
conventionally modelled, then (leaving aside so-called biological variables
such as age and sex) we should be indistinguishable from one another.[18]
Thus, for psychologists, difference can only be a function either of the
sociocultural or the personal. So 'individual differences' are attributable
to 'personality', whose study constitutes a distinct domain and which
refers to a constellation of affective attributes that implicate a personal
history. Of course, the distinctions between individual and society and
biology and culture allow equally well for the converse argument that
emotions are the true 'universals' and that humans differ cognitively as a
function of 'culture', where 'culture' is taken for granted as an analytical
category and as 'a variable' in the effort after a cognitive model of mind.[19]
But this poses no problem to those who are intent on claiming science as
peculiarly their own – after all, it takes only a little circular thinking to
arrive at the position whereby the claim to objective analysis is itself a
sufficient guarantor of rationality.

Thus the distinction between rationality and emotion as understood
by psychologists implies a particular subject-object relation between the
self and lived experience. Further, this distinction points to the paradox
that lies at the heart of the idea of the individual that informs classical
economics theory and its contemporary transformations. Given limited
means, the individual is understood to make rational choices among

theoretically unlimited wants; but one's wants or desires are intrinsically affect-laden, so how can one's choices ever be quite rational?

Introspection suggests that our folk psychological model of mind, itself predicated on a distinction between emotion and rationality, makes our sense of ourselves as active subjects reside not in the domain of rationality but in the domain of emotion; it is a folk personality model. In this model of the person I, Christina, am one who last week got angry with so-and-so because he attempted to put me down, who felt pleased when making a meanly clever riposte, who was charmed when someone else paid me a compliment, who was depressed by my own inadequacies, who is involved in writing this chapter . . . and so on. Were I to be passionate about logical problem-solving, or making money, then my sense of self might be understood to reside in that.

In interrogating these passions of the self, we become objects to ourselves and others in respect of the way we and they characterize our subjectivity, and subjects to the extent that we assert ourselves in the face of that characterization. Our notions of ourselves as particular persons reside precisely in this defiant assertion of self as consciously feeling and as having the right to those feelings as expressions of who we are. The 'individual' comes into being as a function of his or her wants and desires and it is in this domain of emotion, of the non-rational, that we are supposed to make rational choices. As 'individuals', then, we are understood to be responsible for the choices that we make, indeed we *are* the artefact of those choices.

Fijians, by contrast, hold to a theory of the person that rests not on individual choice, but on recognition of one's relations to others and the obligations that reside in these relations. One distinguishes oneself not in assertion of individuality, but to the degree that one demonstrates who one is as a function of what one is given to be in relation to others. The Fijian term for kin, *weka*, may be extended to include all ethnic Fijians and kinship terms are routinely used in both reference and address; with the exception of the relation of competitive equality between cross-cousins, all kinship relations are hierarchical. Elsewhere I have shown how, in the development over time of love relations across sex, desire and compassion (the two most salient forms of love for Fijians) implicate one another and become the site of a struggle to constitute hierarchy – a struggle that can never be resolved, precisely because, in these cross-sex love relations, compassion is undermined by desire and desire over time gives way to compassion. And in each desiring or compassionate moment of relationship one strives to assert oneself as the subject of one's own acts, one strives *for* oneself and *against* becoming merely the object of the other's manipulation.[20]

The struggle for effectiveness in relation to others is, for Fijians, at once a passionate struggle of opposing wills to control and a willed struggle to render one's own passions as effective. In the Fijian theory of the person no distinction is made between emotion and rationality; Fijians do however distinguish between the passions (*yalo-na*) and the will or wish (*loma-na*). Yalo is often translated as 'spirit' or 'soul', but Fijian usage, while it refers to the immaterial substance of the person that continues to exist after death, suggests that the term refers to the passions that inform human life.[21] Thus *yalo* is used in very many compounds to indicate human qualities e.g. *yalo qaqa*, determined, courageous, *yalo ca*, bad-tempered, *yalo kaukaua*, aggressive, *yalo lailai*, timid, *yalo katakata*, angry (lit. hot-spirited) and so on. These passions of the *yalo* are what binds one to life. *Vakayalo*, lit. 'in the manner of the *yalo*' means to be reasonable, responsible, and in contemporary Christian texts is translated as 'spiritual'. Loma-na may denote the inside of a thing and is often translated as 'mind' or 'intention'. It is used in many compounds to denote intentions towards others, e.g. *loma ca*, malicious, *loma donu*, straight or sincere. As a verb *loma-na* means to love or feel compassion; *velilomani* – literally 'loving one another' – suggests harmony of mind and intention between people.

One's passions (*yalo-na*) and one's will (*loma-na*) are not held to be, as it were, functionally separable from one another; for one's passions are understood to be manifest in what one wishes or wills and what one wishes or wills to be a function of one's passions. It follows that *lomaqu*, my will or my wish and *yaloqu*, my temper or disposition or character are aspects of the same phenomenon.

The struggle for effectiveness in relationship is implicit in hierarchical relations, explicit in relations of competitive equality. That these apparently exclusive relations implicate one another can be seen in the way that *madua* – usually translated as 'shame' – comes to be a crucial experiential dimension of any person's own effectiveness vis-à-vis others. The term *madua* refers to a range of affects having to do with other people's blame or praise of one's actions; at one extreme it denotes a deep and abiding shame and at the other a mild embarrassment or shyness. Madua is not itself understood to be intrinsic to either the passions or the will; it is always a function of the dynamics of particular relationships. Madua is manifested in facial expression, body posture and actions – one hangs one's head, drops one's chin to one's chest, avoids eye contact with others by looking down and off to one side; one's shoulders and body droop; one does not speak and if profoundly *madua* one is likely to get up and flee the company one is in, seeking solitude.

An adult person is especially *madua* when his or her behaviour is brought into disrepute. This is to be ashamed of oneself, but one may be shamed too by others' behaviour. For example, one may be shamed by a younger brother's drunken violence and promiscuity, by a son's laziness and neglect of duty, by a younger sister's illegitimate pregnancy, or a daughter's involvement with a married man; elders collectively may be shamed by drunken behaviour in young men; a paramount chief or clan chiefs may be shamed by their people's poor showing in some community endeavour. In these collective relations, a paramount or a group of clan chiefs may induce shame in their people by publicly berating them. In dyadic relations, for adults and young adults *within* sex, shame gives rise to an angry and/or sorrowful lecture from the senior person – a lecture which is intended to induce shame in the one who is junior. But where a man feels shamed by a woman's behaviour he tends to resort to physical punishment; a husband may beat his wife for dancing, a brother may beat a younger sister for smoking in public or for failing in some responsibility to senior kin, a father may beat his daughter for sexual promiscuity, and so on.

In all cases, shame and anger are aspects of the same experience; this is most clearly seen when the anger can be directed by the person who is shamed towards the one who has done the shameful thing and who is then shamed by being punished for what he or she has done. For this person, that is for the one who is made to be ashamed of him- or herself, the anger that is an aspect of that shame can have no object but the self. Note that in all the examples of shame I have referred to, the senior party rebukes or punishes the junior; if a junior person were to presume to lecture or physically beat one who is senior to him or her this in itself would be a cause for shame and require the junior person ceremonially to ask forgiveness by presentation of *yaqona* root or a whale's tooth, followed by the drinking of *yaqona*. By contrast, *madua* has no acknowledged place in relations of competitive equality between cross-cousins who, both within and across sex, may tease each other unmercifully; to evince *madua* in such a case is to be outdone. In short, *madua* is at once expressive and constitutive of hierarchical relations; it is a crucial existential aspect of the political economy of kinship.

When adults use *madua* in reference to a young child, the term tends to denote shyness rather than shame and is associated with fear (*rere*). Below I attempt to show how, in the Fijian village child's constitution of self, fear, shyness, anger, and shame are constelled together in such a way that, over time, an understanding of what it is to be *madua* comes to inform all one's relations with others.

In my book, *Making Sense of Hierarchy*, I showed how children constituted over time an idea that hierarchy is a principle of social relations by reference to people's disposition vis-à-vis one another in the ritualized spaces of the house, the church, the community hall, and the village itself. An above/below axis describes the internal space of these buildings; it refers to a single plane where one part of the space is called 'above' and the opposite pole of the space is 'below'. So when people are gathered together to eat, to worship, to drink *kava*, or to discuss village affairs, differential status is always apparent; their relative positions accord with an interaction between rank, seniority, and gender that describes hierarchical relations between kin. Above/below is the spatial corollary of the tributary relationship that is constituted in *kava* ritual, where the root of this plant is presented to chiefs, under whose aegis it is made into drink and redistributed to the assembled people. This ritual transforms balanced reciprocal exchange across households and larger collectivities into tribute. Chiefly ritual *appears* to contain, and thus to render non-threatening, equally powerful notions of equality, such that Fijian villagers come to conceive of hierarchy as given. However, chiefly ritual does not encompass the whole of life and the competitive equality that describes relations between cross-cousins is equally important and, as I have shown elsewhere, cannot ultimately be contained by chiefly ritual; rather Fijian social relations have to be characterized in terms of a thoroughgoing antithetical dualism whereby hierarchy and equality are in tension with one another and dependent on one another for their very continuity. Both hierarchy and equality are understood by villagers to be given in the nature of social relations, but *madua* is, as I noted above, a function of hierarchical relations.

Part of the text of *Making Sense of Hierarchy* was devoted to showing *how* a child constitutes its understanding of hierarchical relations with others via its 'recognitory assimilation' of the body posture appropriate to particular situations. Piaget reserves 'recognitory assimilation' – a term that describes a kind of motor recognition – for babies, but I take it to have a more general application insofar as it continues to inform young children's recognition of their own physical being in relation to others and underlies a developmental shift that produces deliberate imitation of certain adult behaviours.[22] Until the age of twelve or so a child is usually literally below – i.e. smaller than – those to whom it is subordinate; nevertheless, a child of four or so, who has begun to imitate the politeness behaviour of adults, makes itself even smaller by walking *lolou* – its body bent over in the posture of respect that is proper as one moves among others who are seated; but the posture of a child who is somewhat older (five to seven) is likely to show a marked and exaggerated shift into respect when the child is required to approach and address an adult, even one who is a member of the child's immediate household. The child will bend right over in walking, or crouch down, or walk on its knees – making itself as small as possible. Five-year-old children are already being sent from house to house to deliver messages or make requests so, by age six or thereabouts, the requirement to adopt this body posture when approaching or addressing adults is frequent as well as routine. Moreover, by this age the child is discriminating among adults, such that married men and women and elders are accorded a more exaggerated bodily deference than are young men and women – who are nevertheless properly respected, for any want of politeness is likely to bring forth a sharp rebuke, if not a blow.

This shift from imitation of others that is found in three- and four-year-olds, to the deliberate and exaggerated bodily respect that is routine in the behaviour of five- and six-year-olds, is not the product of an enlightened understanding of differential status as this is manifested on the above/below axis that describes any space in which people are gathered. Rather it is at once an acknowledgement and a manifestation of *madua* (shyness compounded by fear) which has been inculcated in children in their relationships with those who are senior to them.[23]

A Fijian baby and young child is *yalo wai*, that is to say both its capacity for reason and its disposition are unfixed like water (*wai*). So there is no point in engaging a child in conversation or explaining anything to it; nevertheless the child is early orientated towards others and made aware of their pre-eminence; apart from hunger, a baby is not understood to have demands of its own and ideally the child should not actually experience hunger because it should be fed before it has to cry for food; any explicit teaching of a child is largely directed towards its obligations to others. A baby or young child who is seated on an older person's lap faces outwards, towards the company, and if adults address toddlers and children up to the age of four or so, it is usually to tell them to do, or not to do, certain things. That an action is forbidden (*sa tabu!*) and that the child must sit down (*dabe ra!*) and be quiet (*tiko lo!*) are the remarks most commonly addressed by adults to toddlers and children up to age three or so. By age three or so, disobedience routinely meets with a smart slap or a sharp knock with the knuckles on the side of the head and if the child cries or becomes angry it is ridiculed or the punishment repeated until the crying or display of anger stops. Laughter, ridicule, and mock threats are the common response to any childish distress – even if the child is simultaneously being comforted – and are likely to come from

The Child in Mind

anyone and everyone present who is senior to the child by several years. Thus a child of seven or eight is *in loco parentis* to younger children of three and four and to toddlers. While shame and fear in a child are not precisely disapproved of, their manifestation in a child's inability to speak up in response to questions or in a timid and shrinking posture are invariably commented on loudly in the child's hearing – for example, *Raica! Sa rere o koya!* or *Gone dau madua na gone oqo!* ('Look! he's afraid!' or 'This child is always shy!') Moreover, it is common for older children or young men deliberately to anger a child by stealthily pinching it or teasing it in some other way, and then to laugh and mock at the futility of its angry response until the child begins to cry or creeps away, pursued by laughter and joking remarks on its behaviour.

The child assimilates these engagements with others to its existing schemes of relationship and this assimilation is simultaneously an accommodation; thus the child makes meaning out of the relations in which it is engaged and that meaning bears on the child's place in relation to others; but in taking the others' point of view, the child also comes to be aware of its own status relative to those others. The experience of being rendered *madua* (here meaning 'shy') through fear constitutes the child's bodily submission to others and anger is its inevitable accompaniment; but whether that anger can be directed at others or only at the self constitutes one's status in relation to others. One can direct anger only towards those of lesser status than oneself.[24]

Thus, what we might be tempted to designate as 'merely emotions' have profound political implications.[25] The process of learning what it is to be *madua* is a visceral experience, one that produces a form of knowledge in the body, long before that knowledge is made explicit in an understanding of what, exactly, it means to be rendered *madua*, ashamed, by a failure to acknowledge one's proper obligations to kin. When, later on, the child arrives at a mature grasp of the fine distinctions of differential status, this explicit understanding has been informed by, and will always be dependent on, that knowledge in the body that is *madua*.

Here I should remind the reader that *all* knowledge is embodied because it is always the product of embodied processes; the distinction I am making here is between knowledge that is easily rendered 'in language' and knowledge that is visceral, felt, not easily communicated. This visceral knowledge that is *madua* has its material icon in the routine postures of politeness that are designated by the term *lolou*. So, the five- or six-year-old child who adopts an exaggerated *lolou* posture in approaching adults has only the crudest understanding of how the above/below axis that describes people's relative disposition in space also denotes differential status. But what this child *does* have is a visceral knowledge of what it is to be *madua* – here meaning shy, bashful, with an element of fearfulness; moreover the exaggerated postural politeness suggests that the child judges it wisest to show itself as *madua* as it possibly can, in order to forestall additional experience of the same kind. This is *not* to say that a child who adopts this posture is necessarily *feeling* fearful at the time; rather that it has an embodied knowledge of what it is to feel afraid or, more mildly, to feel shy or bashful, combined with an embodied knowledge that it is best not to draw attention to oneself by putting oneself forward. The *lolou* posture is explicitly understood by adults to evince humility, to be a disavowal of any arrogance or ambition (*viavia levu* literally 'wanting to be big'). Indeed, when a child is rebuked for failure to show a proper awareness of its own inferiority or for a desire to make its own decisions or to put itself forward in some way, or for disobedience, it is usually in terms such as the following: *Gone dau be, sega ni via muria na vosa! Gone viavia levu, gone ca! E tabu me viavia levu – kila?* 'Impudent child, unwilling to do what you're told! Arrogant child, bad child! It is forbidden to act as if you're grown-up – understand?' This Fijian childhood experience leads me to ask what sort of knowledge in the body is pre-supposed by psychological models of child cognitive development.[26]

The child in child development

The models differ as to what capacities the child may be understood to have at birth. But common to them all is the image of the child as a locus of insatiable demands – not merely for bodily comfort, but for love, attention, and, above all, for more and more knowledge. This child demands to know. Parental responsibility is to meet this demand by providing a multiplicity of means via which the child is able momentarily to feed its demand to know by acting on the world.[27] In this perspective the child is understood to act too upon its mother and other care-givers, and in so doing actively to manipulate the care-giver's responses. In brief, the child is understood to gain control of the world of objects (including other people) through knowledge of it.

This child is orientated to a world of objects, rather than of relationships.[28] Its subject/object relation to the world is constituted in a crude distinction such that this child is ideally always the active subject.[29] In this absolute splitting between the child as active subject of its behaviour and the world of objects that are acted upon, other people can easily be rendered as things. But, given that, in the psychological perspective, everyone is an 'individual' and 'social relations' may be relegated either to 'the emotions' as the artefactual domain of these relations, or to 'culture' – both of them domains of error, separate from rationality as such – the struggle for rational control over one's emotions is simultaneously a struggle for control over others. The implication of models of cognitive development is that in gaining control over her/his emotions, the child or the person becomes as it were free to manipulate the world of things. So we arrive, by virtue of a teleological certainty, at the concept of the person as an individual who, by virtue of an ideal disconnection from relations with others, is able to act directly upon the world and thus to gain an uncontaminated empirical knowledge of it.[30]

The point of my comparison between the Fijian and the psychological models of the person has been to suggest, as I pointed out at the outset, how ideologically loaded are *all* our models. It is not intended to 'disprove' psychological models but rather to demonstrate how embedded they are in an idea of person and sociality that is no more nor less partial, no more nor less self-evident, than the Fijian idea. I admit to caricaturing somewhat – but only somewhat – cognitivist psychological models of mind and of child development (including those posited by evolutionary psychologists).[31] As I noted above, it is now understood that affect is a dimension of problem-solving and that emotion inevitably implicates cognition; but it is still true that, by and large, rationality and emotion are treated as functionally separate domains. Thus natural science models of cognition postulate a pre-given world and a pre-given subject – that is to say, the rational subject, who is capable of objective analyses that are guaranteed by empirical evidence, even if they may sometimes be contaminated by error attributable to bias that is itself explained as either sociocultural or personal.[32]

My own perspective on these matters is a different one – it entails an attempt to derive a model of mind that is scientifically valid *because* it is at once phenomenologically and empirically valid: one that recognizes that while we cannot hope to escape from history we may, nevertheless, come to understand something of its embodiment in ourselves and others by virtue of a comparative study of the processes by which we make meaning over time.[33]

In this perspective, each one of us is the locus of manifold relations with others that inform the endogenous constitution of embodied cognitive schemes; so each one of us constitutes cognitively the social relations of which we are the transforming product. Humans have a common biology, are subject to the same general physical conditions and the same physiological processes; and all of us are compelled to make meaning of the world by virtue of engaging with the meanings others have made and are making (for language is a condition for what we call mind). And it is because we have, all of us, to live in and through the world that we constitute our categories as guarantors of the world in which we live – that is, as valid. So while we all live the same world, we have no choice but to live it autonomously as a function of our own, always unique, histories as particular persons. It is common to us all, therefore, to be different from one another.[34]

This assumption of the commonality that resides in our difference informs participant observation as the fundamental research method of anthropology. Moreover, it brings us to the heart of the human existential dilemma: that we assume and act on the assumption that meanings made by others (and especially by intimate others) can be rendered as ours; but it is in the nature of mind that this can never entirely be achieved. Nevertheless, because sociality is the very condition of our human autonomy, we *can* come to understand others, even radically different others, to the extent that we allow their understandings of the world to inform, and thus transform, our own.

Thus any given person is at all times at once a manifestation of his or her history and an historical agent. He or she at once maintains the continuity of meanings and transforms them by virtue of actively constituting an understanding of the world in and through relations with others (see for example Toren 1993b). So the systematic study of *how* children constitute the categories in whose terms adults represent what they know of the world can be extraordinarily revealing. It can give the anthropologist access to what children know; that is, to at least a partial understanding of what adults – who are becoming to their children and their children's children what their own parents and grandparents were to them – know without knowing, or know and attempt to deny.

In this perspective, where humans are biologically social creatures, subjectivity is predicated on inter-subjectivity and *all* knowledge of the world is mediated by relations with others, there can be no useful analytical distinction between emotion and rationality. Rather the challenge is to describe and delineate as precisely as possible the historical constitution of our own models of human being and thus of mind as a function of human being (with particular reference to their politico-economic implications). We shall then be in a position to chart the transformations in these models as a function of our studies of how children constitute their understanding of the world and the implications of this process for our analyses of collective social relations.

So, in contemporary anthropology, distinctions between body and mind, individual and society, biology and culture are beginning, at last, to be discarded as inadequate to encompass the complex data with which anthropologists have to deal; and a new analytical vocabulary is being forged to address new formulations of the anthropological endeavour. A growing awareness of the central importance of ideas of the person for ethnographic analyses have made anthropologists more generally aware that their own analyses are bound to implicate a particular, western, theory of person and mind. Thus our attempts to explain ideas of the person and of mind held by others throw into relief the necessity for a re-examination of our own taken-for-granted human science concepts.

Notes

1. Thus the driving force of Husserl's phenomenology was his concern that 'science as a valid systematic theory' must, despite humanity's 'historicity', be possible. Historicity gives rise to the relativism that Husserl's phenomenology, his 'philosophy as rigorous science' sought to escape. Philosophy should be able to make apparent the under-pinnings of science, i.e. the workings of human consciousness that makes science possible. This concern required not only that Husserl acknowledge the historical nature of our categories, but that he attack too the naivete of the positivist natural science approach to mind (Husserl 1965:141 and Carr 1970).
2. For the two quotations in this sentence, see Tooby and Cosmides 1992:65 and 55.
3. The reader will note that the kinds of question asked by Ingold and Whitehouse are commensurable with my own, for all that we come up with somewhat different answers. The approach I develop in this chapter and elsewhere (see for example Toren 1993a and 1999) is derived in part from my reading of the various works of Merleau-Ponty (see for example 1962, 1964, 1974), whose commitment to an idea of embodied history has helped me to take further the idea of cognition as a microhistorical process that I put forward in Toren (1990).
4. See for example Plotkin, Chapter Three.
5. For a phenomenological approach to the biology of cognition, from which my own position is in part derived, see Maturana and Varela (1980 and 1987).

6. Thus Sahlins, in his influential attempt to synthesize structure and process refers to a 'cultural totality', which he conceives of as 'the system of relations between categories without a given subject' (1985: xvi–xvii); here cultural categories are received readymade, open to being transformed only when they are 'risked in action'.

7. A conclusion derived from the fascinating diary studies by Melissa Bowerman of her own children's language acquisition (see for example Bowerman 1982). Such studies make it quite plain that 'language' as described in books by linguists and grammarians is an artefact of their own analytical activity, just as 'culture' is the artefact of ethnographic analysis.

8. See Piaget (1971: 113).

9. See Furth (1994).

10. See Mehler and Dupoux (1994), but note that their findings are not uncontroversial.

11. Jerry Fodor was the first, and remains the most influential, contemporary cognitive psychologist to propose a modularity theory (see Fodor 1983). In a review of Plotkin (1997) and Pinker (1998), however, Fodor argues against the idea of massive modularity in large part because 'eventually, the mind has to integrate the results of all those modular computations and I don't see how there could be a module for doing that' (Fodor 1988: 12).

12. Cf. Plotkin, Chapter Three, where he takes the 'poverty of the stimulus' to be self-evident.

13. See for example Trevarthen (1988).

14. For a more detailed explanation of this process and a series of ethnographic demonstrations of its validity, see Toren (1999).

15. See Toren 1990 and 1999.

16. Tooby and Cosmides (1992) assert that their evolutionary psychology offers a unified perspective on the human condition and castigate other psychologists and anthropologists who hold to the 'standard social science model (SSSM)' which rests on the Cartesian distinction between body and mind. Apparently they fail to perceive as artefacts of the SSSM their own similarly misconceived distinctions which, for example, locate particular forms of mental phenomena (which are themselves conceptual artefacts derived from an analysis of what people say and do) in particular regions of the brain – a proceeding that in their view allows them not only to retain the distinction between so-called 'levels of analysis', but to differentiate, for example, 'social knowledge' from, say, 'perception'. By contrast, I argue that human autopoiesis entails that sociality informs all our

cognitions, such that social relations enter into the very structuring of attention and perception cannot ever be neutral – the challenge, then, is to understand how the history of social relations enters into the cognitive constitution of meaning over time. Barkow *et al.* can pretend to having done away with Cartesian distinctions only by virtue of a sleight of hand that makes what is 'cultural' at once synonymous with what is 'relative' and the by and large only trivially interesting artefact of a set of 'universal evolved psychological mechanisms' located in the heads of 'individuals'. In other words they resuscitate in their very analytical vocabulary the distinctions they claim to have done away with.

17. See for example Buck (1986), LeDoux (1986), and the discussion of 'what are the minimal cognitive prerequisites for emotion?' in Ekman and Davidson (1994).

18. This holds too for Tooby and Cosmides (1992) for whom it applies to contemporary newborn babies and to humans in general as they evolved to meet the adaptational demands of Pleistocene environmental conditions.

19. See for example Altarriba (1993) and my review (Toren 1997a).

20. See Toren (1994).

21. I prefer to use 'the passions' as an over-arching term here, rather than other, less powerful possible alternatives (e.g. disposition, attitude, character) because the term implies that what psychologists call 'emotions' are always an artefact of inter-subjectivity, and because the *yalo* that binds one to life and lives on after death apparently comes into being as a function of an engagement with others.

22. See Piaget (1962: 78–86) and Piaget and Inhelder (1969 [1966]: 52–63) for an analysis of imitation.

23. For an analysis of the place of prescriptive injunctions by adults to children in the constitution over time of an idea of hierarchy as principle in Fiji, see Toren (1995).

24. For further analysis of the relation between anger and shame and its political implications, see Toren (1997b).

25. I wrote this material before I had read the excellent ethnography by Lutz (1988) on Ifaluk and the collection of essays concerning 'the politics of emotion' in a variety of ethnographic areas by Lutz and Abu-Lughod (1990), but it will be apparent to the reader who knows these texts that in what I have said so far, and in what follows, there is a good deal of overlap in our observations. For example, I agree heartily with Lutz that 'emotion experience, both in the West and on

Ifaluk, is more aptly viewed as the outcome of social relations and their corollary world views than as universal psychological entities' (Lutz 1988: 209). Where we differ is in the models of human being in whose terms we argue our respective cases. Lutz (1988) argues for a social constructivist model and Lutz and Abu-Lughod (1990) adopt a version of Foucauldian 'discourse' as an analytical tool. Neither of these approaches seems to me to be adequate for explaining how humans come to be so remarkably similar to one another in the ways they are different, and so remarkably different in the ways they are the same – to do this, I argue, one has to be able to demonstrate that ontogeny is a genuinely historical process (see Toren 1999).

26. Plotkin says in Chapter Three that he fails to understand this question – 'the language use being unconventional to say the least'. Perhaps, but given that mind and body are aspects of one another rather than separable systems, it seems important to me not only to emphasize that knowledge is inevitably embodied, but also to ask what kind of knowing is supposed to be given in the child at birth. My point in investigating the idea of the child that is central to models of child development is to demonstrate that this idea and the model of mind it entails are no more nor less immune from the ideological weight of history than are Fijian ideas of person and mind.

27. See for example Bandura (1981) and Vye *et al.* (1988).

28. The corollary of this is that 'social cognition' constitutes a separate domain of investigation (see for example Higgins, Ruble and Hartup 1983, Flavell and Ross 1981, and Hirschfeld 1994).

29. Behaviourists do not take this view, but while behaviourist models are still with us, they do not dominate contemporary developmental psychology. The following perspective is more common: '[W]e had fallen into the habit of thinking of the child as an "active scientist" . . . But this active, constructing child had been conceived as a rather isolated being, working alone at her problem-solving. Increasingly we see now that, given an appropriate, shared social context, the child seems more competent as an intelligent social operator than she is as a 'lone scientist' coping with a world of unknowns' (Bruner and Haste, 1987:1). At first sight, this idea of 'the active constructing child' would seem to contradict another prevailing idea – that of 'socialisation'. Not so, for in this simplified Vygotskian perspective the child is 'socialised' by virtue of learning to speak. In this view the categories the child uses '. . . are not invented by the child: they are the common currency of the culture, the framework that determines the boundaries of the child's concepts'. Vygotsky's idea

that 'internalisation' is an inherently transformative process allows for the possibility of a genuinely historical theory of cognitive development; unfortunately this challenge has yet to be met. (See for example Scribner 1985 and Toren 1999 for a discussion of what Vygotsky has to contribute to the project of understanding how we become who we are.)

30. So, for example, the idea of differentiation through functioning that is central to Piaget's genetic epistemology means that the child in his model inevitably assimilates knowledge and in so doing accommodates to a world that pushes back, as it were, forcing further assimilation and accommodation until an equilibrated knowledge structure is produced. So the child is bound to become, like its parents, an 'intuitive scientist' even if 'bias' (attributable of course to 'culture') remains something of a problem (see Ross 1981). By contrast, Fodor's 'modularity thesis' argues for 'input systems' that are innate 'hardwired neural structures' – 'domain specific', 'mandatory' and 'informationally encapsulated'; central systems (which govern processes such as the fixation of belief) look at what the input systems deliver and compute knowledge about the world (see Fodor 1983). One can, because of his concern with biological validity, rather easily render Piaget's model historical; this is somewhat more difficult with Fodor's model, if only because his 'input systems' are characterized in such a way that they would appear to be entirely immune from the mediation that is an inevitable function of inter-subjectivity.

31. Given that this admission appears to be open to easy misunderstanding (see Plotkin, Chapter Three, p. 101), I should point out that to caricature somewhat a theoretical position is to emphasize its characteristic traits, perhaps at the expense of subtle deviations from them. The reader of these notes, however, will have become aware that insofar as there are any subtle deviations from a cognitivist position, I've addressed these too.

32. My remarks here are of course pertinent to the general cognitivist project. Here I should perhaps point out, as I have elsewhere (Toren 1993a), that certain domains of meaning, e.g. 'colour' or 'living kinds', may indeed be a function of specific cognitive processes. From an anthropological standpoint this idea becomes problematic only when domain specificity is taken to imply a relative absence of social mediation and thus of historical variation (see also footnote 9 above). It is, of course, in the interests of the cognitivist endeavour and their implicit (and mysterious) claim to be the only users of an

empirical method, to argue a case in which historical processes (in their terms 'culture') can be treated as an external variable rather than as intrinsic to the constitution of mind over time. It is by virtue of this intellectual sleight of hand that they are able to avoid addressing the historical nature of their own epistemological assumptions.

33. The reader is directed to Toren (1990) which remains, so far as I know, the only systematic empirical study of how people come to be 'enchanted' (as Bourdieu would have it) by an idea they themselves have made. For Fijian adults, hierarchy is a taken-for-granted principle of social organization; that it should be so is an idea crucial to Fijian political economy. Two-thirds of this full-length monograph concern adult ideas and how these are expressed in everyday ritualized behaviour proper to domestic, chiefly, communal and church contexts. The final third looks at ideas of status differentiation (systematically collected using a variety of techniques) held by 67 Fijian village children attending the local primary school. The analysis of these data shows that children have cognitively to constitute the idea of 'hierarchy as principle' and that this micro-historical process is crucially informed by their intersubjective relations with others.

34. Given autopoiesis, one can of course just as well argue that we are all different in the ways we are the same. Natural science models of mind, because they ignore history, emphasize 'sameness' and minimize, or explain away, 'difference'. I am arguing here for a model of mind as a function of the whole person in inter-subjective relations with others in the environing world – that is to say, for a model that is capable of coping with sameness and difference at one and the same time. This is not a model of 'transmission' or 'socialization' or 'cultural construction' – terms that are quite happily used by cognitivists. This has to be a model in which the cognitive constitution of meaning is embedded in inter-subjectivity, for it is in this constituting process that meanings are at once maintained over time and transformed.

References

Altarriba, J. (ed.), (1993), *Cognition and Culture: A Cross-Cultural Approach to Cognitive Psychology*, North Holland: Elsevier.

Bandura, A. (1981), 'Self-referent thought: a developmental analysis of self-efficacy', in J.H. Flavell and L. Ross (eds), *Social Cognitive Development*, Cambridge: Cambridge University Press.

Barkow, J.H., Cosmides, L., and Tooby, J.(1992), *The Adapted Mind: Evolutionary Psychology and the Generation of Culture*, New York: Oxford University Press.

Bowerman, M. (1982), 'Reorganisational processes in lexical and syntactic development', in E. Wanner and L.R. Gleitman (eds), *Language Acquisition: the State of the Art*, Cambridge: Cambridge University Press.

Bruner, J. and Haste, H. (1987), 'Introduction', in J. Bruner and H. Haste (eds) *Making Sense: The Child's Construction of the World*, London: Methuen.

Buck, R. (1986), 'The psychology of emotion', in J.E. LeDoux and W. Hirst (eds) *Mind and Brain. Dialogues in Cognitive Neuroscience*, Cambridge: Cambridge University Press.

Carr, D. (1970), 'Introduction', in Edmund Husserl (ed.), *The Crisis of European Sciences and Transcendental Phenomenology: An Introduction to Phenomenological Philosophy*, Evanston: Northwestern University Press.

Ekman, P. and Davidson, R.J. (1994), *The Nature of Emotion: Fundamental Questions*, Oxford: Oxford University Press.

Flavell, J.H. and Ross, L.(eds) (1981), *Social Cognitive Development*, Cambridge: Cambridge University Press.

Fodor, J.A. (1983), *The Modularity of Mind*, Cambridge, Mass.: MIT Press.

—— (1988), 'The trouble with psychological Darwinism', in *London Review of Books*, 20: 11–13.

Furth, H.G. (1994), 'The child's entry into the symbolic order: A developmental-societal interpretation of J. Lacan', in *Social Development*, 3: 158–84.

Higgins, E.T., Ruble, D.N. and Hartup, W.W. (eds), (1983), *Social Cognition and Social Development*, Cambridge: Cambridge University Press.

Hirschfeld, L.A. (1994), 'Is the acquisition of social categories based on domain-specific competence or on knowledge transfer?', in L.A. Hirschfeld and S.A. Gelman (eds.) *Mapping the Mind: Domain Specificity in Cognition and Culture*, New York: Cambridge University Press.

Husserl, E. (1965), *Phenomenology and the Crisis of Philosophy*, trans. with notes and intro. by Quentin Lauer, New York: Harper Torchbooks, Harper and Row.

—— (1970), *The Crisis of European Sciences and Transcendental Phenomenology: An introduction to Phenomenological Philosophy*, trans. with intro. by David Carr, Evanston: Northwestern University Press [Orig. 1954, The Hague: Martinus Nijhoff].

Le Doux, J.E. (1986), 'The neurobiology of emotion', in J.E. LeDoux and W. Hirst (eds), *Mind and Brain: Dialogues in Cognitive Neuroscience*, Cambridge: Cambridge University Press.

Lutz, C.A. (1988), *Unnatural Emotions: Everyday Sentiments on a Micronesian Atoll and their Challenge to Western Theory*, Chicago: University of Chicago Press.

—— and Abu-Lughod, Lila (eds) (1990), *Language and the Politics of Emotion*, Cambridge: Cambridge University Press.

Maturana, H.R. and Varela, F.J. (1980), *Autopoesis and Cognition: The Realisation of the Living*, Dortrecht: D. Reider.

—— (1988), *The Tree of Knowledge: The Biological Roots of Human Understanding*, Boston: Shambhala.

Mehler, J. and Dupoux, E. (1994), *What Infants Know*, Cambridge: Blackwell [Original, 1990].

Merleau-Ponty, M. (1962), *Phenomenology of Perception*, trans. by Colin Smith, London: Routledge & Kegan Paul [Original, 1945].

—— (1964), *Signs*, trans. and with intro. by Richard C. McCleary, Evanston: Northwestern University Press.

—— (1974), *Phenomenology, Language, Society. Selected essays*, ed. J. O'Neill, London: Heinemann Educational.

Piaget, J. (1962 [1946]), *Play, Dreams and Imitation in Childhood*, New York: Norton.

—— (1971 [1969]), *Structuralism*, London: Routledge & Kegan Paul.

—— and Inhelder, B. (1969 [1966]), *The Psychology of the Child*, Routledge & Kegan Paul.

Pinker, S. (1998), *How the Mind Works*, London: Allen Lane.

Plotkin, H. (1997), *Evolution in Mind*, London: Allen Lane.

Ross, L. (1981), 'The intuitive scientist formulation and its developmental implications', in J.H. Flavell and L. Ross (eds), *Social Cognitive Development*, Cambridge: Cambridge University Press.

Sahlins, M. (1985), *Islands of History*, Chicago: University of Chicago Press.

Scribner, S. (1985), 'Vygotsky's uses of history', in J.V. Wertsch (ed.), *Culture, Communication and Cognition*, Cambridge: Cambridge University Press.

Tooby, J. and Cosmides, L. (1992), 'The psychological foundations of culture', in J.H. Barkow, L. Cosmides and J. Tooby (eds) *The Adapted Mind: Evolutionary Psychology and the Generation of Culture*, New York: Oxford University Press.

Toren, C. (1990), *Making Sense of Hierarchy: Cognition as Social Process in Fiji*, London: Athlone Press.

—— (1993a), 'Making history: the significance of childhood cognition for a comparative anthropology of mind', *Man* (N.S.), 28: 461–78.

—— (1993b), 'Sign into symbol, symbol as sign: cognitive aspects of a social process', in P. Boyer (ed.), *Cognitive Aspects of Religious Symbolism*, Cambridge: Cambridge University Press.

—— (1994), 'Transforming love, representing Fijian hierarchy', in P. Gow and P. Harvey (eds) *Sexuality and Violence: Issues in Representation and Experience*, London: Routledge.

—— (1995), 'Ritual, rule and cognitive scheme', in P. Wohlmuth (ed.), *The Crisis in Text, Vol 6 of Journal of Contemporary Legal Issues*, San Diego: University of San Diego.

—— (1997a), 'Review of Jeanette Altarriba (ed.), *Cognition and Culture: A Cross-Cultural Approach to Cognitive Psychology* (1993)', *British Journal of Psychology*, 88: 174–5.

—— (1997b), 'Cannibalism and compassion: transformations in Fijian concepts of the person', in V. Keck (ed.), *Common Worlds and Single Lives: Constituting Knowledge in Pacific Societies*, London: Berg.

—— (1999), *Mind, Materiality and History: Explorations in Fijian Ethnography*, London: Routledge.

Trevarthen, C. (1988), 'Universal cooperative motives: how infants come to know the language and culture of their parents', in G. Jahoda and I.M. Lewis (eds), *Acquiring Culture: Cross-cultural Studies in Child Development*, London: Croom Helm.

Vye, N.J., Delclos, V.R., Burns M.S. and Bransford, J.D.(1988), 'Teaching thinking and problem solving: illustrations and issues', in R.J. Sternberg and E.E. Smith (eds), *The Psychology of Human Thought*, Cambridge: Cambridge University Press.

Steps to an Integration of Developmental Cognitivism and Depth Psychology
Charles W. Nuckolls

When one speaks of natural ontologies, their postulation and violation, the model of the mind advanced assumes that existential assumptions follow from the observation of perceived regularities. The mind records these regularities, and whether or not this capacity is innate (Boyer and Sperber) or task-derived (Ingold), the process itself unfolds in predictable succession. The developing mind violates naturally observed and associated regularities, and this induces conceptualization of superhuman agencies, the basis of all organized religions. While providing significant insight, the developmental cognitivism of Boyer and others (for example Lawson and McCauley 1990) is rooted in a long tradition – the tradition that begins with the question of why 'natural' rationality, based on the perception of associated regularities, subverts itself in apparently irrational religious belief. Developmental cognitivism resides intellectually in the world of eighteenth-century rationalism, and the answer it gives preserves one version of the Enlightenment ideal of mind, leaving it unconflicted and without the deep and troubling desires Freud introduced over a century later.

Nevertheless, running through responses to the cognitivist project (for example Toren, Chapter Five) is the criticism that it neglects the relevance of affect and deep motivation. In his conclusion to this book, Whitehouse suggests that schema formation is always affect-dependent, and that the greater the affect the more likely it is that a new schema will be constituted and remembered (pp. 213–16). This is surely correct. But, if so, it is hard to understand why cognitive anthropologists do not recognize that psychoanalysis has something to say on the subject. If the cognitive account of religious propositions needs to consider motivation, then simple economy of effort should lead it to an encounter with depth psychology – not in the form of clinical stories and anecdotes, but of experimental research of the sort cognitive science itself touts.

Charles W. Nuckolls

'Cognitivism' here refers to a concern with the encoding, storage, retrieval, and application of knowledge – in a word, with 'processing', broadly conceived. There are diverse forms of cognitivism, from the schema-theoretic work of D'Andrade (1995), to Lakoff's metaphor-based linguistics (Lakoff and Johnson 1999), to the connectionist-inspired 'cultural models' of Strauss and Quinn (1997). Important distinctions notwithstanding, most forms of cognitivism share one trait in common: the processing of interest to them rarely involves attention to deep motivation, or the conflicts and ambivalences which inhabit the unconscious. Typically, motives are formulated in individualistic terms, with an emphasis on the agent's desire to master the environment, control his or her actions, seek self-realization, or manipulate power relations (Deci and Ryan 1985; Lutz 1988, 1992; Rodin 1990; Ryan and Connell 1989). Recently there have been attempts to breach the impasse, by locating motivation in the structures of cultural knowledge and calling it 'goals'. Such goals possess directive force, acting as motivators of behaviour (for example D'Andrade and Strauss, 1994). While this represents a welcome departure from the utilitarian individualism of other approaches, the attempt to reconcile cognition and desire by locating motives in cultural models cannot be considered completely satisfactory. It is difficult to account for conflict between motives, and for the fact that such conflict itself might be highly motivating. It is also developmentally superficial by failing to relate enduring motivational complexes to features of childhood experience which may be recurrent across broad sections of society. Does it matter? While the answer could be no, I will argue here that a cognitivist account – whatever its brand or flavour – benefits from attention to psychoanalysis. That is because the phenomenon we are interested in – postulated superhuman agencies that systematically flout intuitive perceptions – can be more fully explained as cognitive constructions shaped by deep motivational conflict – 'deep cognition', in other words.

Developmental cognitivism holds that the common properties of culturally postulated superhuman agencies, of the sort found in all religions, derive these properties from systematic violations of intuitive assumptions. Boyer hypothesizes in Chapter Two that religious representations (to be defined as such) always postulate the existence of superhuman beings that violate intuitive assumptions about the existential processes associated with persons, artefacts, animals, or plants.

Spirits and ghosts are commonly represented as intentional agents whose physical properties go against the ordinary physical qualities of embodied agents. They go through physical obstacles, move instantaneously, etc. Gods have non-standard physical and biological qualities. For instance, they are immortal, they feed on the smell of sacrificed foods, etc. Also, religious systems the world over include counter-intuitive assumptions about particular artefacts, statues for instance, which are endowed with intentional psychological processes. They can perceive states of affairs, form beliefs, have intentions, etc. (Boyer, Chapter Two, p. 59).

One might concede this point but at the same time ask, what makes a violation of intuitive assumptions attention-demanding rather than simply implausible? Boyer limits his discussion to counter-intuitive assumptions, yet other assumptions seem to be equally well remembered. How, then, does one account for them? Finally, if all counter-intuitive assumptions are equally memorable, why are only some (out of all that are possible) recurrent?

The answer proposed in this chapter is that the Boyer hypothesis does not recognize, and cannot theorize about, the emotionally complex origin of the assumptions described as 'intuitive'. It misses the most salient of these assumptions by neglecting emotional attachment and the conflicts resident in deep cognition. It is the violation of these assumptions – as natural as any Boyer describes – which explains the development of religious propositions. The reason is that the most important natural expectation violated by religious propositions is the expectation that early emotional attachments, formed in childhood, will continue forever. The expectation is almost always thwarted in normal development, since childhood attachments cannot continue if adult autonomy is to be achieved. Is it possible to have it both ways – attachment and autonomy? As Boehm (1989) points out, the paradox is inherent in primate evolution, and there is good evidence that the ambivalence it causes is not confined to humans. Tensions among satisfaction quests might even have an adaptive significance, in that they prepare the organism to respond more flexibly in multi-contingency environments (Campbell 1965). Therefore, if Ingold in Chapter Four and Plotkin in Chapter Three are correct, and evolutionary processes must be considered in the development of social constructions, we should focus on the development of attachments, the conflicts that arise, and the ambivalences that result. This leads, inevitably, either to encounter with Freud or to an avoidance of him that pointlessly stunts and limits the development of a cognitive theory of religion.

Now, for those not familiar with the difference between cognitive theory and psychoanalysis, or the historical antipathy that divides them, the fact that both have something to contribute to the understanding of religious beliefs might seem obvious. While cognitive psychology (broadly conceived) describes the processes of information-encoding and -retrieval, psychoanalysis considers the relationship between information and internal models of self and other. Clearly they share a lot in common (Horowitz 1988; Nuckolls 1995; Westen 1991, 1992, 1998). *Both* agree that there is an unconscious. *Both* agree that knowledge systems tend to become organized during specific sensitive developmental periods, and that such systems constitute templates or schemas used later and more generally. *Both* agree that childhood-derived systems of knowledge influence the construction of religious propositions, requiring a methodology of developmental reconstruction. Most significantly, both accept the argument that properties of mind are shaped by human evolution. (See also Plotkin, Chapter Three.) With such broad areas of agreement in common, is it not possible to specify the phenomenon in question in such a way that both developmental cognitivism and psychoanalysis might be useful?

Toward a simple rapprochement: deep cognition

Let us posit the existence of a repertoire of relational schemas which contains archaic components, many formed in childhood, that can never be erased. Such early schemas of self and others are constrained by mature concepts of self which contain and integrate immature self-schemas. Nevertheless, in a kind of parallel processing, earlier forms continue an unconscious appraisal of current events, possibly following primitive association and the logic of the 'primary process'. This is what I am calling deep cognition. The link between the dynamic unconscious and cognitive schematic could then be stated as follows:

> Access to conscious symbol-systems, including cultural images, words, and action scenarios, might occur only through the information organized by unconscious schemas, such that to instantiate one is to instantiate the other.

Unconscious relational schemas conflict, either because they represent mutually unfulfillable desires, or because the desires they represent are opposed by mature thought and culturally normative demands. If higher-order cultural-knowledge structures are accessible only by activating lower ones, in the dynamic unconscious, then it is possible that higher-order structures reproduce in their form and function the conflicts of the lower-order relational structures. In principle, there is nothing in this proposition at odds with the cognitivist account, for as Boyer remarks in Chapter

Two, 'adult representations . . . seem to become more complex by gradual enrichment of principles that can be found in the pre-schooler' (p. 63). The difference is in the nature of the principles, and the extent to which these bear the imprint of early and ambivalent attachment to one's caregivers.

Unresolvable conflict, this chapter claims, is a natural outcome of human development in the representation of attachment. At this level, unconscious relational schemas produce ambivalence and the need to deal with it – or in psychoanalytic terms, defend against it. There come into being cultural-knowledge structures, including beliefs about superhuman agencies, which both reproduce conflicts and attempt to resolve them, in a mutually reinforcing way. To prove this, it must first be shown that the cognitive unconscious is conflicted and that conflicts have their origin in the nature of relational attachment and, second, that attachment conflicts give rise to relational schemas that inform the construction of superhuman agencies.

The first step: transference and Core Conflict Relational Themes

The properties of mind most relevant to a psychological understanding of religious propositions depend on a central assumption – that thoughts and ideas can have an active influence on people's minds even when they are not conscious, and sometimes precisely because they are not conscious. To the first part of this statement most of the contributors to this volume will agree. No one claims that the assumptions violated by supernatural beliefs are conscious assumptions open to inspection by those who hold them. That is the point of calling them 'intuitive'. As to the second part of the statement, that exclusion from consciousness is actually vital to religious propositions, this is more debatable. Here I shall argue that unconscious conflict between relational schemas is basic to the development of a belief in superhuman agencies, because such agencies represent and partially resolve the conflicts that arise in relation to conflicted childhood attachments.

First, is there evidence that relational patterns shaped in childhood can be applied, or 'transferred', to adult relationships? Freud (1958) described transferences as 'stereotype plates' or representations of early interpersonal relationships that shape and influence current ones. On the surface, this is to suggest no more than what the literature on psychological priming experiments has demonstrated repeatedly – that we tend to perceive new people based on mental representations of significant others in the past. One study, typical of many in the cognitive literature, can be cited here. Anderson and Cole (1990) found that when a fictional character resembling a significant other was presented to subjects, the subjects tended to distort their recollections of the fictional character to conform to the template already established by their memory of the significant other. (See also Anderson *et al.* 1995.) Interestingly, such distortions appear to signify more than the matching of experience to cognitive schema, or the instantiation of template or script. They also have strongly affective attributes. When Anderson and Baum (1994) presented subjects with fictional characters who resembled the subjects' own negative significant others, they found that subjects reacted with depressive and negative feelings, indicating that a transference had occurred.

Probably the most important experimental work on transference and related psychodynamic concepts has been done by Lester Luborsky. Over the last thirty years, Luborsky and his colleagues (Luborsky 1976, 1977; Luborsky and Crits-Christoph 1990; Barber and Crits-Christoph 1993) have developed a method for abstracting interpersonal relationship patterns that appear in patient narratives during psychotherapy sessions. Typical narratives are about father, mother, brothers, sisters, friends, bosses, and the therapist. Luborsky developed a method for analysing these narratives in terms of their repeated basic constituents, which he calls a 'core conflict relationship theme'. The CCRT describes the relationship patterns and conflict in terms of three components: wishes, needs, or intentions toward the other persons in the narrative, as expressed by the subject; expected or actual responses from others; and responses of self. Within each component the types with the highest frequency across all relationship episodes are identified, and this combination constitutes the CCRT. Luborsky and his colleagues hypothesized that important themes, because they had been shaped early in life, would tend to recur, making for a powerful transference effect.

Subjects' interview material contains many relatively concrete descriptions of interpersonal relationships. The CCRT method begins with a collection of these descriptions, usually at least ten in number for each subject. Independent judges read the narratives and identify each of the three components: wishes, responses from others, and responses from the self. For each component, the types with the highest frequency across all relationship narratives are identified, and their combination constitutes the CCRT formulation. The interjudge agreement on identifying relationship themes (Bond, Hansel and Shevrin 1987) and rating their completeness (Crits-Cristoph, Luborsky, *et al.* 1988) has been shown to be acceptable. The results offer support for the basic tenets of Freud's transference hypothesis on the following three points.

First, on the number of transference patterns, there seems to be one main relational theme, as Freud predicted. Averaging across one sample, for example, the main wish was judged to be present in 80 per cent of each patient's narratives, whereas a secondary wish was present, on the average, in only 16 per cent of each patient's narratives (Luborsky, Crits-Christoph and Millon 1986). Moreover, there is strong evidence early in treatment that 60 per cent of patients who relate a narrative about the investigator describe a pattern that is similar to a theme evident in narratives about a significant other (Connolly, Crits-Christoph, *et al.* 1996: 122). One could object that psychodynamically oriented therapy probably tends to elicit this kind of response, and thus skew the results. But the same result is evident in patient narratives from non-psychodynamic treatment settings (Connolly, Crits-Christoph, *et al.* 1996: 1220).

Second, on the consistency of the theme over time, investigators compared CCRTs scored from sessions early in treatment with the same patient's CCRTs scored from sessions later in treatment, about one year later. Considerable consistency over time was detected (Luborsky, Crits-Christoph, *et al.* 1985). This suggests that relational schemas are strongly encoded, and increases the likelihood that when established in childhood they remain active well into adulthood, shaping and constraining new relational information.

Third, on the question of themes' early origins, the hypothesis states that there should be a parallel between the relationship pattern with the therapist and the one with early parent figures. Luborsky and his colleagues compared CCRTs scored from narratives involving a memory of an interaction with an early parental figure versus the overall CCRT score from all other narratives. A high degree of similarity was evident for early-memory-of-parents CCRTs paired with the same patient's overall CCRT (see Luborsky, Crits-Christoph and Millon 1986; Barber and Crits-Christoph 1993). Now, it could be argued that since Luborsky and his colleagues have not done long-term studies, the hypothesis of early childhood origins remains speculative. This has always been a problem with research that purports to demonstrate the validity of psychodynamic processes. But that is changing, and work in the development of attachment styles provides strong evidence that patterns of childhood associations do constitute templates for adult relationships (Brennan and Shaver 1998, Hazen and Shaver 1987; see also Kirkpatrick and Hazen 1994; Feeney and Noller 1996).

Transference, in short, is an ordinary fact of life. Even Boyer concedes as much, when he acknowledges that 'a whole domain of ritual action is based on assumptions that *transfer* properties of live organisms to a non-living natural objects' (p. 64, emphasis mine.) But what remains to be considered is the question of why in the case of relational transferences its origins are for the most part repressed, and its outcomes in conscious-ness so varied and different. Here we must focus not only on transference, but on the nature of the relationships shaped early in childhood.

The second step: core conflicts and attachment theory

Simply put, 'attachment' refers to the relationship between infants and their care-takers, and according to John Bowlby, constitutes part of universal human endowment. Attachment theory is essentially a theory of the microprocesses of development that emphasizes the daily inter-actional exchanges between parent and child and the developing internal working model of the child (Bowlby 1969, 1973). It is not a theory of cross-cultural human development, even though one of the earliest studies in attachment took place in Africa (Ainsworth, *et al.* 1978). Nor does it readily accommodate the observation that attachment templates might be internally contradictory, like CCRTs, even though Bowlby himself acknowledges that the templates can be mixed (Bowlby 1969). Attachment theory shares with contemporary psychoanalytic theories a shift in the conceptualization of the unconscious – from a repository of repressed instinctual wishes, to a structure comprising representations of self, or object, and of prototypic interactions between the two. The emphasis on unconscious representations is most clearly expressed in the centrality of the concept of internal working models, similar to the core conflictual relationship themes above. Bowlby notes that people may have more than one internal working model and suggests that different working models may conflict with each other. This fact is crucial to the development of belief in supernatural agencies.

Observational data reveal that attachment to particular care-takers is recognizable at around six months of age and appears to be fully developed at one year. A significant attachment figure (usually the biological mother) serves as a secure base for the infant, a place where the child can seek refuge and from which begin to explore the environ-ment. Attachment behaviour is behaviour that has proximity to an attachment figure as a predictable outcome and whose evolutionary function is protection of the infant from danger. Such behaviour is not confined to human beings, of course, and the fact that it is found among most primates is strong evidence for its adaptive significance. For example, Harlow and Zimmermann's classic study of cloth-covered and wire-covered 'surrogate mothers' (1959) demonstrated that rhesus monkeys require secure attachment in childhood in order to develop normally. Clinging contact with the mother was important, not only as a behavioural prerequisite for the infant that was at least as salient as nursing but also as the basis for the development of a secure base for subsequent exploration of the environment. Hinde also focused on the normative development of mother–infant relationships in rhesus monkeys (for example Hinde and Spencer-Booth 1966) The consistent finding through-out the history of this research has been that mother–infant relationships in Old World monkeys and apes involve common behaviour patterns, follow similar sequences of developmental change, and appear to be subject to the same set of influences, all of which provide empirical support for the basic tenets of Bowlby's attachment theory.

Bowlby assumed that mothers were usually the primary care-givers, but recent research demonstrates that infants and young children can establish relationships with more than a single individual. (Neither Bowlby nor Ainsworth argued otherwise.) From the nature of attachment, it follows that dyadic patterns of relating are more resistant to change than individual patterns because of reciprocal expectancies. In general, the more the infant's relationships to such individuals or objects prior to separation resemble that of the typical mother–infant attachment, the more closely their separation reactions follow the prototypical patterns previously described. Thus the relationship between infant and primary care-giver generates a template, used to understand (via the mechanisms of trans-ference) future relationships in adulthood. There is no reason to think that these relationships necessarily involve only people; they might also involve gods and goddesses, spirits and ghosts, and all the other super-natural agencies of interest to Boyer. If one is starting from what every child experiences, then attachment surely ranks as high as the perception of solidity or continuity which Boyer considers the bedrock of the intuitive ontologies later flouted by spirit beliefs.

The third step: conflict in attachment and its vicissitudes

Human infants are primed to seek out a primary attachment, and in most cases this attachment is to the mother – a bond mediated by intimate physical contact (Spiro 1997). The assumption is that this contact will continue, but the assumption must sooner or later be violated, as the child individuates and the mother withdraws. This is a universal process, and no exceptions have ever been noted, although the method and outcome of this transition vary between social groups because of the different values placed on emotional fusion and autonomous individuation. From the beginning, these different valuations play a direct role in the process, making it wrong to assert, as early psychoanalysts did, that human development is the same everywhere or subject only to minor variations. At the same time, it is no less misleading to assert, as some cultural relativists have done, that the process is infinitely variable or unconstrained by developmental urgencies.

For example, American child-rearing (especially in white middle class families) generally pushes children to early individuation (Bellah, *et al.* 1985; Choi, Nisbett and Norenzayan 1999; Hsu 1981). Parents strive to inculcate greater autonomy in children, and reward them for display of individual achievement and accomplishment. 'My child started . . . ing' (fill in the blank with the relevant skill, from walking to talking to playing an instrument) is the usual way parents make judgements about themselves and others, as they compare early acquisition of autonomy skills (Kakar 1978). Such skills may or may not be important in themselves. But as markers in the development of the supreme value – autonomy – they are crucial, and children who do not measure up are singled out for special remediation or therapy, not uncommonly involving prescription drugs.

Which comes first, the early development of individuation or the cultural value we call 'individuality'? If the question seems to be of the chicken-and-the-egg variety, it is precisely that: there is no point in assigning priority to either one, except in one sense. All children must achieve some degree of individuation from their primary care-takers, but the extent to which this true – and the meaning assigned to it – is dependent on cultural values (Spiro 1984). Once established, the value of individuation selects for and prefers parenting styles which lead to the development of personal autonomy. Now, there is another side to this process. No one would argue that 'independence' is the only value American culture seeks to maximize. There is also the value of home and community, of shared dependency and common purpose, and this value also finds expression. American cultural values contradictorily emphasize both individuation and dependency (Bellah, *et al.* 1985; Raeff 1997), and people must try to balance them or, if they cannot, to adjust to the conflict that accompanies the inability to choose. There is therefore a dialectic of contradictions, developmental and cultural, that is mutually supportive and continuous (Nuckolls 1998).

Particular cultural patterns, like the case above, are interesting, but Boyer is correct when he says that the purpose of his theory is not to explain the particularities of religious beliefs. To adumbrate a series of particularistic illustrations, therefore, in the manner of most ethnographers does not constitute a strong critique of developmental cognitivism. The critique must be able to state that the relevant properties of superhuman agencies are better explained in universalist terms using a different theoretical framework. By 'relevance' I mean transmissibility and memorability, the criteria Sperber in Chapter One holds up as basic to the endurance of a set of beliefs. We must take as given the cognitivist point of departure and their insistence that these attributes demand explanation.

A South Indian case study

The case to be described resists the criticism that it represents only a particular instance because it exemplifies tendencies that are widely distributed across many social groups. It is equivalent, thus, to Boyer's study of the Fang, except that the processes I call attention to concern the nature of attachment, its relationship to ambivalence, and the salience of religious propositions. Specifically, the case study exemplifies the tendency to view women ambivalently, both as providers of succour and destroyers of male potency, and as models of the divine. The contradiction is found in many places (see Spiro 1997) including Greece (Friedl 1967), Java (H. Geertz 1961; Jay 1969; Brenner 1995), Spain (Gilmore and Gilmore 1979), Portugal (Hollos and Lies 1985), France (Rogers 1975; Rapp 1975; Segalen 1983), Italy (Cornelisen 1976) and southern Europe generally (Saunders 1981), among the Kafyar of Nigeria (Netting 1969), the Swahili of Mombasa (Swartz 1982), the Mundurucu (Murphy and Murphy 1974), and India (Carstairs 1957; Nuckolls 1996; Obeyesekere 1981, 1984, 1990).

Like most societies, the Jalaris of South India (a Telugu-speaking community of the southeastern coast) postulate the existence of superhuman agencies that violate a number of intuitive assumptions. Such agencies cannot be seen in ordinary waking experience; they never die, or if they do, usually come back to life; and they have the power to move objects at a distance. There are other assumptions they *could* violate, and no doubt if the Jalaris wished to, they could enumerate them. For example, the spirits defy gravity and move through solid objects, but one would have to elicit this information; the Jalaris would not volunteer it, and indeed, to most Jalaris of my acquaintance, it would seem ridiculously trivial to point it out. So why are some intuitions selected for systematic violation and reference and not others? And how do we know that violations are important in constituting these beings, rather than simply

Charles W. Nuckolls

incidental trappings – descriptions, that is, attached to superhuman agencies only as a consequence, not a cause, of their postulation?

Starting from the observation that Jalari spirits violate some, but not all, developmentally expected intuitions, we can, in the manner of Boyer, explain some of their attributes. For the purposes of this account, in fact, we can accept the whole of Boyer's explanatory hypothesis. What we *cannot* explain, however, is the fact that the Jalaris always and invariably define these spirits as 'mothers'. This definition is by no means unique to the Jalaris, and a similar belief is one of the most widely encountered facts of anthropological fieldwork. From the fact that they are mothers, all of their other powers and attributes derive, including some of those considered 'violations' of developmentally intuitive assumptions. Mother goddesses nurture, as real mothers do, but they also punish and kill. They are sexually voracious, unlike real mothers are supposed to be, and they can take control of living human bodies through possession. From the perspective of explanatory social science, which is more important: the fact that Jalari spirits violate cognitive assumptions of physical regularity (which they do), or that they are all mothers, in relationship to whom ordinary living people are like children?

The Jalaris posit the existence of a variety of spirits, most of them female, known collectively as *ammavallu* or 'mothers' (Nuckolls 1996). These spirits possess all the qualities Boyer and Sperber (as well as Lawson and McCauley 1990) say they should, fulfilling the criteria for supernatural agencies who defy intuitive conceptions. These are supposed to endow them with, to use Boyer's phrase, 'attention-grabbing' attributes (Chapter Two, p. 59), which also explains their memorability and transmissibility across generations. It is curious, however, that with exposure to so many other similarly posited agencies, including those of mainstream Hinduism (not to mention Christianity and Islam), the Jalaris show remarkably little interest in incorporating most candidates. This is not true across the board, however. Twice in the recent past new goddesses have arrived in the village, both times accompanied by epidemic diseases. In both cases, it was the disease (smallpox and cholera) that got people's attention, and when they reflected on its origin, they inferred the intervention of a mother goddess.

The Jalaris associate terrible calamities, and dramatic events of all kinds (good and bad), with divine females classified as 'mothers'. Goddesses are binary, made up of two aspects, one malign and the other benign. Sometimes goddesses do good things and sometimes they do bad things, but predicting which they will do is impossible. They are fickle. Nevertheless, one must act toward them as if their behaviour could be influenced, and that means giving them regular offerings of good things (meat, new clothes, and occasionally alcohol or even marijuana). People regularly forget to do these things, and so, when a goddess attacks and punishes them by inflicting disease or interrupting the fish catch, they say it's because she felt neglected. But would it have made any difference if they had made the offerings, in the correct amount and on time? The Jalaris doubt it.

Ambivalence of this sort is characteristic of both the goddesses themselves and the people who worship them. The goddess is good and bad; people love them and hate them; no one is sure what to do, only that something must be done. When new calamities befall, as during the epidemic diseases, people interpret events according to the schema just described. It is shot full of conflicted images and emotions; and this, I will argue, is related both to the circumstances of Jalari childhood and to the structure of Jalari cosmology. Moreover, ambivalence is not merely something 'added on' to a supernatural template already constituted by other means. A psychoanalytically informed model of development is better than the cognitivist model at this level and for this purpose – in short, it explains the features of Jalari goddess beliefs that are most salient to their construction and transmission from one generation to the next.

An interesting case in point is the vocabulary concerning 'possession', that is, the belief that the goddesses can temporarily inhabit a human consciousness and invest it with new purposes. The vocabulary is strongly physical, with references to holding and handling. It has often seemed to me, in listening to the Jalaris describe possession experiences, that I was listening to a description of the actions of a parent toward a small child: the picking up, the handling, the directing are all highly reminiscent of the way parents treat their children. A Jalari parent, in fact, expects children to exercise little control or direction on their own part until an age Americans would consider very late (Kakar 1990; Kurtz 1992; Nuckolls 1996). Even then, the demonstrations of independent initiative and personal responsibility American parents love to praise are almost wholly absent. Is it possible that the vocabulary of possession in Jalari culture represents, through transference, values and attitudes originally associated with the relationship between mother and child, and thus support the hypothesis that psychodynamic mechanisms mediate language forms and cultural constructions (Nuckolls 1997)?

Recent work from all over South Asia indicates that ambivalence is central to the relationship between mother and child and especially mother and son (Kakar 1978, 1982, 1989; Nuckolls 1991, 1993, 1996; Obeyesekere 1981, 1984, 1990; Roland 1988; Trawick 1990). On the one hand, a boy is drawn by memories of his mother's nurturing (far more long-lasting and intense in India than in the West) to idealize the feminine. On the other hand, fear that the mother may reject him or, worse, exploit him for the fulfilment of her own sexual needs compels him to constrain the feminine in order to keep its power to envelop him under control. This constitutes what Luborsky and his colleagues term a core conflict relational schema – a pattern formed in childhood that becomes a template for understanding future relationships. It is not unique to South Asian societies, but it is present with special prominence.

Let us assume, then, that conflict in the nature of the mother–child relationship exists and that it is unresolvable in any permanent sense. This is consistent with what we know about child development in Hindu India (Kurtz 1992). How do people deal with the ambivalence that might result? Professional possession-mediumship offers one culturally sanctioned solution, differently symbolized for the men and women who undergo the experience. Ambivalence in the maternal relationship resolves itself among the men in possession by goddesses, a role which normatively allows certain men to immerse themselves in a nurturing feminine role identity and at the same time to control that identity through the practice of possession-mediumship. The position of the women who become possession-mediums is similar, but reversed. Wanting sons is natural in a culture where fulfilment of a woman's role is contingent on the production of male offspring. But in having sons, a Jalari mother must eventually acknowledge losing them to wives, who will supplant her, and (in South Indian culture) to a set of affines who become competitors with her for her sons' attention and support. Under some circumstances, ambivalence in the maternal role – between wanting mature sons and knowing that their maturity means some degree of disaffection from her – is intensified and then resolved in the experience of possession by her own dead sons. As a medium, the mother regains total control over her son, whom she incorporates as her permanent tutelary spirit. The son never grows up; he can never leave; and he can never be alienated (Nuckolls 1996).

Resolution of cultural ambivalence in the relationship of sons and mothers is thus possible in different ways. The first way is through symbolic transformation of the son to make him less problematic for the mother. The second way is through symbolic transformation of the mother to make her less problematic for the son. Male possession-mediums resolve the ambivalence in favour of the son. The 'son', as it were, recovers the mother through his own symbolic transformation and then complete immersion in a female persona which becomes (for him) a controlled object of devotion. Female possession-mediums resolve the ambivalence in favour of the mother, who then recovers the son through a process of re-absorption into herself. In both cases, the significant other in the mother–son relationship is returned and simultaneously relieved of its ambivalence-generating nature through symbolic transformation into an inalienable possession as well as into a source of divinatory power. Although these possession experiences are best exemplified in professional mediums, the same dynamic is to be found more generally, since possession is something most people in Jalari culture experience at one time or another.

To be 'caught', 'come to', or 'got down upon' by a possessing spirit called 'mother' is to refer to a relationship that has its origins in childhood. This is no simple thing, because all goddesses – like all mothers – have two aspects: one benign and the other malign. This is one aspect of the ambivalence. If the possessing goddess is in her benign form, and the experience pleasant and useful, then the 'mother' is nurturant. Her purpose in possessing is to do good. If the goddess is in her malign form, and the experience of possession painful, then the 'mother' is angry. Her purpose is to punish and inflict pain. Through regular worship and occasional (male) animal sacrifice, people aim to control the goddesses and insure that the form they most often reveal is the benign one. But they always forget to perform these tasks, with the result that the goddesses become angry and attack.

There are probably many reasons why people forget to make sacrifices to the goddess, but chief among these might be ambivalence. Villagers need the goddess, but they fear she will envelop them, and the fear makes them want to shun her. Doing so directly, however, is too dangerous – and in any case, one should only express devotion to the goddess. 'Forgetting', therefore, while not exactly deliberate, is one of the few means available to express hostility to a supreme being. Seen in a wider context, the relationship between goddesses and devotees is no less problematic and generative of ambivalence than the mother–son relationship, but the transactive language of worship at least affords some measure of action. One can curse the goddess for her failure to provide sustenance; think of her as either nurturant or punishing, encouraging one and limiting the other; and even imagine sex with her in the appropriate idiom of worship. Of course the goddess never ages or dies, so the relationship can be prolonged forever. When Jalaris speak of possession by the goddess, using the vocabulary of mother–child interaction, they have transferred the latter and transformed it into the former, where the conflict it generates can be managed in a religious idiom while at the same time retaining its ambivalence-generating power.

This chapter has argued that fundamental religious propositions violate intuitive emotional structures in two ways, first by asserting that the model of early care-giving will continue forever, even though it cannot do so without putting at risk the development of autonomy, and second by claiming that the model will not continue, even though the development of secure attachments in adulthood depends on it. Religious propositions of the kind cognitivists consider fundamental are violations of developmentally derived models of attachment, but since these models are conflictual, religious propositions both represent and attempt to resolve basic contradictions in human experience.

Conclusion

This chapter began with the comment that developmental cognitivism has a long history, with resonances to forms of eighteenth-century rationalist assessments of religious thought. This is true in a broader sense as well. The history of thought in the West (especially England and France) usually takes contradictoriness to be a weakness or failure. To be at variance with what one also desires could be taken to be symptomatic of the irrational or the insane. Against monism stands a long tradition of dialectical thinking, especially prominent in Germany, which questions the existence of things in themselves in preference to complex relations, and the interaction between these relations and the perceiving consciousness. Paradox is embraced, and understood as the powerful dynamic that drives and develops systems of knowledge, both those that are conscious and those that are unconscious.

The view advanced in this chapter supports the dialectical view, and holds that many features of culture – including religious beliefs – result from structural contradictions. They are insoluble by design. One of the most basic assumptions violated in human development is the assumption that the maternal relationship will continue in its earliest form. At first the child is in close physical proximity to the mother, and the sole object of her affection and attention. Then the child is weaned, and the privileged position it once enjoyed must now be shared with others. The expectation that the relationship would continue forever is shown to be false, and the child must grow up knowing that its most basic expectation about the world is not inviolable. At the same time, the wish itself is contradictory: the desire for continued dependency on the primary attachment figure is opposed by the desire to develop some degree of autonomy. As Spiro notes, 'it is a psychological truism that children's experientially acquired conceptions of their microsocial world of the family form the basis for their initial cognitive orientations to the macrosocial world' (1997: 150). Somehow the contradiction between early experientially derived expectations and their violation in normal development must be resolved, even if it is the form of a paradox that acknowledges no permanent resolution.

Religion as a 'culturally constituted defence mechanism', to use Spiro's (1965) phrase, offers one route to resolution of conflicted attachment wishes. The 'mother' deity, as we have seen, represents at the same time as it partly resolves the conflict over childhood-derived wishes for dependence and autonomy on the part of the child as well as the mother. Conflicted wishes are transferred to the image of the goddess, where they can be dealt with through the transactive language of worship. The fact that such wishes are never fully and completely realized, of course, partly explains the continuity (transmissibility) of such a belief system. Nevertheless, they promise resolution, even if at the same time they make that impossible. This is a paradox, perhaps, but as I have written elsewhere, culture itself can be understood as a paradox, or problem that cannot be solved (Nuckolls 1998).

This chapter has not questioned the starting point of the Boyer hypothesis: that the violations of intuitive assumptions inform or direct the construction of superhuman agencies and their attributes. It does question their source. If the development of conflicted attachment is a human universal, or nearly so, then it would be surprising if ambivalence played no role in the genesis of religious propositions. Indeed, if my argument is correct, then it might even play the primary role, and the ontological expectations adduced by Boyer might function only as enabling conditions. I make no argument as to primacy, however. The point is simply that the human attachment and its inevitable contradictions are too important to overlook in any theory that claims that development and religious beliefs are related.

References

Ainsworth, M., Biehar, M., Waters, E., and Wall, S. (1978), *Patterns of Attachment: A Psychological Study of the Strange Situation*, Hillsdale: Erlbaum.

Anderson, S. and Baum, A. (1994), 'Transference in interpersonal relations: inferences and affect based on signficant-other representations', *Journal of Personality*, 62: 459–97.

—— and Cole, S. (1990), '"Do I know you?": the role of significant others in general social perception', *Journal of Personality and Social Psychology* 59: 384–99.

——, Glassman, N., Chen, S., and Cole, S. (1995), 'Transference in social perception: the role of chronic accessibility in significant other representations', *Journal of Personality and Social Psychology*, 69: 41–57.

Barber, J. and Crits-Christoph, P. (1993), 'Advances in measures of psychodynamic formulations', *Journal of Consulting and Clinical Psychology*, 61: 574–85.

Bellah, R., Madsen, R., Sullivan, W., Swidler, A., and Tipton, S. (1985), *Habits of the Heart*, New York: Harper and Row.

Boehm, C. (1989), 'Ambivalence and compromise in human nature', *American Anthropologist*, 91: 921–39.

Bond, J., Hansel, J., and Shevrin, H. (1987), 'Locating a reference paradigm in psychotherapy transcripts: reliability of relationship episode location in the Core Conflictual Relationship Theme (CCRT) method', *Psychotherapy*, 24: 736–49.

Bowlby, J. (1969), *Attachment and Loss: Vol. 1. Attachment*, New York: Basic Books.

—— (1973), *Attachment and Loss: Vol. 2: Separation*, New York: Basic Books.

Brennan, K. and Shaver, P. (1998), 'Attachment styles and personality disorders: their connections to each other and to parental divorce, parental death, and perceptions of parental caregiving', *Journal of Personality*, 66: 835–78.

Brenner, S. (1995), 'Why women rule the roost: rethinking Javanese ideologies of gender and self-control', in A. Ong and M. Peletz (eds), *Bewitching Women, Pious Men: Gender and Body Politics in Southeast Asia*, Berkeley: University of California Press.

Campbell, D. (1965), 'Ethnocentric and other altruistic motives', in D. Levin (ed.), *Nebraska Symposium on Motivation*, Lincoln: University of Nebraska Press.

Carstairs, G. (1958), *The Twice Born*, Bloomington: Indiana University Press.Choi, I., Nisbett, R., and Norenzayan, A. (1999), 'Causal attribution across cultures: variation and universality', *Psychological Bulletin* 125: 47–63.

Cornelisen, A. (1976), *Women of the Shadows*, Boston: Little, Brown.

Crits-Christoph, P., Luborsky, L., Dahl, L., Popp, C., Mellon, J., and Mark, D. (1988), 'Clinicians can agree in assessing relationship patterns in psychotherapy: the Core Conflictual Relationship Theme method', *Archives of General Psychiatry*, 45: 1001–4.

D'Andrade, R.G. (1995), *Cognitive Anthropology*, Cambridge: Cambridge University Press.

—— and Strauss, C. (1994), (eds), *Human Motives and Cultural Models.* Cambridge: Cambridge University Press.

Deci, E. and Ryan, R. (1985), *Intrinsic Motivation and Self-Determination in Human Behavior*, New York: Plenum.

Feeney, J. and Noller, P. (1996), *Adult Attachment*, Thousand Oaks: Sage.

Friedl, E. (1967), 'The position of women: appearance and reality', *Anthropological Quarterly*, 40: 97–108.

Freud, S. (1958 [1912]), 'The dynamics of transference', in J. Strachey (ed.), *The Standard Edition of the complete psychological works of Sigmund Freud* (Vol. 12, pp. 99–108), London: Hogarth Press.

Geertz, H. (1961), *The Javanese Family*, Glencoe: Free Press.

Gilmore, M. and Gilmore, D. (1979), 'Machismo: a psychodynamic approach (Spain)', *Journal of Psychological Anthropology*, 2: 281–300.

Harlow, H. and Zimmermann, R. (1959), 'Affectional responses in the infant monkey', *Science*, 130: 421.

Hazen, C. and Shaver, P. (1987), 'Romantic love conceptualized as an attachment process', *Journal of Personality and Social Psychology*, 52: 511–24.

Hinde, R. and Spencer-Booth, Y. (1966), 'Effects of six-day maternal deprivation on rhesus monkeys', *Nature* 210: 1021–3.

Hollos, M. and Lies, P. (1985), 'The hand that rocks the cradle rules the world: family interaction and decision making in a Portuguese rural community', *Ethos*, 13: 346–57.

Horowitz, M. (1988), *Cognitive Psychodynamics. From Conflict to Character*, New York: John Wiley & Sons.Hsu, F. (1981), *American and Chinese: Passages to Differences*, Honolulu: University of Hawaii Press.

Jay, R. (1969), *Javanese Villagers*, Cambridge, Mass.: MIT Press.

Kakar, S. (1978), *The Inner World*, Delhi: Oxford University Press.

—— (1982), *Shamans, Mystics, and Doctors*, New York: Knopf.

—— (1989), 'The maternal-feminine in Indian psychoanalysis', *International Journal of Psychoanalysis*, 19: 355–62.

—— (1990) 'Stories from Indian Psychoanalysis: Text and Context,' in J. Stigler, R. Shweder and G. Herdt (eds) *Cultural Psychology: Essays on Comparative Human Development*, Cambridge: COP.

Kurtz, S. (1992), *All the Mothers are One*, New York: Columbia University Press.

Lakoff, G. and Johnson, M. (1999), *Philosophy in the Flesh*, New York: Basic Books.

Lawson, T. and McCauley, R. (1990), *Rethinking Religion*, Cambridge: Cambridge University Press.

Luborsky, L. (1976), 'Helping alliance in psychotherapy: the groundwork for a study of their relationship to its outcome', in J. Claghorn (ed.), *Successful Psychotherapy*, New York: Burner/Mazel.

—— (1977), 'Measuring a pervasive psychic structure in psychotherapy: the core conflictual relationship theme', in N. Freedman and S. Grand (eds), *Communicative Structures and Psychic Structures*, New York: Plenum Press.

—— and Crits-Christoph, P. (1990), *Understanding Transference: The Core Conflictual Relationship Theme Method*, (2nd edn), New York: Basic Books.

—— Crits-Christoph, P. and Millon, T. (1986), 'Advent of objective measures of the transference concept', *Journal of Consulting and Clinical Psychology*, 54: 39–47.

Lutz, C. (1988), *Unnatural Emotions: Everyday Sentiments on a Micronesian Atoll and their Challenge to Western Theory*, Chicago: University of Chicago Press.

Murphy, Y. and Murphy, R. (1974), *Women of the Forest*, New York: Columbia University Press.

Netting, R. (1969), 'Marital relations in the Jos Plateau of Nigeria', *American Anthropologist*, 71: 1037–45.

Nuckolls, C. (1991), 'Culture and causal thinking: Diagnosis and prediction in a South Indian fishing village', *Ethos,* 19: 3–51.

—— (1993), 'The anthropology of explanation', *Anthropological Quarterly,* 66: 1–21.

—— (1995), 'The misplaced legacy of Gregory Bateson: toward a cultural dialectics of knowledge and desire', *Cultural Anthropology*, 10: 368–96.

—— (1996), *The Cultural Dialectics of Knowledge and Desire*, Madison: University of Wisconsin Press.

—— (1998), *Culture: A Problem that Cannot be Solved*, Madison: University of Wisconsin Press.

Obeyesekere, G. (1981), *Medusa's Hair*, Chicago: University of Chicago Press.

—— (1984), *The Cult of the Goddess Patini*, Chicago: University of Chicago Press.

—— (1990), *The Work of Culture*, Chicago: University of Chicago Press.

Raeff, C. (1997), 'Individuals in relationships: Cultural values, children's social interactions, and the development of an American individualistic self', *Developmental Review*, 17: 205–38.

Rapp, R. (1975), 'Men and women in the South of France: public and private domains', in R. Reiter (ed.), *Toward an Anthropology of Women*, New York: Monthly Review Press.

Rodin, J. (1990), 'Control by any other name: definitions, concepts, and processes', in J. Rodin, C. Scholler, and K. Warner Schjaie (eds), *Self-Directedness: Cause and Effects throughout the Life Course*, Hillsdale: Erlbaum.

Rogers, S. (1975), 'Female forms of power and the myth of male dominance: a model of female/male interaction in peasant society', *American Ethnologist*, 2: 727–56.

Roland, A. (1988), in *Search of the Self in India and Japan*, Princeton: Princeton University Press.Ryan, R. and Connell, J. (1989), 'Perceived locus of causality and internalization: examining reasons for acting in two domains', *Journal of Personality and Social Psychology*, 57: 749–61.

Saunders, G. (1981), 'Men and women in Southern Europe: a review of some aspects of cultural complexity', *Journal of Psychoanalytic Anthropology*, 4: 435–66.

Segalen, M. (1983), *Love and Power in the Peasant Family: Rural France in the Nineteenth Century*, Chicago: University of Chicago Press.

Spiro, M. (1965), 'Religious systems as culturally constituted defence mechanisms', in M. Spiro (ed.), *Context and Meaning in Cultural Anthropology*, New York: Free Press.

—— (1984), 'Some reflections on cultural determinism and relativism with special attention to reason and emotion', in R. Shweder and R. LeVine (eds), *Culture Theory*, Cambridge: Cambridge University Press.

—— (1997), *Gender Ideology and Psychological Reality*, New Haven: Yale University Press.

Strauss, C. and Quinn, N. (1997), *A Cognitive Theory of Cultural Meaning*, Cambridge: Cambridge University Press.

Swartz, M. (1982), 'The isolation of men and power of women: sources of power among the Swahili of Mombasa', *Journal of Anthropological Research* 38: 26–44

Trawick, M. (1990), *Notes on Love in a Tamil Family*, Berkeley: University of California Press.

Westen, D. (1991), 'Social cognition and object relations', *Psychological Bulletin*, 109: 429–55.

—— (1992), 'The cognitive self and the psychoanalytic self: can we put ourselves together', *Psychological Inquiry*, 3: 1–13.

—— (1998), 'The scientific legacy of Sigmund Freud: toward a psycho-dynamically informed psychological science', *Psychological Bulletin*, 124: 333.

Whitehouse, H. (1996), 'Jungles and computers: neuronal group selection and the epidemiology of representations', *Journal of the Royal Anthropological Institute* (N.S.), 2: 99–116.

Conclusion: Towards a Reconciliation
Harvey Whitehouse

Are the arguments about mind, evolution, and culture, advanced in the two parts of this volume, fundamentally intractable?[1] Clearly, some of the contributors think so. Nevertheless, the distance between the perspectives of Parts One and Two, although reflecting widely and deeply held differences of approach between cognitive scientists and social anthropologists respectively, is partly an artefact of style rather than of substance.

A certain amount of rhetorical posturing obscures opportunites for exploring middle ground. For instance, in critiquing *tabula rasa* models of cognitive development, Plotkin claims in Chapter Three that 'no psychologists worth their salt now believe that previous theorists like Skinner and Piaget contributed much to our understanding of language and language acquisition' (p. 140). Arguably, however, Plotkin overstates the situation, exaggerating the difficulties of partial compromise or synthesis between at least some aspects of the approaches in Parts One and Two. The rather more moderate views of Karmiloff-Smith are instructive. In place of a notion of mental modularity, she argues for a process of 'modularization', requiring us to combine certain insights of both Piagetian and Chomskean/Fodorian models. The resulting picture envisages learning as a recurrent process of phased development, begin- ning with the achievement of 'behavioural mastery' and involving successive processes of 'representational redescription' as domains of knowledge become, through experience, progressively more accessible to conscious analysis and verbal expression. Although accounting for a high degree of domain specificity, consistent with the arguments of Part One of this volume, Karmiloff-Smith's theory of representational redescription produces a developmental account that strongly recalls certain aspects of the perspectives advanced (and the terminology preferred) in Part Two. Thus, Karmiloff-Smith endorses Piaget's view that 'both gene expression and cognitive development are emergent properties of a self-organizing system' (1992: 9). And she goes on to criticize Fodor's perspective for failing 'to help us to understand the way in which children turn out to be active participants in the construction of their own knowledge' (1992: 10). In these and many other passages, Karmiloff-Smith's views (and her terminological choices) are noticeably closer to Ingold's and Toren's than to Sperber's, Boyer's, and Plotkin's.

The respectability of Karmiloff-Smith's approach within cognitive and developmental psychology calls into question Plotkin's claim with regard to psychologists 'worth their salt' and, more importantly, his assertion that 'the case of language alone blows a hole in the notion of a *tabula rasa* . . . big enough for a large coach and horses to be driven through' (p. 139). Although Karmiloff-Smith does not, strictly speaking, put forward a *tabula rasa* theory of mind, she does at least demonstrate that it is possible to account for the development of some key aspects of domain specificity (e.g. in relation to language, physics, number, theory of mind, etc.) without according causal primacy to genes in the construction of developmental trajectories (see Ingold, Chapter Four, pp. 168–71). Indeed, the only element of genetic prespecification Karmiloff-Smith allows is a limited set of initial attention biases in the neonate's input systems.

I am not suggesting that Karmiloff-Smith's model of representational redescription offers the only possible middle ground between the arguments advanced in Parts One and Two of this volume, or indeed that this model necessarily fits, more substantially than any other approach, available evidence (psychological, ethological, biological, anthropological, etc.) with respect to the relationship between mind, evolution, and cultural transmission. What I *am* suggesting is that the positions taken up in this volume sometimes exaggerate the incommensurability of the two sets of projects being advanced. This tendency is even more apparent in some of the Part-Two chapters.

Ingold and Toren firmly reject a number of assumptions of orthodox approaches in biology and cognitive science. The details of what an alternative programme might look like, however, are not very elaborately or precisely specified. Ingold's chapter, which makes only general suggestions as to how we might proceed, tends to collapse developmental processes into an undifferentiated bundle of elements. As the dichotomies between evolution and history, genes and environment, nature and nurture, competence and performance, and planning and implementation come crashing down, no structures appear to be left among the rubble. Even the distinction between mental and public events is abolished as part of the insidious Cartesian regime that must be toppled (Chapter Four, p. 197).

Where I carried out my fieldwork in Papua New Guinea, people often alluded to the fact that one cannot divine the thoughts of others. Thoughts, sensations, and feelings could be tentatively inferred but not directly perceived. Private fantasies, plans, hopes, and fears were construed as a separate domain from public actions, the two impacting upon each other in more or less intelligible ways. I find it hard to imagine a culture in which this is not the case. Surely people everywhere sometimes think before they act, or at least engage in silent contemplation?

Imagine a simple scenario in which one is sitting on a park bench, privately debating whether to buy an ice-cream from the nearby vendor. The plan and its implementation are surely distinct from a phenomeno-logical point of view. They are distinct in the sense that the former can only be experienced by the one unique actor (i.e. is private) whereas the latter directly impinges on the perceptual apparatuses of others (i.e. is public). But they are also distinct by virtue of operationalizing different systems of memory. The plan involves semantic memory and explicit, verbally stateable computations, such as the projected cost of an ice-cream, the amount of money in one's pocket, the possible implications for being able to buy a bus ticket on the way home, and so on. By contrast the act of getting up, walking over, finding the money, and so forth, entail skills of an embodied nature, including finely tuned sensorimotor skills, feats of orientation, balance, and perception. This process of implement-ation involves the use of implicit knowledge, the activation of which is rapid and automatic (see Mandler 1985). Ingold, however, is surely correct that all skills develop through *practice*. This applies both to explicit, non-automatic planning and implicit, automatic implementation, and indeed to cognitive processes more generally. I would argue, however, that we do not need to deny the highly structured character of cognition in order to make this point (see also Strauss and Quinn 1997: 29–34.)

To a large extent, I think that many of Ingold's and Toren's specific arguments about the primacy of development in understanding the relationship between mind, evolution, and culture are substantially supported by established approaches in cognitive science, such as Esther Thelen's examplary work on dynamic systems (Thelen and Smith 1995), Gerald Edelman's theory of neuronal group selection (Edelman 1992; see below), and a number of connectionist models of parallel processing in networks (for example Sejnowski and Rosenberg 1987). With the possible exception of Edelman's work, which remains somewhat con-troversial in cognitive science (less so in neuroscience), these approaches are at least as 'orthodox' as Sperber's, Boyer's, and Plotkin's. This makes Ingold's apparent opposition to cognitivism in general,[2] and Toren's explicit refusal to incorporate any discussion of 'Western science models of mind' into the main body of her chapter, seem rather unnecessary.

These rhetorical stances enable Plotkin to observe, reproachfully, that '(r)ather than somewhat mysteriously and arbitrarily disapproving of the widely agreed views of a neighbouring discipline, our colleagues in the human sciences outside of psychology need to be telling psychologists precisely where and why their data contradict psychological theory' (p. 141).

Probabilistic versus qualitative approaches

The contributors to Part Two of this volume are highly critical of cognitive models of cultural transmission, apparently for very different reasons. Ingold is critical mainly on the grounds that cognitive approaches, in common with models of evolution under natural selection, place certain theoretical entities (e.g. genes, modules, etc.) in an executive position with regard to the causation of recurrent features of human development and culture. Toren rejects cognitive models on the grounds that they unreflexively promote the categories of Western folk psychology to the status of scientific 'facts', whereas a distillation of more diverse ethno-psychological knowledge may avoid some grosser forms of intellectual imperialism and have greater applicability cross-culturally. Nuckolls is critical on the grounds that cognitive science explains very much less than it might, not especially because it is ethnocentric but because it excludes a body of data available within its own institutional setting, namely evidence from fields of depth psychology (such as psychoanalysis).

On the face of it, these indeed appear to be very different objections. Nevertheless, behind all of them may be detected a common antipathy to the accordance of causal primacy to any given entity or process on *probabilistic* grounds, a procedure that is fundamental to real-world sciences but not to social/cultural anthropology. For instance, Ingold's argument that genes either have to explain 100 per cent of the variance in a particular phenomenon or they explain nothing, seems to dismiss out of hand the grounds on which causal properties are accorded to genes in theories of natural selection. The argument advanced by both Toren and Nuckolls that affect cannot be separated off from processes of concept-formation seems to follow a similar trajectory. Cognitive science does not rule out affectivity in principle but only for the purposes of making probabilistic claims, for instance about recurrent patterns of concept-formation, taken as a *theoretically* distinguishable set of processes. The distrust of such reasoning, uniformly exhibited by Part-Two contributors, is understandable when it is viewed in the context of ethnographic perspectives.

Ethnographic research is primarily concerned with detailing all the possible factors that contribute to a particular range of social and cultural phenomena, usually within a relatively small population. Smallness of scale, obviously, is an artefact of qualitative research methods – within the space of one or two years of fieldwork, there is a limit to the number of people you can get to know really well. Such microscopic studies of human sociality reveal the extreme complexity of the processes by which behaviour and meaning are generated and transmitted. To most ethnographers, it seems absurd to account for a particular religious belief in terms of universal cognitive dispositions or susceptibilities since it is obvious that the expression of a particular belief is caused much more directly and substantially by other prevalent beliefs, ideas, and cultural 'maps', by complex personal motives, emotions, and intentions (both conscious and unconscious), by political and economic forces and constraints, by discursive conventions and embodied habits, and by a host of other distinctive contextual factors. These factors, moreover, are manifestly shaped by wider (e.g. regional, national, and global) events and processes, both contemporary and historical. Ethnography these days is largely judged by the extent to which it addresses all these causes, influences, precipitating conditions, constraints, and so forth. Thus, the anthropological 'instinct' is to mistrust probabilistic notions of partial causality and to seek instead more encompassing, qualitative accounts of social/cultural phenomena, in which what appears to be general turns out to be particular (locally distinctive) after all.

The contrasting methodological procedures of naturalistic science and ethnography, however, may open up more fruitful opportunities for cross-fertilization than most contributors to this volume are prepared to concede. The authors in Part One are, on the whole, resigned to the incommensurability of the two sets of projects, while those in Part Two tend to regard naturalistic approaches as irretrievably misguided. Nuckolls, however, points out in Chapter Six that cognitive science stands to be improved by attending to ethnographic perspectives and vice versa. I share this view.

Locating the causes of mental activity

Nuckolls suggests that, by tending to construe cognitive causes in rather narrow terms (for example, excluding deep motivational conflict), the contributors to Part One unnecessarily limit the strength and breadth of the hypotheses they advance. In a similar vein, I would argue that restricting the cognitive project to the identification of causes *internal to organisms* impoverishes the explanatory potential of psychological models.

Boyer makes a persuasive case that certain simple violations of intuitive knowledge, such as a notion of 'ghost' which combines standard psychology and counter-intuitive physics, are more likely to recur in any society than a set of extremely complex doctrinal representations, for instance concerning the mystery of the Holy Trinity. Boyer is surely right about this, and gives a precise and well-substantiated account of the cognitive foundations of counter-intuitive representations. This does not mean, however, that the concept of ghost is more 'natural' than the idea of the Holy Trinity. Rather, it suggests that the sociocultural conditions for the transmission of ghost-concepts are more widespread than for elaborate theological ideas. The latter tend to arise in literate and highly routinized doctrinal traditions, where learning and memory are greatly assisted by texts, repetitive sermonizing, and theological debate. These sociocultural conditions are emphatically not universal. Indeed, in many non-literate societies, where religious representations are transmitted in very infrequent climactic rituals, we often find a marked diminution of doctrinal and exegetical discourse (see Whitehouse 2000).

Interestingly, the periodic but very intense rituals of many tribal societies do not focus on the transmission of counter-intuitive concepts, but rather on the violation of cultural schemas. Rites of inversion and initiation, for instance, are concerned more commonly with the temporary violation of authority relations, sexual mores, kinship obligations, and so on, rather than with the violation of intuitive ontological knowledge. The sorts of counter-intuitive representations with which Boyer is concerned flourish somewhere in the middle of a continuum between advanced doctrinal schemas, reproduced in semantic memory through routinized transmission, and multivocal ritual imagery, established in episodic memory through the violation of cultural schemas and the evocation of intense affective states in rare and climactic acts of ritual transmission. (See Whitehouse 1995, 1996b.) Ghosts and other counter-intuitive concepts are, by contrast, prominent in mundane, everyday discourse, which is supported neither by a body of codified doctrine nor by extremely arousing, revelatory, and memorable ceremonies (Whitehouse 1996c).

Thus, the representations which interest Boyer belong to a particular set of sociocultural conditions of cognition and transmission and it is in relation to this set that experimental data on recall for counter-intuitive representations is likely to produce the strongest results. Boyer's theoretical perspective could, perhaps, be profitably expanded so as to incorporate the socially situated character of cognition and, thereby, identify stronger relations of causality between cognitive processes and distributions of representations.

As soon as we acknowledge that the causes of all mental activity are located simultaneously within *and among* organisms, we are obliged to take on board some of the most important insights of both parts of this volume. The fact that I remember something long enough to create what Sperber calls a 'public representation' of it cannot be explained in terms of properties of my mind *per se* but only in terms of properties of my mind *in its environment*, which includes socially regulated cycles of prior transmission. The probability of a given human being 'taking in' and 'passing on' any particular information can only be poorly estimated with reference to the fiction of a generic human mind. Claims about selective pressures on the evolution of mental architecture, and consequently about evolved neural mechanisms, require much stronger predictions, and these are only possible if we are prepared to specify relevant social conditions of mental activity, including culturally distinctive patterns of prior learning and affectivity.

In the next section, I describe Edelman's (1992) theory of neuronal group selection, and highlight the challenges it presents to the nativist epistemology advanced in Part One of this volume. Edleman's theory does away with the distinction between 'innate' and 'acquired' mental capacities; it presents the possibility of a unitary theory of the formation of *all types* of representation; it does this by situating mental activity in a social and historical context, thereby establishing a bridge connecting neurology, psychology, and sociology; it integrates cognitive and affective processes. This theory, it seems to me, is a more promising starting place for an epidemiology of representations.

The theory of neuronal group selection

One of the most striking discoveries of the brain sciences is the diversity of potential patterns of neuron firings in the brain. Humans possess approximately a hundred billion nerve cells, and the number of potential firing patterns is greater than the number of particles in the known universe. According to Edelman, learning is a process of natural selection within a potential population of virtually infinite firing patterns. To express this in concrete terms, we might imagine random firing patterns in neural centres governing motor activity to produce random behaviour, such as that exhibited by newborn babies. Sperber's version of the modularity thesis presupposes that child development follows a genetically specified schedule, such that appropriate structures for various forms of competence are pre-programmed. Edelman's theory, however, suggests that the developmental sequence results from the reinforcement of certain firing patterns through experience, and the weakening or elimination of others. This is why the potential number of firing patterns has to be as great as it is – learning is a process of elimination, of selecting out unwanted firing patterns, and continuously accumulating repertoires of more desirable ones. According to this view, classification of the environment is not a process of *instruction* (as in conventional cognitivism) but of *selection*.

Edelman describes his theory as the 'theory of neuronal group selection' (TNGS). TNGS is founded on three basic tenets. The first is 'developmental selection' (1992: 83), producing the topobiological dimensions and divisions of the nervous system. Edelman shows that even the neuroanatomy of organisms is not genetically programmed. DNA strings set constraints on brain formation (from foetal development onwards) but the eventual topobiological distribution of nerves in a given brain is the unique outcome of selectional processes. Thus, in genetically identical animals (including human monozygotic twins) neuroanatomical circuitry is never identical. Moreover, the 'wiring' of an organism is constantly changing. Edelman describes these ever-changing links between nerve cells as a 'primary repertoire', constituting (at a given point in time) the range of links between which synapses could, in principle, occur.

The second tenet is 'experiential selection' (1992: 83–4), resulting in actual synaptic connections (as opposed to potential ones). Edelman shows that particular connections become established through regular bio-chemical reinforcement in conjunction with the organism's behaviour. The resulting set of functioning circuits, established through somatic selection, is described as a 'secondary repertoire'.

The third tenet is 'reentrant mapping' (1992: 85), consisting of the interactive processes between firing patterns (or 'brain maps'). The firing patterns involved in perceptual processes involve many different parts of the brain. In order to produce the experience of 'seeing' something, maps relating to shape, focal hues, motion, and so on are simultaneously activated in different sectors of the neural system, and these sectors must be interconnected and coordinated. This process of coordination (i.e. reentrant mapping) is also established through somatic selection. Recursive reentry across neural sectors is reinforced in the same way as experiential selection. All three processes are linked to motor behaviour (producing inputs to the system or 'sensory sampling') via a process of 'global mapping' (1992: 89).

With these general principles in mind, let us briefly consider one of a string of experiments in artificial intelligence, pioneered by a team of scientists in California and inspired by Edelman's theory. The experiment parallels more or less perfectly Sperber's toy example about 'protorgs' and 'orgs' (Chapter One, pp. 28–9), but it involves a process of learning based on natural selection, as opposed to any form of instruction.

The experiment involves a motor-driven automaton with a primitive visual system linked up to a supercomputer. The automaton is equipped with a specific primary repertoire (equivalent to a very primitive neuro-anatomy) in the circuitry of the supercomputer. This circuitry impels it to move around and take visual samples of its environment randomly. The automaton is also endowed with circuitry that reinforces specific perceptions, but not others. Separate circuits detecting stripy objects and bumpy objects are separately reinforced. Placed in an environment with a wide variety of objects, the automaton begins by sampling all objects randomly. Through experience, however, a 'secondary' repertoire of reentrantly connected circuits is established enabling the automaton to track only stripy or bumpy objects. The automaton shows that it is able to learn to distinguish stripy or bumpy objects from those that are neither, but also to distinguish those that are stripy *and* bumpy from those that have only stripes or only bumps. This is achieved through the selectional formation of global mappings. Although the automaton is a computer-based machine, it functions more like a brain than a computer: 'it categorizes only on the basis of experience, not on the basis of prior programming . . . [It] carries out categorization on value in a fashion that might be called embodied . . . Of course, the brain of a real animal has the capacity to assemble many more mappings of this kind' (Edelman 1992: 93, emphasis removed).

The automaton in this experiment is like the protorgs and orgs in Sperber's toy example because it is concerned with identifying two discrete variables and their simultaneous occurrence. But the automaton, unlike the modular orgs and protorgs, is not programmed to do this. It is an artificial animal capable of learning through a simulated process of neuronal group selection. In contrast with orgs and protorgs, the auto-maton does not have to know in advance that there exist objects which are stripy but not bumpy, bumpy but not stripy, stripy and bumpy, and neither stripy nor bumpy. But if it is 'rewarded' for finding stripy and bumpy objects, it can proceed to make all these distinctions through processes of experiential selection. The dispensation of rewards in real brains is obviously a crucial mechanism for the TNGS.

Edelman argues that in *real* brains, synaptic connections are strengthened by ascending diffuse emissions from the hedonic centres and limbic
system. These neuroanatomical sectors are described as 'value systems',
and they are linked to particular regulatory functions such as feeding,
circulation, respiration, sexual arousal, and so on. The biochemical
emissions from the brain's value systems give rise to the experience of
affective states (which of course affect regulatory functions as well as
the nervous system itself). Edelman's argument is that certain configurations of firing patterns trigger emissions from the brain's value systems
so as to reinforce the synaptic connections entailed in those configurations.
Thus, an emotionally stimulating configuration of firing patterns, for
example, would stand a greater chance of being repeated than a 'neutral'
configuration. (See Strauss and Quinn 1997.) In concrete terms, a baby
may have the goal of transferring a hand-held object to its mouth; the
infant's cortex receives no pleasant impulses in response to random
movements of the limbs, and so the random firing patterns in sensorimotor
sectors are not reinforced. But when a particular random movement of
the hand results in the object touching the baby's lips, the synaptic
connections involved in this behaviour are strengthened. A particular
configuration of firing patterns is thus cumulatively selected through
experience. Note that the baby is in no sense 'programmed' to put things
in its mouth, but has merely stumbled upon one of a range of potential
behaviours that is satisfying. According to this theory, we are programmed
for nothing, save to explore the potentialities of our bodies and environments via a process of learning by neuronal group selection.

In arguing against nativist construals, Edelman does not have to
overlook or deny recurrent, species-specific cognitive patterns. Thought
processes are constrained but in no sense 'programmed' by DNA segments.
For sure, the range and the nature of human mental life are substantially
different from those of a chimpanzee, and massively different from those
of a frog; moreover, all humans probably think much more like other
humans than like any non-human species. But these outcomes of neural
development in each individual are not genetically specified; they are
the outcomes of processes of natural selection through embodied experience of the world and the evolution of our species. Edelman (necessarily)
argues that both somatic and natural selective systems are interconnected.
Neuronal group selection in the brain occurs on a time-scale of minutes
and hours, whereas in generations of organisms natural selection occurs
over millions of years. But the principles are the same and each process
gives shape to the other: 'a small loop consisting of the events in neuronal
group selection leads to diverse phenotypic behaviours in different

Conclusion

individuals of a species. These diverse behaviours provide the basis for
ongoing natural selection in the grand loop of evolution. The two selectional systems, somatic and evolutionary, interact' (Edelman 1992: 97).

According to Edelman, human brains do not come pre-equipped with
modules for classifying the world, for acquiring grammars, or for any
other mental function. Rather, they are equipped with a mass of ever-
changing circuitry that is capable of endlessly creating new maps (and
new configurations of maps) through neuronal group selection. None of
the firing patterns appropriate to the construction of a sentence is specified
in advance – they come about by a process of gradual reinforcement
through experience. In this respect, neural activity is rather like the massive
hive of activity in a jungle (Edelman 1992: 69). There is no design or
programme that directs the growth of plants or the behaviour of animals.
Adaptations to this ever-changing environment are not planned in advance,
but they occur through the random discovery of fortuitous matches.
Edelman describes the study of this selective process as 'the science of
recognition', and this is the science which he considers proper to the
analysis of brain functions: 'In considering brain science as a science of
recognition I am implying that recognition is not an instructive process.
No direct information transfer occurs . . . Instead, recognition is selective'
(1992: 81).

Neuronal group selection and memory

For Edelman, the creation of memories is a gradual process in which
particular configurations of firing patterns are strengthened through partial
(but significant) duplication. As he puts it (1992: 102):

> The TNGS proposes . . . that memory is the specific enhancement of a
> previously established ability to categorize . . . This kind of memory emerges
> as a population property from continual dynamic changes in the synaptic
> populations within global mappings . . . In such a system, recall is not
> stereotypic. Under the influence of continually changing contexts, it changes,
> as the structure and dynamics of the neural populations involved in the original
> characterization also change . . . Memory, in this view, results from a process
> of continual recategorization. By its nature, memory is procedural and involves
> continual motor activity and repeated rehearsal in different contexts . . . Unlike
> computer-based memory, brain-based memory is inexact, but it is also capable
> of great degrees of generalization.

Edelman's argument fits quite well with theories of 'semantic memory'
– for example, *general scripts* for familiar situations, such as going to

the doctor or to a restaurant. We all know, for example, that restaurant scripts involve variations on a sequence (e.g. entering, being shown to a table, consulting a menu, ordering, eating, paying, tipping, departing). The scope for variation is quite limited (for example you cannot depart before you enter, or eat before you order, etc.) but there are differences between most fast-food restaurants (where you pay before eating, for instance) and more conventional establishments. Scripts for these kinds of events are usually formed gradually, through experience and observation. One feature of these general scripts is that they tend to take precedence over our memories of *actual* episodes. If I eat at a particular restaurant every week, for example, I may be able to remember some unique details of my last meal but as time passes the meals seem to 'fade' into each other. I couldn't tell you anything unique about my meal six months ago, even though I could infer many general details about that experience from a typical script. In Edelman's terms, the available script at a given point in time is presumably a configuration of firing patterns which have been cumulatively reinforced – the common denominators of repetitive experiences.

But there are other types of remembering which do not work like this. Some memories, in fact, seem to be created in an instant, rather than cumulatively over time. Everybody can remember unique episodes from their pasts, some of which may have a remarkable vividness. I can remember numerous childhood incidents, for example, with great clarity. These sorts of memory are referred to by cognitive psychologists as 'autobiographical' or 'episodic' memories. Particularly vivid and detailed memories of one-off events can even have a canonical structure in which location, activity, source, affect, and aftermath seem to be recalled quite predictably. (See for example Winograd and Killinger 1983.) In cognitive psychology, this phenomenon is sometimes referred to as 'flashbulb memory'. Kulik and Brown (1982), who coined this term, argued that the formation of flashbulb memories involved the activation of a particular neural mechanism.

From Edelman's viewpoint, this presents a problem. Natural selection in the brain involves a diverse population of firing patterns, with numerous recurrences of 'advantageous' patterns eventually establishing scripts (i.e. particular configurations of firing patterns). Flashbulb memory does not appear to fit with this model because it suggests that just one set of firing patterns can be enough to produce a script. Clearly, neither of the models is adequate for a general theory of memory. If every set of firing patterns had the character of flashbulb memory, we would remember every moment of our lives with absolute clarity. And if every set of firing patterns were integrated into a cumulative process of selection, we would have no autobiographical memories – only general scripts for repetitive events.

It therefore seems necessary to distinguish episodic and semantic memory. (See Tulving 1972.) But how might these types of memory be integrated into a theory of the brain? It is possible that the answer lies partly in the diversity of affective states. There is a massive discrepancy between the mild irritation or anxiety occasioned by bumping into a boring acquaintance and the terror of being threatened by an armed killer. The former is likely to evoke standard scripts for evasion, whereas the latter is likely to establish a script of its own, never to be forgotten. One of the features most commonly associated with 'flashbulb memories' is intensity of emotion. Extreme sensations of fear, lust, anger, horror, and so on seem to make the episodes in which they are evoked more memorable as one-off autobiographical events. Thus, the terrifying ordeal, the first kiss, the violent confrontation, and the shocking violation of morality, all appear to 'engrave' themselves on our memories. It is as if these emotive types of event burn an indelible firing pattern into the brain. The ascending diffuse emissions of the brain's value systems seem to be more intense on these occasions than on others. (This, at least, is what one might expect if these emissions are the biochemical correlates of emotional states.)

Following an extensive review of the literature on emotion and memory, Christiansen (1992) concludes that there seems to be a positive correlation between the intensity of affective states and the vividness and longevity of episodic memories. Nevertheless, this could only be part of the story, if only because some affective memories decay faster than others.

In addition to strong emotional content, a classic feature of 'flashbulb memories' is that they are triggered by *surprising* events. A surprising event is one that does not conform to our normal expectations; in other words, it is an event which is incongruent with existing semantic scripts. There would be nothing memorable about the sight of a woman riding her bicycle up King's Parade in Cambridge. It would, however, be hard to forget the sight of her riding a bicycle up the aisle of King's College Chapel during Holy Communion.

Wright and Gaskell (1992) argue that the experience of 'flashbulb memory' can be explained in terms of a cognitive processing loop. They suggest that when an event is perceived, the cognitive apparatus searches for a relevant script; if none is found the search continues until at last a reasonably adequate approximation to the event is remembered. The new event can then be attached to an existing script. Abnormal events would go around the loop many times before a suitable script is located. It is proposed that flashbulb memories result from the failure to locate an adequate script: the cognitive apparatus becomes exhausted and settles for the creation of an entirely new script, in which all kinds of indiscriminate details are encoded.

It would be possible to modify Edelman's theory of neuronal group selection to accommodate the flashbulb phenomenon. Let us suppose that ascending diffuse emissions from the brain stem reinforce select firing patterns in different degrees, depending on the 'strength' of these emissions (i.e. 'strength of emotion). We could envisage two main classes of neural response to any kind of affective stimulus.

Response 'A' would involve the substantial reproduction of already established firing patterns (i.e. scripts in semantic memory). Because of the cumulative reinforcement of certain parts of these firing patterns in the past, these would remain the most reproducible parts of the new firing patterns. We might refer to these particularly reproducible parts as a 'primary firing pattern'. 'Secondary' aspects of the new firing pattern (i.e. ones that have not been cumulatively reinforced in the past, or not to the same degree) would not be repeated, or would be repeated weakly or infrequently and eventually decay. These would be aspects of our experience which are either not remembered or soon forgotten.

Response 'B' would involve the establishment of radically new firing patterns, reinforced by strong emissions from the brain stem which fail to correspond to already established firing patterns. This would account for the particularly vivid and enduring character of certain episodic memories, especially the flashbulb phenomenon.

Neurology, psychology, and social theory

At this point, it is possible to see the *potentiality* for a theory of transmission that integrates neurological, psychological, and sociological perspectives. The *actual* integration of neurological and psychological theories is clearly a long way off. A comprehensive neurological account of 'simple' perceptual processes is not yet possible, let alone such an account of, say, a public oration. Nevertheless, if Edelman's line of thinking is broadly correct, a great deal of psychology starts from the wrong premises – of which perhaps the most pervasive is the assumption that at least some aspects of cognitive architecture are genetically prespecified. Nativist assumptions do not necessarily affect the quality of the data collected in psychology and linguistics, but they may lead to invalid inferences from these data. Detailed examples are provided in Edelman's eloquent critique of Chomsky's notion of a 'language acquisition device' (1992: 241–52). Edelman argues that theories of 'cognitive semantics' (Langacker 1987; Lakoff 1987) are much more substantially consistent with neurological research than is any notion of genetically specified mechanisms. Following Edelman's reasoning, 'hard-wiring' is not a factor in the memorability of representations. All representations are created through integrated processes of engagement with the environment and, since the most stimulating aspects of the human environment are *social*, we are obliged to envisage all processes of transmission in terms that are simultaneously sociological, psychological, and neurological. Let us consider an example of how we might proceed from here.

In two recent monographs (Whitehouse 1995, 2000), I have argued that divergent modes of ritual action engage different processes of memory. Highly routinized practices, such as liturgical rituals and daily temple offerings, are substantially encoded in semantic memory. Each ritual performance follows a familiar, repetitive script. Participants could not possibly remember specific performances last year, or the year before that – they could only infer from their general, semantic knowledge that they probably performed a certain ritual at a certain time on a certain day.

By contrast, the infrequent and highly traumatic rituals found (for example) in systems of initiation and sporadic cult activity, engender primarily episodic memories. In many cases, these episodic memories are experienced as a direct violation of existing semantic knowledge. In a traumatic instant, one's everyday assumptions are challenged and overturned. These moments of intense religious revelation are recalled as one-off, autobiographical events. These contrasting modes of ritual action involve very different assessments of relevance.

Consider, as an example of a routinized practice, formulaic responses in the Catholic Mass. The Priest recites a set of familiar words or phrases, to which the congregation responds with fixed answers or repetitions. This, at least, is the general script. Although cognized as a repetitive, predictable sequence of behaviours, the reality is that no two performances could be identical. Nevertheless, subtle differences between performances are consistently bracketed out as irrelevant, so that the impression is of behavioural replication. Let us suppose, for example, that on one occasion the Priest stutters over the penultimate 'amen'. Although members of the congregation would claim that they are repeating the Priest's utterance, it would be unthinkable for any of them to repeat the stutter. The stutter is not part of the script and so it is disregarded as irrelevant. Few people (barring perhaps the mean-minded) would be able to recall the Priest's slip of the tongue a few weeks later. We are dealing with a system of communication in which relevance is determined more or less exclusively in terms of general scripts.

As an example of the infrequent, traumatic mode of ritual action we might consider initiation rites in any number of Papua New Guinea societies. For example, among the Baktaman of inner New Guinea, first degree novices are snatched from their parents' homes in the middle of the night and taken to a secluded place in the forest, where they are made to rub dew and pork fat on their bodies (Barth 1975: Chapter 4). Among the Orokaiva of Northern Papua, novices are blindfolded with barkcloth hoods, mercilessly beaten by men disguised as spirits, and corralled onto a ceremonial platform (Williams 1930; Schwimmer 1973; Iteanu 1990).

In the Baktaman case, novices have no prior knowledge of the initiation process. Their abduction in the middle of the night and the whole sequence of events which follows fail to conform to any semantic scripts available to them. Not only are these experiences utterly mystifying and unfamiliar, they are profoundly frightening. In these circumstances, novices inevitably hunt in vain for recognizable forms of behaviour among their abductors. In neural terms, this presumably involves a massive reinforcement of novel firing patterns. I have elsewhere linked these sorts of episode to the formation of flashbulb memories (for instance, Whitehouse 1995: 195, 206), as has Gilbert Herdt in his discussion of Sambia religious experience (1989: 115).

In the course of the initiation process, it becomes clear to novices that their ritual experiences are pregnant with meaning. But, according to Barth (1975, 1987), this is not a process which corresponds to 'everyday' knowledge (i.e. semantic memory) but refers to a secret corpus of knowledge engendered in the enduring episodic memories of initiation ritual. It is the nature of flashbulb memories that everything in the perceptible environment is encoded; nothing can be 'bracketed out' as irrelevant, for there is no script against which to determine 'relevance'. As novices advance through the grades of initiation, they begin to observe regularities between one set of episodic memories and the next, leading to the inferential construction of patterns and meanings.

In the case of Orokaiva novices, a certain amount of 'everyday' knowledge is probably brought to bear on the situation. Novices may associate the ceremonial platform, on which they are corralled, with the type of platform used for butchering pigs (Bloch 1992: 9). But being treated like pigs is hardly a familiar situation, and to get a sense of the emotive quality of this experience we could imagine how we might have felt as children, being driven into a giant oven. So even where novices can make working assumptions about the relevance of particular ritual episodes, the process still involves a radically new configuration of scripts (i.e. sets of firing patterns).

In my study of a religious movement in New Britain, Papua New Guinea (Whitehouse 1995), I argued that routinized and sporadic rituals, substantially encoded in semantic and episodic memory respectively, engendered very different political regimes. Routinized performances (such as liturgical rituals) tend to give rise to notions of anonymous, 'imagined' communities, consistent with expansionary ideologies. Particular actors are not specified in semantic scripts for repetitive rituals. By contrast, more sporadic, traumatic rituals tend to evoke enduring memories of experiences shared by relatively small groups of people, promoting localized solidarity and cohesion. This is only the starting point of a much more intriguing and complex story, which leads to a recasting of dichotomous *sociological* theories of religion, from Weber, Gellner, Turner, Barth, and others (Whitehouse 1995: Chapter 8; Whitehouse 2000). The theory I have been developing on the basis of ethnographic research combines psychological and sociological arguments, but it is ultimately assimilable to the theory of brain functions outlined above. It approaches the topic of cultural transmission on the assumption that all neural/mental and social processes are mutually implicated, and neither is reducible to genetically specified hard-wiring.

Most ethnographers can recall moments in the field when it dawned on them that certain of their behaviours in early interactions with locals would (in a native) have been deemed embarrassing, ridiculous, or downright offensive. Fortunately, our informants tend to extend to us the same tolerance normally reserved for very young children, and for this we tend to experience a disproportionate gratitude. But, in a very real sense, we do enter the field as children. Through the establishment of novel, affect-laden scripts, our insights and competences mature. Nevertheless, our susceptibilities to the representations of our hosts are not the outcome of a shared 'bridgehead' of genetically determined cognitive architecture. What we have in common is a capacity for learning, against a rich and intricate background of prior learning. For the ethnographer, this background is usually systematically different from that of his or her 'informants'. In order to carry out successful ethnography, we have to start from the assumption that all the representations of an unfamiliar culture are novel. None of them will (or should) come 'naturally'. We know how hard it can be to get to grips with complex genealogies or cosmologies, but if we think it is comparatively easy to grasp a given concept of extranatural agency, then perhaps we should think again. The flux of representations in a given village is only acessible through the labours of maturation, which is a gradual and cumulative process of learning by recognition, rather than a process of instruction. If Edelman is correct, that the brain is more like a jungle than a computer, then it is also a jungle within a jungle. The hive of activity in the brain is implicated in the hive of activity in society.

Conclusion

A neat summation of the central argument advanced in Part One of this volume is provided in Boyer's opening sentence in Chapter Two (p. 57): 'Cognitive dispositions that result from the evolutionary history of the species account for certain general or recurrent properties of cultural representations.' The crucial question, for Boyer, concerns what we mean by 'certain general or recurrent properties', since the existence of evolved cognitive dispositions appears to be beyond dispute. But this *is* disputed in Part Two. Ingold, in particular, challenges not only the notion of 'cognitive dispositions' but the very foundations of orthodox evolutionary theory. Some of the foundations of Ingold's challenge are themselves problematic, however. For instance, it may be hard to accept that 'organic form . . . arises as an emergent property of the total system of relations set up by virtue of the presence and activity of the organism in its environment' (Ingold, pp. 167–8). True, it would be impossible to account for every detail of my present organic form in terms of 'instructions' contained in my DNA, but the fact that I have four fingers and a thumb on each of my hands surely owes appreciably more to my genetic inheritance than to the presence of breakfast cereal in my environment and my fondness for the activity of eating it. Aspects of organic form may only ever be part-caused by genes, but that does not make every influence on organic form the same, or equally explanatory. But what if the *brain* develops according to biological principles that are different *in kind* from those applying to the development of fingers and thumbs? What if, as Edelman suggests, all properties of brain activity result from processes of recognition and never instruction? That would cast a very different light on what is meant by a notion of 'cognitive dispositions'. It would mean, among other things, that cognitive dispositions are caused by processes located *among* as well as *within* oganisms. In that case, *mentation* (rather than organic form) really could be characterized as an outcome of 'the total system of relations set up by virtue of the presence and activity of the organism in its environment'. Expressed like that, Ingold's idea seems to me both radical and plausible.

Following Edelman, cognitive dispositions, and susceptibilities to representations, would be a function of the affective responses that strengthen configurations of firing patterns but also a function of prior synaptic changes in and between relevant sectors of the nervous system. These two variegated determinants of memory interact with each other through the socially situated development of the human organism. Thus, there are no dispositions or susceptibilities that are cognitive rather than social in origin: all are simultaneously both. From this basic insight springs the possibility of integrated neurological, psychological, and sociological theories. I have given a brief example of how such theories might proceed, but the field remains wide open. These are just the beginnings of an epidemiological model that is as relevant to anthropologists as it is to cognitive psychologists.

I agree with the authors of Part Two that cognition is socially and historically constituted. Mental activity is an *adaptive* process which encompasses neural, mental, social, and cultural phenomena. Perhaps the compulsion, among many social anthropologists, to envisage cognition this way derives from the experience of ethnographic research. Ingold's extensive fieldwork among hunter-gatherers, Toren's detailed developmental studies of Fijian children, Nuckolls' fine-grained studies of Indian and American communities, and my own work in Papua New Guinea have sensitized us to the bewildering adaptability and complexity of human mental life and culture rather than to the simpler and more recurrent principles that might seem to lurk beneath this diversity. As Plotkin in Chapter Three is the first to admit, 'culture . . . is the most complicated thing in the known universe' (p. 94). But, following Plotkin, we should not despair, in the face of this complexity, of finding ways to carve up our subject matter at the joints, and of seeking ever more precise descriptions of the relations between the parts we have been able to differentiate. Cognitive science may need to modify some of its models and methods in the light of ethnographic perspectives and social science may need to understand that mental life is more richly structured than its practitioners have generally appreciated, but that should improve rather than foreclose the possibility of fruitful dialogue and collaboration between our various disciplines.

Notes

1. I should like to thank the Royal Anthropological Institute for permission to reproduce in this chapter slightly modified text from pages

105–14 of my article in the *Journal of the Royal Anthropological Institute*, 1996, Vol. 2, No. 1, pp. 99–116, entitled 'Jungles and computers: neuronal group selection and the epidemiology of representations'.
2. At the beginning of Chapter Four, Ingold suggests that his critique is mainly directed at 'classical' cognitivism, but his subsequent remarks on cognitivism are not similarly qualified.

References

Barth, F. (1975), *Ritual and Knowledge among the Baktaman of New Guinea*, New Haven: Yale University Press.
—— (1987), *Cosmologies in the Making: a generative approach to cultural variation in inner New Guinea*, Cambridge: University Press.
Bloch, M. (1992), *Prey Into Hunter: the politics of religious experience*, Cambridge: Cambridge University Press.
Christiansen, S.A. (1992), 'Emotional stress and eyewitness memory: a critical review', *Psychological Bulletin*, 112: 284–309.
Edelman. G. (1992), *Bright Air, Brilliant Fire: on the Matter of the Mind*, London: Penguin.
Fodor, J.A. (1988), 'Modules, frames, firdgeons, sleeping dogs, and the music of the spheres', in J. Garfield (ed.), *Modularity in Knowledge Representation and Natural-Language Understanding*, Cambridge, Mass.: MIT Press.
Herdt, G. (1989), 'Spirit familiars in the religious imagination of Sambia shamans', in G.H. Herdt and M. Stephen (eds), *The Religious Imagination in New Guinea*, New Brunswick: Rutgers University Press.
Iteanu, A. (1990), 'The Concept of the Person and the Ritual System: an Orokaiva view', *Man* (n.s.), 25: 35–53.
Karmiloff-Smith, A. (1992), *Beyond Modularity: A Developmental Perspective on Cognitive Science*, Cambridge, Mass.: MIT Press.
Kulik, J. and Brown, R. (1982), 'Flashbulb Memory', in U. Neisser (ed.), *Memory Observed: Remembering in Natural Contexts*, San Francisco: W.H. Freeman.
Lakoff, G. (1987), *Women, Fire, and Dangerous Things: What Categories Reveal about the Mind*, Chicago: University of Chicago Press.
Langacker, R.W. (1987), *Foundations of Cognitive Grammar*, Stanford: Stanford University Press.
Mandler, G. (1985), *Cognitive Psychology: an Essay in Cognitive Science*, Hillsdale: Erlbaum.

Conclusion

Schwimmer, E. (1973), *Exchange in the Social Structure of the Orokaiva: Traditional and Emergent Ideologies in the Northern District of Papua*, London: Hurst.

Sejnowski, T.J. and C.R. Rosenberg (1987), 'Parallel networks that learn to pronounce English text', *Complex Systems*, 1: 18–211.

Strauss, C. and Quinn, N. (1997), *A Cognitive Theory of Cultural Meaning*, Cambridge: Cambridge University Press.

Thelen, E. and L.B. Smith (1995), *A Dynamic Systems Approach to the Development of Cognition and Action*, Cambridge, Mass.: MIT Press.

Tulving, E. (1972), 'Episodic and semantic memory', in E. Tulving and W. Donaldson (eds), *Organization of Memory*, New York: Academic Press.

Whitehouse, H. (1995), *Inside the Cult: Religious Innovation and Transmission in Papua New Guinea*, Oxford: Oxford University Press.

—— (1996a), 'Jungles and computers: neuronal group selection and the epidemiology of representations', *Journal of the Royal Anthropological Institute* (N.S.), 2: 99–116.

—— (1996b), 'Rites of terror: emotion, metaphor, and memory in Melanesian initiation cults', *Journal of the Royal Anthropological Institute* (N.S.), 2: 703–15.

—— (1996c), 'Apparitions, orations, and rings: experience of spirits in Dadul', in J.M. Mageo and A. Howard (eds), *Spirits in Culture, History, and Mind*, London: Routledge.

—— (2000), *Arguments and Icons: Divergent Modes of Religiosity*, Oxford: Oxford University Press.

Williams, F.E. (1930), *Orokaiva Society*, London: Humphrey Milford.

Winograd E. and Killinger, W.A. (1983), 'Relating age at encoding in early childhood to adult recall: development of flashbulb memories', *Journal of Experimental Psychology: General*, 112: 413–22.

Wright, D. and Gaskell, G.D. (1992), 'The construction and function of vivid memories', in M.A. Conway, D.C. Rubin. H. Spinnler, and W.A. Wagenaar (eds), *Theoretical Perspectives on Autobiographical Memory*, Netherlands: Kluwer Academic Publishers.

Index

Abrahamsen, A. 5
Abu-Lughod, L. 173–4n25
Ainsworth, M. 188–9
Altarriba, J. 173n19
Anderson, S. 186
Antel, E. 61
anthropomorphism 64
artificial intelligence 6, 211
Astington, J. W. 47, 62
Atran, S. 26, 34, 45, 51n12, 61
attachment theory 188–91
autopoiesis 16, 156–60, 176n34

Baillargeon, R. 61
Bandura, A. 174n27
Barber, J. 187
Barkow, J. H. 78
Barkow, J., L. 6, 50n3
Baron-Cohen, S. 61–2, 106
Barrett, J.L. 67, 74–5, 84n7
Barth, F. 218–9
Bartlett, F. C. 67, 70
Bastien, J.W. 64
Bateson, G. 135
Bauer, P. 61
Baum, A. 186
Bechtel, W. 5
Becker, A. H. 61
behaviourism 4–5
Bellah, R. 190
Bellugi, U. 7
Berlin, B. 26
Bernstein, N. A. 135
Bertoncini, J. 7
Bloch, M. 218
Bloom, P. 51n10
Boehm, C. 183
Bohm, D. 94, 146
Bond, J. 186
Bourdieu, P. 141–2, 149n13, 176n33

Bowerman, M. 172n7
Bowlby, J. 188–9
Boyd, R. 75, 104
Boyer, P. 2–3, 6, 9, 14–17, 41, 44–5,
    57–9, 63, 67, 73, 75, 83n3, 84n4, 123,
    132, 181–3, 184–5, 189–92, 197, 205,
    208–9, 220
Brennan, K. 187
Brenner, S. 191
Brown, A. 50n3
Brown, R. 214
Bruner, J. 174n29
Buck, R. 173n17
Burge, T. 51n5

Campbell, D.T. 94, 183
Carey, S. 26, 61
Carr, D. 171n1
Carstairs, G. 191
Cavalli-Sforza, L.L. 75, 104
Chase, W. 4
Choi, I. 190
Chomsky, N. 6–7, 15, 33, 98–101, 203,
    216
Christiansen, S.A. 215
Clark, A. 6, 31, 101, 114, 133, 138, 142,
    148n10
Clark, J.E. 135
Cohen, J. 122, 124, 147n4, 148n11
Cole, S. 186
Coley, J.D. 34, 45
competence and performance 134–5
Connell, J. 182
Connolly, M. 187
Cornelisen, A. 191
Cosmides, L. 6–7, 27, 46, 78, 82, 105,
    117–8, 125–8, 147n6, 171n2, 172n16,
    173n18
Costall, A. 136–7
Crits-Christoph, P. 186–7

Index

Cross, P. 62
Curtis, S. 7

d'Aquili, E. 148n11
D'Andrade, R. G. 139, 182
Darwin, C. 2, 5, 96, 102, 114, 118,
 120–1, 123, 125, 147n3
Davidson, N.S. 45
Davidson, R. J. 173n17
Dawkins. R. 12, 75
Deacon, T. 101
DeCasper, A. 147n7
Deci, E. 182
Dehaene, S. 46
Dennett, D. 51n6
Dent, C. H. 130, 147n7
development 60–3, 103, 129–38, 165–70,
 188–91
Dickenson, A. 101
divination 64–6
domain specificity 3–5, 26, 29, 31, 32,
 33, 36–9, 43–4, 57–63, 78
Dretske, F. 51n6
Dreyfus, H. L. 134–5
Dreyfus, S. E. 134–5
Dunbar. R. I. M. 6, 106, 123
Dupoux, E. 172n10
Durham, W.H. 12, 75, 93
Durkheim, E. 113

Edelman. G. 5, 82, 205, 209–17, 220–1
education of attention 138–43
Ekman, P. 173n17
Elman, J.L. 9, 101
emotion 2–3, 16–18, 57, 160–8, 181–97
epidemiology 10–13
Estes, D. 62
ethnography 63–6, 72, 136–7, 162–9,
 173n25, 191–5, 206–7, 218–20
evolutionary biology 5–16, 26–50, 79–82,
 91–107, 114–25
 and cognitive specialization 5–9, 26–
  50, 104–7, 118–20
 criticisms of 13–16, 79–82, 91–103,
  106–7, 120–5, 155–6, 206
 and culture 9–13, 42–50, 75–82, 103–
  6, 114–18
 developmental systems approach
  102–3, 123–5

and history 120, 133, 155–60 passim,
 169–71
and natural selection 5–9, 27–39, 91–4,
 96, 98–102
and *tabula rasa* approaches 5, 97–102,
 116–17, 203–4
 see also modularity
experimental data 44–5, 66–71, 83n3,
 84n4

Fang 63, 79, 191
Feeney, J. 187
Feldman, M.W. 75, 104
Flavell, J.H. 174n28
Fodor, J. A. 7–8, 23–7, 30, 47, 49, 51n7,
 98, 100–1, 172n11, 175n30, 203–4
Freud, S. 104, 181, 183, 185
Friedl, E. 191
Furth, H.G. 172n9

Gall, F.J. 6
Gallistel C.R. 46, 61
Gaskell, G.D. 215
Gatewood, J. B. 141, 143
Geertz, H. 191
Gellner, E. 58, 85n8, 219
Gelman, S.A. 4, 26, 33, 34, 45, 46, 61–2,
 118
Gibson, J. J. 15, 142–3
Gilmore, D. 191
Gilmore, M. 191
Goodwin, B. C. 124
Gopnik, A. 62, 106
Gottlieb, G. 98
Gould, S.J. 102
Greenfield, P.M. 105, 147n8
Grice, H.P. 48
Guillaume, P. 149n13
Guthrie, S. E. 72

Hanko-Summers, S. 61
Hansel, J. 186
Harlow, H. 189
Hartup, W.W. 174n28
Haste, H. 174n29
Hatano, G. 61
Hazan, C. 187
Herdt, G. 218
Higgins,E.T. 174n28

Index

Hinde,R. 189
Hirschfeld, L. A. 4, 26, 33, 44–5, 78, 118, 174n28
Hollos, M. 191
Horowitz, M. 184
Hsu, F. 190
Husserl, E. 171n1
Hutchins, E. 133, 149n14
Hutchinson, J.E. 45

Inagaki, K. 61
Ingold, T. 2–3, 14–15, 17, 79–80, 95, 131, 135, 137, 142, 144, 145–6, 147n5, 171n3, 181, 183, 203–4, 220–1, 222n2
Inhelder, B. 173n22
intuitive ontology 11–12, 41–2, 58–75, 181, 191–2
Iteanu, A. 218

James, W. 64
Jay, R. 191
Johnson, M.H. 61, 182
Johnson-Laird, P.N. 125, 146n2
Jusczyk, P. W. 7

Kakar, S. 190, 193
Karmiloff-Smith, A. 4–6, 203–4
Keating, D.P. 61
Keil, F. C. 3–4, 26, 34, 37, 42, 62, 74–5
Kellman, P. J. 6
Kelly, M. 42
Killinger, W.A. 214
Kitcher, P. 104
Kroeber, A. 114–6, 144
Kugler, P.N. 131
Kulik, J. 214
Kurtz, S. 193–4

Lakoff, G. 182, 217
Laland, K.N. 96
Langacker, R.W. 217
language 5–7
Laughlin, C.D. 148n11
Lave, J. 134, 138
Lawson, T. 181, 192
Le Doux, J.E. 173n17
Leekam, S. R. 62
Lehrman, D. 123
Leslie, A.M. 26, 47, 106

Leudar, I. 136–7
Lies, P. 191
Lock, A. 130
Luborsky, L. 186–7, 194
Lumsden, C.J. 75
Lutz, C. A. 173–4n25, 182

Métraux, A. 64
Mandler, J. 61
Manktelow, K. 31
Markman E.M. 34, 45, 62
Massey, C. 61
maternal deprivation 189
Maturana, H.R. 171n5
Maynard Smith, J. 96, 102, 104, 147n3
Mayr, E. 96
McCauley, R. 181, 192
McDonough, L. 61
McManus, J. 148n11
Medin, D. 34
Mehler, J., G. 7, 172n10
Meltzoff, A. 61–2, 149n13
Merleau-Ponty, M. 141, 149n13, 171n3
metaphysics 94
Millikan, R.G. 51n6
Millon, T. 187
modularity 6–10, 13, 23–50, 101, 116–18, 125–9, 175n30
    and cultural diversity 39–50
    degrees of 23–6, 172n11
    and domain specificity 26, 46
    and evolution 27–39, 81, 98–102, 118–20, 125–9
    functions of 36–9
    and initialization 33–4, 44
    and language 42–3, 46, 99–102, 216–17
    and meta-representations 47–50
    and relevance 35–6
modularization 131, 203–4
Morton, J. 61
Murphy, R. 191
Murphy, Y. 191

Netting, R. 191
neural networks 2, 5, 8, 205
neuronal group selection 209–17
Nisbett, R. 190
Noller, P. 187

Index

Norenzayan, A. 190
Nuckolls, C.W. 3, 16–18, 184, 190,
    191–4, 197, 207, 221

Obeyesekere, G. 191, 193
Odling-Smee, F.J. 96
Ortony, A. 34
Over, D. 31
Oyama, S. 102–3, 123–4, 131, 147n4

Papineau, D. 51n6
Perner, J. 62
phenomenology 79, 155
Piaget, J. 4–5, 8, 99, 101, 102, 158–9,
    165, 172n22, 175n29, 203
Piatelli-Palmarini, M. 51n4
Pinker, S. 6, 51n10, 99, 100, 132, 172n11
Plotkin, H. 2, 9–10, 13 15, 92, 97, 99,
    104, 119–20, 124, 131, 148n9, 171n4,
    172n12, 174n26, 175n31, 183–4,
    203–4, 205–6, 221
poverty of the stimulus 9, 98, 158
Premack, D. 34
Putnam, H. 51n5
Pye, D. 135

Quinn, N. 182, 212

Raeff, C. 190
Ramble, C. 67, 83n3, 84n4
Rapp, R. 191
rationality 160–2, 181, 196
Recanati, F. 51n5
Richerson, P. 75, 104
Ridley, M. 95
Rodin, J. 182
Rogers, S. 191
Roland. A. 193
Rosch, E. 149n16
Rosenberg, C.R. 5, 205
Rosengren, K. S. 62
Ross, L. 174n28, 175n30
Rozin, P. 50n3
Rubin, D. 135, 145
Ruble, D.N. 174n28
Ryan, R. 182

Sahlins, M. 172n6
Saunders, G. 191

Schmidt, S.R. 68
Schull, J. 50n3
Schwimmer, E. 218
Scribner, S. 175n29
Searle, J.R. 105
Segalen, M. 191
Sejnowski, T. J. 5, 205
Severi, C. 64
shamanism 64–5
Shanks, D. 101
Shaver, P. 187
Sherif, M. 105
Shevrin, H. 186
Shore, B. 132, 148n11
Shubin, N. 103
Simon, H. 4
Skinner, B.F. 5, 99, 101, 203
Slobin, D. 7
Smith, L. B. 82, 205
Sober, E. 45
social force 105–6
Spelke, E. S. 5–6, 26, 61
Spence, M. 147n7
Spencer-Booth, Y. 189
Sperber, D. 1, 2, 6, 8–14, 17, 23, 35, 41,
    48–9, 77, 113–14, 115–20, 126–7,
    130–1, 134–5, 137, 139–46, 148n12,
    148n15, 181, 191–2, 205, 209–11
Spiro, M. 189–9, 196–7
Springer, K. 62
Starkey, P. 61
Stewart, I. 122, 124, 147n4, 148n11
Stich, S. 51n4
Strauss, C. 182, 212
Suchman, L. A. 136
Sugiyama, K. 61
Swartz, M. 191
Symons, D. 50n3
Szathmary, E. 96, 104

Thelen, E. 82, 124, 131, 135, 148n10,
    205
Thompson, E. 149n16
Tonkin, E. 146n1
Tooby, J. 6–7, 27, 78, 82, 105, 117–8,
    125–8, 147n6, 171n2, 172n16, 173n18
Toren, C. 2–3, 16–18, 79, 101–2, 106–7,
    165, 170, 172–6 passim, 181, 204, 205,
    221

Index

transference 185–8
Trawick, M. 193
Trevarthen, C. 172n13
Tulving, E. 215
Turner, V. 219
Turvey, M.T. 131

unconcious 3, 17–18, 182–97 passim

Varela, F. J. 149n16, 171n5
Vye, N.J. 174n27
Vygotsky, L.S. 174–5n29

Waddington, C.H. 92, 102
Walker, S. 73
Ward, T. B. 61

Weber, M. 219
Wellmann, H. 62
Westen, D. 184
Whitehouse, H. 72, 82, 130, 146n1,
    171n3, 181, 208, 217, 219
Whiten, A. 13, 62
Williams, F.E. 218
Wilson, D. 8–9, 35, 48
Wilson, E.O. 75
Wimmer, H. 62
Winograd, E. 214
Wright, D. 215

Zimmermann, R. 189
Zukow-Goldring, P. 129, 143